GOD'S BABIES

God's Babies

Natalism and Bible Interpretation in Modern America

John McKeown

OpenBook
Publishers

http://www.openbookpublishers.com

Digital material and resources associated with this volume are available at http://www.openbookpublishers.com/isbn/9781783740529#resources

ISBN Paperback: 978-1-78374-052-9
ISBN Hardback: 978-1-78374-053-6
ISBN Digital (PDF): 978-1-78374-054-3
ISBN Digital ebook (epub): 978-1-78374-055-0
ISBN Digital ebook (mobi): 978-1-78374-056-7
DOI: 10.11647/OBP.0048

Cover image: Anonymous, *The Flood* (1450-1499), oil on panel. Rijksmuseum Amsterdam. https://www.rijksmuseum.nl/en/search/objecten?q=flood&p=1&ps=12&ii=0#/SK-A-3418,0

All paper used by Open Book Publishers is SFI (Sustainable Forestry Initiative) and PEFC (Programme for the Endorsement of Forest Certification Schemes) Certified.

Printed in the United Kingdom and United States by Lightning Source for Open Book Publishers (Cambridge, UK).

Contents

Acknowledgements   vii

Foreword   ix
David Clough

1. Natalism: A Popular Use of the Bible   1

2. Protestant Natalism in the U.S.   31

3. Martin Luther: Forerunner of Natalism?   77

4. The Old Testament Context   109

5. Augustine on Fruitfulness   145

6. An Ecological Critique of Natalism   177

7. Conclusion   209

Appendix   215

Abbreviations   223

Works Cited   227

Index   247

Acknowledgements

This book could not have been completed without help from many people. Many thanks to David Clough, Celia Deane-Drummond, Eric Christianson, and John Bimson for help and encouragement during research. Thanks also to Kristin Johnston Largen, Tom Greggs, and my proof-reader Karen Vincent. The staff of Open Book Publishers in Cambridge have helped greatly in turning the text into a book: my thanks to Alessandra Tosi, Catherine Heygate, Bianca Gualandi, and Rupert Gatti.

The University of Chester generously provided the bursary which enabled the years of research for this book. Thanks also to friends in the John Ray Initiative, a group linking Christianity, science and environmental issues, for their support. Also thanks to Peter Francis, warden of the Saint Deiniol's Library (now Gladstone's Library) which awarded me the Richard L. Hills Scholarship. My thanks are also due to staff at university libraries in Cheltenham, Chester, Oxford, at Tyndale House in Cambridge, and to Michael Gale at the Queen's Foundation.

This book is part-funded by a Kickstarter campaign (kck.st/1s53DWd), which ended on 8 October 2014. Generous supporters have helped offset the Open Access publisher's costs and thanks are due to the following people: Dr. Anthony Hereward, Dr. Caitlin Kight, Helen Haran, Richard Grossman, Karin Kuhlemann, Derek McKeown, Professor Tom Tregenza, Ruth O'Brien, Ben Toulson, Dr. Andrew Cowley, Caroline Pomeroy, Dr. Ian McKeown, Emily Herberich, Dr. Matthias Becher, Colin Bell, and Samuel T. Dangremond.

Finally, this book is dedicated to my wife Lynda whose encouragement over the years has made this possible.

Foreword

UN projections indicate that the global human population is likely to increase by nearly 50% in the first half of the 21st century, from 6 billion to 9 billion (United Nations 2004). This staggering and unprecedented growth deserves much greater attention from Christian ethicists and the church at large. A concern for the welfare both of human beings and other creatures provides good reasons to think that Christians should give strong support to measures that would result in a slowing of this projected growth, notwithstanding concerns about reproductive liberty and the ethics of contraception. In this book, however, John McKeown draws attention to the uncomfortable truth that Christian engagement with this issue needs to start further back. As he shows, many Protestant Christians in the US believe that having larger than average families is biblically mandated, and statistics indicate that this is having an impact on birth rates in the country where per capita impact on scarce resources is greatest.

McKeown's book engages constructively and critically with the arguments of the natalists who believe that the Bible requires them to have large families. He does so by situating a careful and painstaking analysis of the hermeneutical arguments that are put forward in favour of this position alongside an equally well-informed account of how the texts they reference have been interpreted by Christian theologians at key points in the Christian tradition. Reflection on this juxtaposition makes clear that the modern arguments put forward in favour of large families are poorly grounded in Christian readings of these texts, and that taking the Bible seriously on this issue is likely to lead to very different interpretations of Christian responsibility.

I very much hope that this book finds an audience among those Christians it most obviously addresses and those in dialogue with them. Christians may finally not be able to agree on this and other issues of biblical interpretation, but they at least owe one another the time to listen to interpretations with which they disagree, in order to consider whether they need to learn to read the Bible differently. This is especially the case when the case for change is argued as clearly, carefully, and persuasively as McKeown does in this book.

David Clough, Professor of Theological Ethics,
University of Chester, UK

1. Natalism: A Popular Use of the Bible

"Because we're Christians, we believe our commandment is to be fruitful and multiply ... big families are what God would have us to do."
(Strand)[1]

Should I choose to have a large family and add even more people to a crowded planet? ... I think that we can safely count 'be fruitful and multiply' among the few divine commands that we have fulfilled.
(Sleeth)

Diverse interpretations and applications of particular Bible verses have shaped American Christian ideas about a religious duty to reproduce biologically, and concepts of ideal family size. This book compares historical and contemporary Christian receptions of Old Testament verses that speak about human fecundity. The receptors initially capturing my attention were Protestant Evangelicals advocating larger family size (an ideology that I call "natalism") in contemporary America. Having found over a dozen popular books from that genre I observed that the verses cited most often are "be fruitful and multiply, fill the earth" (Genesis 1:28), and the verses from Psalm 127 quoted below.

> Sons are a heritage from the LORD, the fruit of the womb a reward. Like arrows in the hand of a warrior are the sons of one's youth. Happy is the man who has his quiver full of them! He shall not be put to shame when he speaks with his enemies in the gate. (Psalm 127:3-5, RSV)

---

1 The interviewee was Rod Dreher, assistant editor, *Dallas Morning News*.

http://dx.doi.org/10.11647/OBP.0048.01

The natalist books and articles also cite over a hundred other Old Testament verses that portray human fecundity as a blessing. I refer to these collectively as the "fruitful verses," and they are listed in the appendix. I explore some of them in detail later.

Definition and distinctions

Natalism is an ideology that advocates a high birth rate within a community.[2] The central message is that parents should have additional children. That is the most obvious manifestation, but there are various parameters that affect birth rates and efforts to influence these can also be part of the natalist agenda.[3] Demographers call these the proximate determinants of fertility and they concern women's lives. Given that women typically have childbearing potential for about thirty years, the main parameters are the number of years in which women are susceptible to pregnancy and the time interval between successive births. These are determined by the age at which childbearing starts and the spacing between births.

In traditional societies the parameters were governed by the proportion that never marries, the age at marriage,[4] the interval before widows remarry, physical infertility, and duration of the decline in fertility immediately after birth (postpartum infecundability), which can be extended by prolonged breastfeeding. How much other methods of family planning were used in pre-modern societies is uncertain (Jutté 29-38). In the last half century new contraceptive technologies have become very significant, but other factors still contribute to limiting births. Late marriage is less important than it once was because with a small ideal family size most women complete their family despite starting later. But in natalist subcultures aspiring to fecundity, youthful age at marriage again becomes important. All the factors noted above are levers potentially usable by natalists to influence their community's birth rate.

---

2   The synonym "pronatalism" often appears in literature in the fields of history and sociology, for example in the title "Pronatalism, Reproduction and the Family in the United States, 1890-1938" (Lovett). The simple term "natalism" is used by Daniel Maguire in a section titled "The Natalist Thrust of Religions" (316), and is also used by Conrad Hackett. I will use this simpler term.

3   I will ignore determinants such as the age of menopause, maternal mortality, and disease, which either vary little across a modern national population, or are not amenable to change through natalist exhortation at the individual or sectarian level.

4   Phrases such as "age at marriage" continue to be standard terminology in demographic literature, though reproductive relationships other than marriage are included in the data under these euphemistic headings. The term "in-union" is increasingly common.

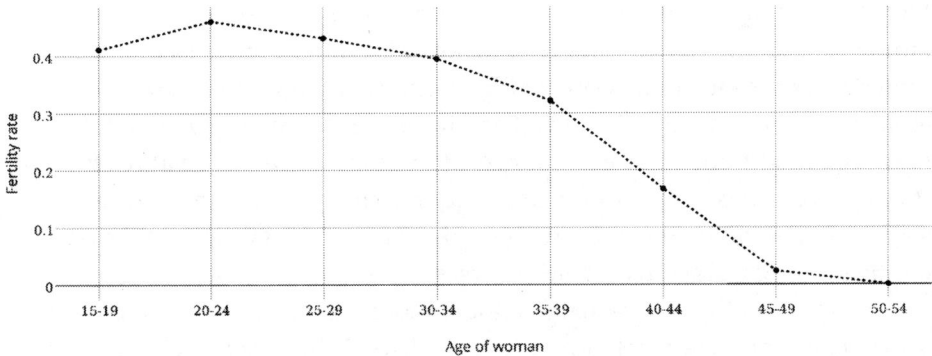

Figure 1. Age-specific fertility rates from Coale and Trussel (Wood 44), illustrating the significance of age at marriage.

A minor factor but one with rising significance is medical treatment of infertility. For example, Susan Kahn finds that a "convergence of pronatalist social pressure, rabbinic permission, and economic accessibility makes fertility treatment all but inevitable for infertile ultraorthodox women in Israel" (294). By contrast, I have not found advocacy of fertility treatment among Protestant natalists, and some oppose it as unnatural.[5]

My use of the word natalism does not include accidental effects on birth rates but only refers to intention[6] and ideology. I make a distinction between effect and motive: described below are ideas which in practice affect birth rates but which are not necessarily intentionally natalist. Any of these ideas can be held independently or in combination with others. The ideas are, first, that marriage is normative, and most people should marry; second, that youthful marriage is the ideal; third, that seeking to reproduce is essential to the constitution of a valid marriage; and fourth, that engaging in a conjugal act without a willingness for that act to result in reproduction is perverted. Also relevant are negative attitudes to particular interventions, notably abortion, artificial contraceptives,[7] and vasectomy. In practice any of

---

5 An exception is vasectomy-reversal, which Protestant natalists recommend.

6 Economists use the word natalist differently to refer to unintentional effects that raise fertility. I am grateful to Tim Meijers (Université Catholique du Louvain) for this example: David de la Croix and Axel Gosseries, "The Natalist Bias of Pollution Control." *Journal of Environmental Economics and Management* 63.2 (2012): 271-87.

7 Arguably this might not necessarily raise fertility, since well-trained practitioners of Natural Family Planning can apparently prevent conception as effectively as users of artificial contraceptives (Zimmerman).

these ideas may increase birth rates, for example by disparaging singleness, lowering the age at first birth, stigmatizing the childless, and hindering family planning. However, they should not be classified as natalist unless the writer's motives include a desire for high fecundity.[8] Any of these ideas could arise from motives other than natalism; for example, advocacy of youthful marriage might only aim at minimising pre-marital sexual relationships. If the expressed concern is only about promiscuity, self-harm, fornication, selfishness, or killing the unborn, then the idea is not natalist, even if based on the same Old Testament fruitful verses.

A small minority of Protestants condemn contraception. Many of these are also natalist,[9] and I call them unlimited natalists.[10] The idea that all conjugal acts must intend reproduction is called procreationism. Kathy Gaca (94, 255) finds its roots in Pythagorean eugenics, as transformed by Philo, adopted by Clement of Alexandria, and moderated by Augustine, for whom fallen marital sexuality is a venial sin excused by the good of offspring. That is far from natalism (Augustine preferred permanent marital abstinence to reproduction, as chapter 5 will show), and modern Catholicism is not even procreationist since it now permits Natural Family Planning (NFP) as implied by *Casti Connubii* in 1930 and clarified by Pius XII in 1951 (Zimmerman 8). *Humanae Vitae* in 1968 contrasts two couples who are both "attempting to ensure that a child will not be born"; that is, both have contraceptive intention, but only the couple using a method of timed abstinence is deemed to be acting morally. The use of NFP is compatible with planning a small family size. Conversely, most Protestant natalists accept the routine use of contraceptives for timing and spacing births while also advocating larger family size.[11]

The condemnation of intentional childlessness is not necessarily natalist. Some modern Protestants believe that the "unitive and procreative ends of marriage" must not be divided, and they argue that this applies at the level of the whole duration of a marriage (Mangina 476). The implication that a deliberately childfree marriage is wrong is emphasized by Thielecke and

---

8   In demography "fertility" refers to the number of births and "fecundity" refers to a potential parent's physical ability to reproduce, whereas in medicine the latter is referred to as fertility. I will use both terms as synonyms referring to the number of births.

9   Sam and Bethany Torode are one example of anti-contraceptive Protestant Evangelical writers who were not also natalist. However, they later publicly disowned their earlier rejection of family planning and converted to Greek Orthodoxy.

10 Many unlimited natalists identify themselves as "Quiverfull" (Joyce 134).

11 The possibility of using contraceptives to increase the surviving number of children (in situations of subsistence poverty) is further indication that anti-contraception is not the same as natalism.

others (Poulson 154). Where that is the only reason, urging such couples to have a child is not natalist, but the same exhortation if rooted in a desire for higher birth rates would be natalist; and it could be a tactical step prior to urging higher reproductivity. The same is true for all of the ideas I noted as incidentally affecting birth rates. When they appear in writings that also advocate high fecundity, they function as part of a natalist agenda.

Why study popular reception of the Bible?

One type of justification is that study of differing interpretations across times and places illuminates the range of possible interpretations. It also enables exploration of hermeneutic issues such as popular awareness of the distance between ancient and modern worlds and how this affects application. More radically, Fernando Segovia calls for "critical analysis of all readers and readings, whether located in the academy or not" and argues that popular reception is "as worthy of analysis and critique as the readings emerging from prominent scholars" (13). The *Blackwell Bible Commentaries* series has shown that for many texts and historical periods the study of reception can be profitable. However, given the huge range of popular interpreters and the extent of Scripture, the choice of material must be justified.

Impact, the real-world effect of reception, is the other type of justification for this kind of research.[12] Elizabeth Schüssler Fiorenza advises that "scholarship must acknowledge the continuing political influence of the Bible" in a world where many people assert "the public claims and values of biblical texts" (16). Beneficial effects of Scripture's reception warrant study, but so do harmful effects. There is an ethical responsibility for scholarship to analyse cultural uses of the Bible. Kenneth Newport, investigating reception of John's Apocalypse[13] by Seventh Day Adventists after the disaster at Waco, finds the "eisegesis continues, and so, in all probability, does the danger of some further flare-up," and so because of potential effects the "scholarly community has a duty to understand this chemistry" (200). The impacts noted by researchers in this genre are not usually quantifiable, and proving causality from biblical reception to behaviour is difficult if not impossible.

---

12 I will not employ Heikki Räisänen's distinction between "effect" and "use" of the Bible. He counts the historical impact of a "plausible" exegesis as an "effect," whereas the impact of a "contrived" exegesis (his example is allegory) he calls a "use" of Scripture (Räisänen 312). This distinction depends on his binary divide between plausible and contrived exegesis, but in my view there is a continuum from more to less plausible.

13 The final book of the New Testament, alternatively titled Revelation.

Different kinds of impact may be of interest to readers depending on their particular concerns or academic discipline. Most of the impacts arise when larger family sizes are achieved, but some arise regardless of that. For example, from a Feminist perspective, Kathryn Joyce and theologian Catherine Keller were concerned at the role natalist ideology plays in reinforcing gender roles within complementarian[14] and patriarchal subcultures. Pastorally, there may be concern that parents who become convinced (through books or other media) that natalism is "biblical" but are unwilling to raise their reproductivity may suffer false guilt. Alternatively, if a couple complies with this perceived duty and achieves high fecundity, then other concerns arise: such as effects on individual women, and on siblings in large families. Among unlimited natalists there may be detriment to women's education, to the care of siblings, and in extreme cases even unsafe pregnancies.

When some types of religiosity more than others are associated with larger family size, over time that affects the composition of the national population.[15] Last century this changed the U.S. religious landscape. A study of the 20th-century shift within U.S. Protestantism from mainline to conservative dominance used GSS data to compare the contributions of causes to that shift (Hout, Greeley, and Wilde). They found that "higher fertility and earlier childbearing among women from conservative denominations" was the primary cause, more important than the combined effect of conversion and changing allegiance (469). Differences in fertility between religious groups in the U.S. continues. A Pew Forum survey in 2007 found the proportion bearing three or more offspring was 6% among "Mainline Protestants," but 9% among "Evangelical Protestants" (Pew, "Religious Landscape" 68). Analysis by Skirbekk, Kaufmann and Goujon (298) of GSS data from 2000 to 2006 also found significant differences.[16] For example, the birth rate of "Liberal Protestants" was lower than that of "Fundamentalist Protestants": the average number of children per woman was 1.84 and 2.13 respectively (298).

---

14 The "complementarian" belief is that men and women typically have different roles. Southern Seminary (where Professor Al Mohler is President), described by Conrad Hackett as "the epicenter of Patriarchal Moderate Natalism" (14), is also headquarters of the Council for Biblical Manhood and Womanhood, a key complementarian advocacy group.

15 Local state populations can also change in composition through differential fertility: a classic U.S. example is the proportion of Mormons in Utah (and neighbouring states).

16 In the U.S. General Social Survey the Protestant categories are fundamentalist, moderate, liberal, and black.

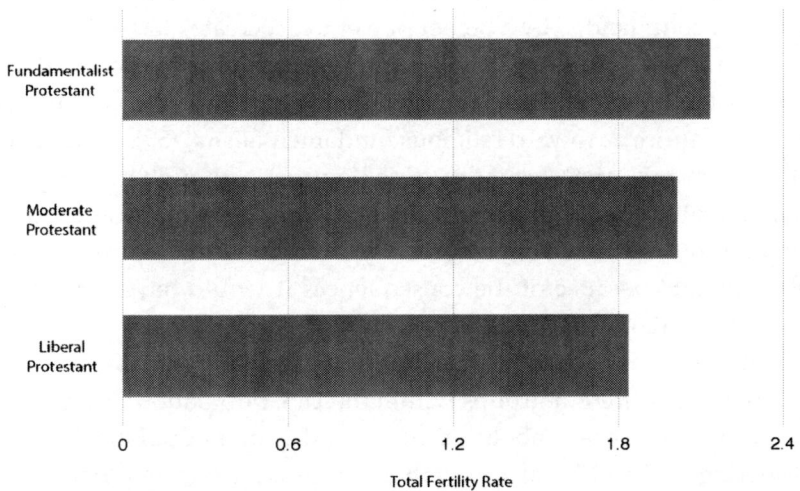

Figure 2. Total Fertility Rate for selected categories of religious affiliation in the U.S., "estimated from GSS data on children ever born to women aged 40 to 59 for the period 2000–2006" by Skirbekk, Kaufmann, and Goujon (297-98).

That may seem a small difference, but within a generation a gap of that magnitude can have a large effect on relative numbers. An earlier study found in 1992 that around half of the Fundamentalist Protestant fertility differential was due to earlier marriage (Mosher, Williams, and Johnson 211).

The discipline of political demography is interested in compositional change within a nation because it can have political consequences. For example, among "white" Americans there was a strong 0.78 correlation between voting in the 2004 election for George W. Bush and having a larger number of offspring (Goldstone, Kaufmann, and Toft 202). However, that Republican white fertility advantage is balanced out by Democratic gains from immigrant support. The "fertility gap would need to widen and persist for the better part of a century before partisanship could be seriously affected" (Kaufmann, Goujon, and Skirbekk, "American Political Affiliation" 54): but long-term higher fertility is exactly what Protestant sectarian natalists plan.

Any subculture with fertility above the national average will, if offspring choose to follow their parents' affiliation, slowly increase its share of the national population. Phillip Longman (an American liberal)[17] laments the

---

17 Phillip Longman is Schwartz Fellow at the New America Foundation.

low birth rate of liberal Americans and contrasts it with those "who believe they are ... commanded by a higher power to procreate" (2004: 5). He warns that "Tomorrow's children ... will disproportionately be descended from ... patriarchal religion," and he claims this "helps explain ... the gradual drift of American culture ... toward religious fundamentalism" (59). Longman calls on liberals to raise their fecundity. Eric Kaufmann, though he also predicts fundamentalist predominance in the U.S., considers that the prospect of "a population footrace between seculars and fundamentalists is a much greater threat" because of the consequences it would have for ecological sustainability (263).

While there has been interest in the effect of religious natalism on relative proportions of different groups within the U.S. population, there has until now been little concern about its effect on the total population. Yet when considering U.S. ecological impact that simple aggregate, population size, is more important than its composition. There are various ways of measuring the ecological impact of consumption, but all place U.S. citizens near the top of the world league. Greenhouse gas emissions in 2010 were 17.6 metric tons per person (World Bank). Multiplied by a U.S. population of 317 million, that amounts to U.S. emissions being roughly a fifth of the world total. In the U.S. there are more births than deaths; in 2008, for example, there were 4.25 million births and 2.47 million deaths (Census Bureau): a large annual natural increase. One contribution to ecological sustainability would be for U.S. births to fall rapidly to population replacement level (Ruether, 2001: 221). I refer here not to a so-called "replacement level" Total Fertility Rate of 2.1 (which the U.S. has had since 1970), but to the actual number of births and deaths becoming equal.[18]

---

18 The anomaly of persistent increase despite "replacement-level" TFR has multiple causes and their relative weight varies from one nation to another. One cause is the tempo effect of the average age of childbearing having risen over recent decades. This stretches the birth total over a longer time period. It means that even if women today had the same number of children as women of an earlier generation, the official TFR would be lower. For example, France in 1985-89 had an official TFR of 1.81, rising to 2.21 if adjusted for tempo. This flaw has been recognized since the 1950s, but none of the proposed alternatives has displaced the established methodology (Bongaarts and Feeney 285). Another cause of persistent growth with a TFR below 2.1 is falling death rates. In most nations, including the USA and the UK, life expectancy has been rising for decades. Since the death rate has been falling, for total births to match deaths the TFR would have to fall below 2 for as long as life expectancy continues rising, and some years after that. A TFR around 2 would only deliver genuine "replacement fertility" (births = deaths) if other factors had been constant (or cancelled out) for decades past.

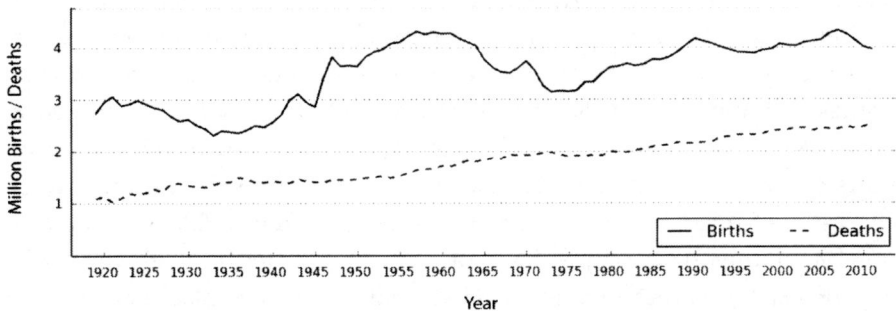

Figure 3. Annual births and deaths in the U.S. (1919-2011). Based on data from the National Center for Health Statistics, with thanks to Robert Anderson and Amy Branum. Graph produced by Alla Hoffman. Data source: http://www.cdc.gov/nchs/data/statab/ natfinal2003.annvol1_01.pdf http://www.cdc.gov/nchs/nvss/mortality_products.htm

Most segments of U.S. society are trending to lower fertility, but Protestant natalism has played a part in keeping the birth rate higher than it would otherwise be. As the graph shows, the number of births has been well in excess of the number of deaths each year in the U.S. The gap narrowed in the periods 1920-35 and 1960-75, but since then progress toward stabilizing U.S. population has been painfully slow.

How many people are persuaded by natalist exegesis, and what effect does it have on ideal family size, or age at marriage? The data to answer these questions numerically does not exist, so I rely on impressions and indirect evidence. Kathryn Joyce estimates the number who self-identify as Quiverfull in the U.S. is in the "low tens of thousands" (Joyce, 2009: 134), but that is only a subset of natalists: those who reject family planning. Broader natalism has been noticed by David Brooks, a *New York Times* columnist, who reported on a "spiritual movement" which he called "natalism ... sweeping across the United States." He observed that they "tend to marry earlier" and "they are having three, four or more kids." He noted that they "attend religious services more often" (a measure of religiosity) and also that "many are willing to move to find places that are congenial to natalist values." The observation of a tendency to marry younger is supported by a 2004 analysis of the National Survey on Family Growth which found that the probability of (first) marriage by age twenty in the U.S. is 17% for Mormons and fundamentalist Protestants, compared to 9% for mainline Protestants, and only 5% for Catholics (Lehrer, 2004: 718). The link between Protestant fundamentalism and the proximate determinants of higher fertility is clear.

The effect of religion on fertility is debated. The "characteristics hypothesis" argues that apparent effects of religion are really the result of a difference between members and non-members in characteristics such as income and years of education. There is also the circular effect by which women with children self-select by attending church more (Hackett, 2008: 6). In the U.S. however multivariate analyses have found that higher fecundity is only partly explainable by characteristics such as occupation, income, place of residence, or education (Hackett; Lehrer; McQuillan; Hayford and Morgan). Religiosity is an independent variable, but the mechanisms of its effect on fertility are unclear. Some point to beliefs relevant to reproduction; others emphasize a religious group's norms for gender and family. Hackett finds the most powerful mechanism is that women participating regularly in church meetings "are exposed to a congregational reference group that influences their thinking about ideal fertility, fertility timing, and motherhood" (8). Obviously this raises a question: why did the group have distinctive thinking in the first place? Natalism plays a part in Protestant fertility as a mechanism, and it is perhaps also an independent factor.

The "doctrine hypothesis" is not easily testable because the large national surveys did not ask about reproductive doctrines. Some social scientists have used "biblical literalism" or "religious intensity" as proxies for such belief, based on their assumption that literalist orthodoxy is natalist, but this is flawed: two people equally literalist and intense may interpret the same biblical text differently. There is little evidence for the role of biblical interpretation, but research by Patricia Goodson and Christopher Ellison is suggestive. A survey of ministerial trainees at ten American Protestant seminaries found that "differences in the interpretation of Genesis 1:28a ... lie at the center of current Protestant debates over family planning" (Ellison and Goodson 514). They tested three statements about how Genesis 1:28a "should be interpreted." The first was "a command from God for people to have as many children as they can." The second was "a blessing from God, and people can decide how many children they wish to or can have." The third was "a general mandate for humans to procreate, and each couple makes their own decision as to how many children they will have" (518).[19] Stronger agreement (on a 1-5 scale) with either the first or second statement

---

19 For my purposes it is unhelpful that in each of the three tested statements an exegesis was combined with an (assumed) application. I would prefer separate testing of these.

was associated with more negative attitudes to family planning. They also found that inerrancy[20] belief strengthened that negative attitude among those choosing the first two interpretive options (520). Only the third statement about Genesis 1:28, as a general mandate, was associated with more positive attitudes to family planning.

It seems likely that currently in the U.S., belief in inerrancy is associated with natalism, but this is not inevitable: it depends on the specific biblical interpretation adopted. That can be shown through an historical example. Donald and Jo Parkerson studied an 1885 town directory from the midwestern U.S. which recorded socioeconomic and religious affiliation data for each woman, and the dates of all children born, not just survivors (Parkerson, D. and Parkerson, J. 55). They classified religious affiliation as pietist (analogous to Evangelicalism), liturgical (Catholic and Episcopal), or unchurched. They found pietist women had a lower fertility at 2.92 compared to liturgical women, who had 3.94 children each. After marriage, pietists delayed their first child longer, for 32 months, and between a second and a third child they delayed over 4 years on average (59). Using diaries and devotional literature they found "causal links between the ideas of 19th-century evangelical pietism and conscious family limitation" (50), specifically the women's desire to gain time for personal sanctification, a duty of intense Christian upbringing that resulted in "fewer children of greater spiritual quality," and a confidence that evangelism would grow the church (61). Those pietists were as inerrantist as any Evangelical today, but they were also pioneers of family limitation. This suggests that biblicism[21] does not necessarily lead to natalism. Biblical inerrancy has no fixed relation to one option in interpretation. For many other verses biblicists accept typological and figurative exegeses, and reception history shows cases in which individuals or large groups of biblicists have altered or abandoned a particular interpretation (Boone 45).

Debating biblical interpretation is not a waste of time. Kathleen Boone notes, with regard to political issues, that many liberal observers assume that conservative Christians are "hiding behind the Bible" and "cynically manipulating a sacred text to garner divine sanction" for their own agenda, but she judges those Christians to be sincere. Similarly, I will take at face

---

20 Inerrancy is the belief that words of the Bible are a gift of the divine inspiration and faultless in all its teachings.
21 Biblicism is a belief in biblical inerrancy, combined with a belief that guidance for all questions of life and conduct today can be found in the Bible, and with willingness to comply.

value natalist confessions that the primary motivator of their belief and practice is the Bible. Kathryn Joyce was told by a leader of the Quiverfull movement that a troubled mother asked their online forum to give her "a reason – besides the Bible – why one should be Quiverfull. The answers were quick and pointed: "apart from Scripture, there's really no reason ... Kids are great and all that, but in reality, it's all about the Bible" (Joyce 169).

Biblical interpretation may be culturally shaped, but it has transformative power in itself. Richard Hornok (a limited natalist who regarded the forbidding of family planning as legalistic and wrong) for his D.Min. project implemented a teaching program, with tests before and after delivery to a class of Evangelicals drawn from local churches.[22] The program resulted in "a significant attitudinal shift toward the biblical perspective" (Abstract) as defined by Hornok. In answer to the question, "Which one factor is most important in determining the number of children one has?," the percentage responses from his "experimental group" were as follows (Hornok 140):

Factor	% Before	% After
Health	22	19
Desire to be a parent	33	38
Financial	15	4
Career	0	0
Age of parents	0	0
Combination of above	11	0
God's Will/Desire	15	27

Even more striking was the change in what they considered to be acceptable reasons for family planning. Whereas before the program the responses had been 77% for "complete freedom" and 23% for "selfless reasons only," after Hornok's classes only 13% chose "complete freedom" and 87% now considered that only "selfless reasons" could be valid (Hornok, 1993: 138). This suggests that without any change in cultural context, the presentation of a new exegesis can change ideas about God's view of reproduction.

The U.S. audience for natalist exegesis is large. The population of the U.S. was 317 million in 2013 (Census Bureau). Around half are Protestant, and (according to a 2011 Gallup poll) among Protestants 41% affirm that "the

---

22 There were 36 people in Hornok's "experimental group" and others in a control group.

Bible is the actual word of God and is to be taken literally, word for word," compared with 46% who affirm that "the Bible is the inspired word of God, but not everything in it is to be taken literally," and 10% who affirm that "the Bible is an ancient book of fables, legends, history and moral precepts, recorded by man" (Jones 2011).[23] The U.S. homeschool movement, among whose teachers the natalist renaissance began, has over a million children within its ranks according to the U.S. Department of Education, and Kathryn Joyce considers this an under-estimate (Joyce ix).

Natalism has been presented as a solution for ecclesiastical anxieties. For example, the *Great Commission Resurgence*, a declaration by the Southern Baptist Convention in 2009, warns in its tenth and final clause that: "Too many Southern Baptists have embraced unbiblical notions about marriage and family. Too often we believe that children are a burden rather than a blessing and smaller families are more 'responsible' than large families" (SBC). The lead author, Daniel Akin,[24] interviewed after its launch, said: "Dr. [Albert] Mohler has pointed out ... You can almost document the decline of baptisms within the Southern Baptist Convention as the decline in the number of children that Baptists have" (Wax). When recruitment is disappointing, natalism can seem attractive to far-sighted church leaders in a context of denominational rivalry and U.S. culture wars.

Natalism is also amenable to secular anxieties and may be co-opted by those concerned about the geopolitics of demography. Nationalists, racists, and nativists[25] desire to strengthen their nation or ethno-linguistic group. Corporations have an interest in growing their pool of labour and customers (Longman, 2004: 41). Birth rates could be raised through progressive policies such as extensive maternity leave and subsidized childcare (Brewer, Ratcliffe, and Smith 261), but those are expensive for governments (Rivkin-Fish 708), so the promotion of natalist ideology may be regarded as a cheaper option. Given that secular appeals to patriotic duty have in recent history been ineffectual in raising fertility, to harness religious natalism could look attractive to secular natalists. Also, alliances of interest might influence family policies in the U.S. (which has given tax credits for additional children since 1998) and that would amplify the influence of natalist preaching.

---

23 By contrast the figures for U.S. Catholics were 21%, 65%, and 9% respectively.

24 Daniel Akin is Professor of Preaching and Theology at Southeastern Seminary, North Carolina.

25 Nativists prefer to maintain a numerical and cultural predominance of "old-stock" inhabitants, i.e. those with an ancestry of a few generations born in that country.

The prospect of Evangelical natalists spreading their ideas in the U.S. is their primary significance, but it is also possible that their example and influence might disseminate natalism to international Evangelical and Pentecostal movements. A pattern of diffusion from U.S. teachers to other nations has been observed in the case of the Prosperity Gospel. For example, the influence of Kenneth Hagin, T.L. Osborn, and other American prosperity teachers has been detected in the UK, Sweden, and Nigeria (Gifford; Coleman 120). Natalism could spread in a similar way; for example, Allan Carlson has organized international events promoting the "Natural Family" (Buss and Herman 3). I have not discovered natalist publications from the UK, apart from a few pages in a book from the Society for the Protection of Unborn Children's (SPUC) Evangelical wing (Anonymous 34-39), but there may be a small UK natalist movement which I have not detected because it has no home-grown literature.

Scope and primary sources

This project does not evaluate all recent natalism that draws on biblical texts. The scope of my search for primary sources was guided by my interest in the recent renaissance of natalism as an articulate ideology among people whose parents and grandparents had small families, and who live in nations that have long experience of low infant mortality. Here I am not interested in the cultural valuation of high fecundity that was ubiquitous in pre-modern societies and persists today in traditional cultures, though it is slowly fading. That is sustained more by kin and peer pressure than by preaching. Examples in the U.S. include the Amish and Hutterites. It persists in some less industrialized nations, but even if I had found natalist reception located in those places,[26] it would have been outside the scope of my project.

My particular concern is the unchallenged spread of natalist teachings among English-speaking Evangelicals in wealthy developed countries whose large ecological footprints make any rise in fertility significant for ecological sustainability. This audience is unlikely to be influenced by sources in languages other than English or with a provenance outside Evangelicalism, so those two criteria guided my scope. Even when I searched in bibliographic databases for natalist Old Testament reception regardless of provenance, the

---

26 There may be natalist preaching among Pentecostals outside the USA (personal communication from Professor John Guillebaud, 13 July 2010).

substantial sources found came from U.S. Evangelicalism. Subsequently my search in "grey literature" concentrated on that sector.

Catholic natalism exists in the U.S. today. In the 19th and early 20th centuries nationalist Catholic natalism was strong in France (Camiscioli; Barusse) and Italy (Ipsen). In recent decades, Catholic natalist publications have been rare and the few instances (e.g. Weigel) do not make substantial use of Old Testament verses. Jason Adams, in a book which carries commendations by three Catholic archbishops, includes Old Testament citations in connection with anti-contraceptive teaching, but not for natalism, which only features in a quotation from the Catechism: "Scripture and the Church's traditional practice see in large families a sign of God's blessing" (Adams 19). The book's collection of homilies by bishops and priests offers one other instance: a claim that small families mean fewer vocations (Adams 111). Even if relevant Catholic sources had been found they would have been outside my scope, but Catholic natalism is a significant topic in its own right.

Eastern Orthodox natalism exists today in Europe and Russia, perhaps having persisted from the early 20th-century manifestation observed by Fagley (Fagley 164), or resurgent because of Orthodoxy's location in states of the former Soviet Union which have the world's lowest birth rates. For example, in 2007 the Patriarch of Georgia, Ilia II, promised to baptize personally any child whose birth order was third or greater, and has been credited with a subsequent increase in Georgia's birth rate (Esslemont). I have found no recent source with substantial natalist Old Testament reception, but Orthodox theologian David Bentley Hart, lamenting U.S. moral decay and commenting on the "culture war," suggests that:

> Probably the most subversive and effective strategy traditionalists might undertake would be militant fecundity: abundant, relentless, exuberant, and defiant childbearing. Given the reluctance of modern men and women to be fruitful and multiply, it would not be difficult, surely, for the devout to accomplish – in no more than a generation or two – a demographic revolution. ... if it is a war we want, we should not recoil from sacrifice. (Hart 81)[27]

My project is limited to reception within Christian communities as my method for evaluation uses comparison with Christian tradition. Therefore, although natalist reception of the Torah by *Haredi* Jews exists, it is outside my scope. Similarly natalism among Mormons (Latter Day Saints) is excluded as they

---

27 Hart's phrase "militant fecundity" was later picked up by natalist bloggers. David Bentley Hart is Professor of Christian Culture at Providence College, Rhode Island.

have distinctive doctrines linking salvation and reproduction, which differ from Protestantism. Secular natalism is resurgent in Russia (Rivkin-Fish, 2010) and Italy (Krause and Marchesi), and often the biblical allusion "go forth and multiply" appears, but it is excluded by my selection principle that Old Testament reception must be substantial.

Even with this limited scope, the quantity of natalist reception of the Old Testament online and in sermons is huge. A general rule for research on modern popular reception is that it cannot be exhaustively surveyed but only sampled. The criteria for sampling must be explicit, and the selection representative. Most natalists have fewer than five children, but those with ten or more are spectacular and attract greater attention.[28] I excluded blogs and other informal online material due to their quantity. The primary sources identified here include all books and journal articles which contain substantial presentation of natalist biblical reception.[29] Some chapters within monographs on other topics were found,[30] but a systematic search for them was not attempted. The sources are all written by conservative Protestants, all from North America.[31] One might expect sources from other strongholds of conservative Protestantism around the world such as Australia and South Africa, but I did not find any. Kaufmann (161-63) mentions the Laestadian Lutherans of Finland, and the Orthodox Calvinists of the Netherlands, as practising what he calls sectarian "endogenous growth," and perhaps future researchers will explore natalist teachings produced outside the U.S.

My primary sources, all those in which natalism is a major theme and is supported with biblical citation and exegesis, are by Mary Pride, Allan Carlson, Charles Provan, Max Heine, Samuel Owen, Calvin Beisner, Rick and Jan Hess, Nancy Campbell, Douglas Wilson, James and Shannon French, Craig Houghton, Steve and Candice Watters, R.C. Sproul Junior, Robert Andrews, Rachel Giove Scott, and Doug Phillips. The sources are mostly from ecclesiastical publishers. Other authors including Albert Mohler, Daniel Akin, Tim Bayly, Richard Hornok, and John Jefferson Davis have produced articles, chapters, or shorter sections of writing that express natalist ideas.

---

28 One reality TV series, *19 Kids and Counting*, about the Duggars, a Quiverfull family, has a weekly average of 1.4 million viewers (Mesaros-Winckles, 2010: 2).

29 The search terms I used in bibliographic databases were fruitful, multiply, fertility, fecundity, reproducti* (asterisk finds alternate suffixes), birth, demograph*, population, contracepti*, family planning, marriage, procreation, sons, and children.

30 The isolated chapters are by Sproul and Davis.

31 All my primary sources were published in the U.S., except the book by Craig Houghton who is based in Canada.

Occupationally, most authors of the natalist sources work as pastors or in Christian education or other ministries. Beisner, Wilson, Owen, Mohler, Akin, and Davis are academics in theology, ethics, or history, based at Christian seminaries and colleges.[32] Carlson is an academic historian currently leading a think-tank. Sproul, Wilson, Bayly, and Hornok are ministers. Some work in media, for example Heine was a newspaper editor, and Campbell edits the women's magazine *Above Rubies*. Geographically the authors are almost all based in the U.S., in states that include Tennessee (Campbell), Alabama (Heine), Texas (Hornok), Kentucky (Mohler, Watters), North Carolina (Akin), Virginia (Sproul), and Washington (French). So they are better represented in the Southern states, less so in the Northeast, and only one was outside the U.S.: Craig Houghton in Canada. Denominationally, many natalists belong to congregations that are independent or affiliated to small connexions. Of those with links to larger established denominations, there are strong contingents of Presbyterians (Beisner, Sproul, Phillips), Southern Baptists (Mohler, Akin, Watters) clustered at seminaries under neo-Calvinist influence, and Lutherans (Carlson, Provan). Craig Houghton is an Evangelical Baptist, and Nancy Campbell's husband is a Pentecostal pastor. Doctrinally all are conservative Evangelicals, and many are associated with Calvinism. Many are post-millennial, but Hornok is pastor of a church affirming pre-millennial doctrine.

This project adopts a categorization proposed by Daniel Doriani.[33] He observes that Christians fall into "three camps," which are first, those who consider family size a matter of personal preference; second, those who commend larger family size but allow family planning; and third, those who say "let God plan your family" and also "stridently lobby for large families" (Doriani 26). The second and third camps are both natalist. Doriani offers the labels "large but limited" and "unlimited" for these two camps. The former are planned natalists, or rather plain natalists who do not also subscribe to anti-contraceptive ideology. Of the seventeen writers listed above, I classify eight as unlimited natalists: Pride, Provan, Hess, Campbell, Scott, French, Houghton, and Sproul.[34] The remainder advocate

---

32 I prioritized academics and denominational leaders, therefore Albert Mohler was included even though his articles on this topic are only published online.

33 Daniel Doriani is Professor of Theology at Covenant Theological Seminary, Missouri (http://www.covenantseminary.edu/the-thistle/dr-dan-doriani-to-return-to-covenant-seminary-in-fall-2013/). All links to online resources were active at time of publication, unless otherwise stated.

34 They reject this label, as what they commend is direct family planning by God.

large-but-limited families: Carlson, North, Owen, Beisner, Heine, Hornok, Wilson, Davis, Watters, and Mohler.

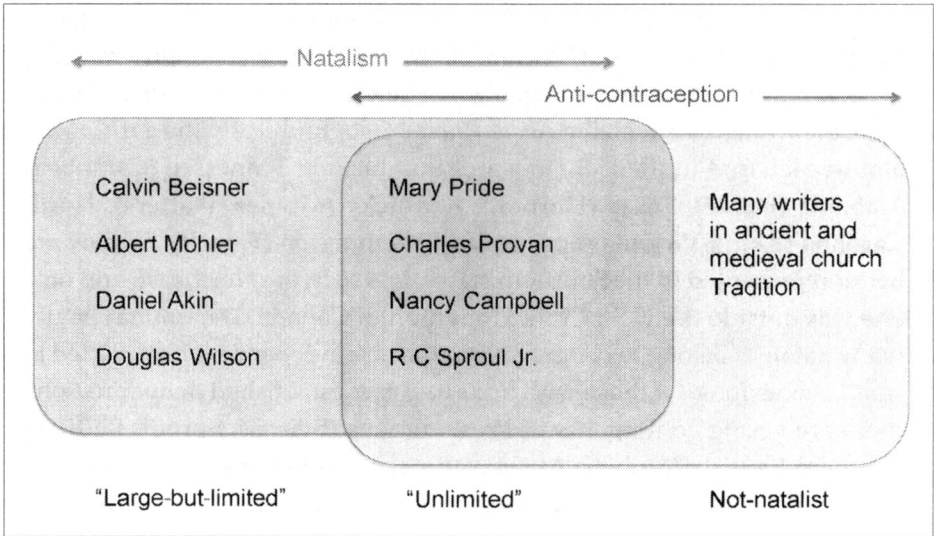

Figure 4. Venn diagram illustrating the difference between the two ideologies: natalism and anti-contraception.

Conrad Hackett classifies U.S. Christians in four categories with regard to natalism. Two of his categories correspond to what I call unlimited and limited natalists: Hackett calls them "Extreme Patriarchal Natalists" and "Moderate Patriarchal Natalists" (Hackett, 2008: 11). Hackett identifies a third group which he labels as "Religious Malthusians" exemplified by the U.S. Episcopalian presiding bishop Jefferts Schori and the Southern Baptist minister Oliver Thomas (13). A fourth group, the silent majority of U.S. Christians, is labelled by Hackett as "Implicit Natalists" because they "do not explicitly promote a particular fertility ideal" but they do "implicitly encourage childbearing" (17), and if there are "women in the congregation who are steadily advancing in their childbearing years without producing any children, other members may ask when they plan to have children, thus promoting the unwritten natalist ethic" (18). Since those in the "Implicit" category do not articulate any natalist interpretation of Bible verses, they are outside the scope of this book.

Do the primary sources have any influence in persuading people to natalism or reinforcing their practice? One test, albeit only relevant to the unlimited type, was a survey of posts from a Quiverfull forum over a two-year period ending in January 2011. These include testimonies of how individuals became convinced and recommendations of books for enquirers.[35] Hess, Pride, and Campbell feature, for example one writing "I read the book [by Hess] and was convinced" (September 2009); and another mentioning "This book [by Pride] was such a God-send. It answered so many of my questions" (December 2010). One wife read the books by Campbell and Hess to her husband and "halfway through *A Full Quiver* he was convinced" (February 2010). Often the books are part of a long enquiry: Pride's *"The Way Home* was the start of a lot of thinking for us" (September 2010). A list of books recommended by the forum included those mentioned here and also the audio version of Charles Provan's book (April 2010). However, the Bible is cited far more than any other source as the decisive influence.[36]

There is a small secondary literature on a few of these primary sources, limited to those published before 1990. There are two critical articles[37] focused on individual natalist sources: Mary Pride's book was critiqued by Jeffrey Meyers[38] in 1997, and Charles Provan's book by James Jordan[39] in 1993. Pride, Provan, and Hess (all three writers from the unlimited camp) are critiqued by Daniel Doriani, and briefly by Patricia Goodson ("Ethics"). The critics focus on the sources' condemnation of family planning, which from a pastoral perspective they regard as legalistic and harmful. Jordan emphasizes that "nowhere does the Bible forbid family planning" (Jordan, 1993: 3). Meyers warns that Pride "continues to provide the intellectual foundation" of a movement to forbid family planning and "because of Pride's book this subject has become a controversial and divisive issue in American Evangelical and Reformed churches" (Meyers, 1997: 4, 9). The widest coverage of natalist sources is in Richard Hornok's D.Min. thesis, which gives most attention to Pride but also looks at Provan, Heine, Owen, and Davis (the last two being limited natalists). Hornok's question is whether it is "permissible to space and limit the number of children one has?" (Hornok, 1993: 4), and since he is himself a limited natalist it is not surprising that while Hornok critiques legalism, he does not criticize the core of natalist ideology, the advocacy of large family size.

---

35 The 1000+ posts were mostly about practical matters of childbirth and childrearing.
36 Biblical citations in the forum were not systematically analysed, but it seems the range of verses cited is similar to those appearing in Hess, Pride, Campbell, etc.
37 Both originally appeared in the periodical *Contra Mundum*, which is published by a conservative Protestant ministry (http://www.biblicalhorizons.com).
38 Jeffrey Meyers is Senior Pastor at Providence Reformed Presbyterian Church. He has a doctorate from Concordia Theological Seminary and is the author of a commentary on Ecclesiastes, published by Athanasius Press in 2007.
39 James B. Jordan is the Director of Biblical Horizons. He has a Th.M. from Westminster Theological Seminary. He is a conservative: his books include *Creation in Six Days. A Defense of the Traditional Reading of Genesis One.* He has also co-authored with Gary North, a leading Reconstructionist.

The fruitful verses and Christian reproduction

While there is little secondary literature specifically on the primary sources, other commentators do look at Christian reception of the Old Testament fruitful verses and consider what might be appropriate for modern application. Raymond van Leeuwen,[40] writing in *Christianity Today* in 2001, warns readers against those who claim that God has "commanded married people to have children," who "claim Genesis 1:28 … as a proof text," and who also "argue on the basis of the created order" (Leeuwen, 2001: 59). Leeuwen's main concern, however, is their forbidding of contraception (Leeuweun, 2001: 60) rather than their natalism.

Kenneth Magnuson[41] writes out of pastoral concern for infertile couples who feel obliged to pursue fertility treatments due to a belief that not doing so would disobey God. He quotes a Jewish woman who lamented that "I am an *akarah* – a barren woman … I hear the words … *P'ru ur'vu*. God's command to be fruitful and multiply has been given again." He finds that "a similar understanding of Genesis 1:28 is held by some Christians" (Magnuson, 2000: 26, 38).

Those who have considered interpretation of the fruitful verses in connection with the issue of population include Richard Fagley[42] in 1960, David Yegerlehner in 1974, and Susan Power Bratton[43] in 1992. None of them cite any recent natalist advocates (and the first two predate all of my natalist sources), but they allude to natalist arguments and biblical reception from earlier years.

Fagley begins with problems of global demography and development. He surveys attitudes to family planning in world religions before turning to the Bible, and then to a history of ideas in Christianity's major branches. He considers the rate of population growth (in the 1950s) too rapid and calls for "responsible parenthood" (Fagley, 1960: 5). He commends Protestantism for adapting to demographic reality, but sees problems in other religious groups. He cites a 1937 pro-fertility Orthodox writing from Greece (164) and refers to a "fertility cult" in 1950s Catholicism, supplying three examples

---

40 Raymond van Leeuwen is Professor Emeritus of Biblical Studies at Eastern University, Pennsylvania.
41 Kenneth Magnuson is Professor of Christian Ethics at Southern Seminary, Kentucky.
42 Richard Fagley was Secretary of the Commission on International Affairs of the World Council of Churches, a theologian, and a Congregational minister.
43 Susan Bratton is faculty chair of Environmental Science at Baylor University, Texas. She has a doctorate in Botany with Plant Ecology and an MA in Theology.

(180, 185). These "would serve as a mother lode of valuable material. I refrain from exploiting it, however, since I cannot convince myself that it is more than a passing aberration" and also, as a Protestant, he is "reluctant to make sectarian points" (184). Of the arguments of the "pro-fertility parties," he briefly observes that they hope for "economic miracles" and "fall back on trust in divine providence" (184), but he does not say whether they use Old Testament texts.

Yegerlehner, a Methodist minister, observed in the early 1970s that "abundant human fertility is a cause for great alarm" (2), and so there is "little room for 'Be fruitful and multiply' ... in contemporary theology." He aims to discover "possible meanings for our generation" rather than simply ignoring this "word of God" (3), and he continues that "we are by no means free to assume that the commandment to 'be fruitful and multiply' no longer applies ... or that it can now simply be overlooked as 'fulfilled.'" He knows his readers are wary of "an enthusiastic literal understanding" but reassures them that the "Old Testament ideal ... need not be thrown in our faces as a text which prohibits population control" (211).[44] In his later chapter surveying "Contemporary Reactions," he alludes to natalist writers.

Bratton developed a "Christian ethic for human population regulation" (26). Her book is mostly concerned with demographic history and sustainability, but a chapter entitled "Abraham's Seed: The Bible and Reproduction" observes that "in favor of large families, Christians often confidently cite God's instructions to Adam and Eve ... [and] a superficial application to family life suggests that Jews and Christians should have as many children as possible" (42). Elsewhere she critiques five arguments whose provenance is "specifically Christian," including a claim that to limit one's family size "disobeys biblical commands to be fruitful and multiply and disregards biblical valuing of children," but Bratton cites no source (130-31). The only natalist writing that she cites is by Harold Brown in a 1985 *Christianity Today* editorial where he "criticized denominations with declining birth rates and suggested Christians from industrial nations ought to meet biblical mandates to reproduce" (Bratton 124). The interval since 1992 would alone

---

44 Yegerlehner identified 101 "fruitfulness verses," but some are secondary allusions, e.g. "For though your people be as the sand of the sea, only a remnant of them will return" (Isaiah 10:22). Some do not mention fertility, e.g. "the multitude of men and cattle within it" (Zechariah 2:4), and a few lack any reference to quantity, e.g. "I will bring forth descendants from Jacob" (Isaiah 65:9). My comparison with the verses used by natalists shows overlap, though a few are not used while many others not on Yegerlehner's list are.

justify revisiting this topic as there have been developments in Near Eastern archaeology, Biblical Studies, and ecological footprint analysis since then.

Theory and methodology

I derived the methodology used here first by looking at examples of academic engagement with popular interpretation of the Bible, and second from discussions of theoretical issues associated with this genre. At a consultation outlining a framework for a commentary series on biblical reception published by Blackwell, John Sawyer pointed to Hans Jauss and *Rezeptionsaesthetik* as offering a theoretical basis, and David Parris has worked on adapting those ideas from literary disciplines for use in biblical reception.[45] However, the methodology is not yet well established and one practitioner, Stefan Klint, writes of "reception criticism" that "how this is to be done in practice is far from self-evident, since no specific methodology or theoretical framework yet exists" (Klint 89). That is especially true for any effort to not only analyse but also evaluate popular reception. Such combinations are rare. On the one hand, some scholars signal that their work was provoked by popular reception of certain Scriptures, but without discussing those receptions directly they move to construct alternative interpretations.[46] On the other hand, those who analyse popular biblical reception usually refrain from evaluating it exegetically. I will consider approaches to analysis now, and afterward will return to the question of how one might evaluate a popular interpretation of Bible verses.

Analysis of reception

The foundational task is to examine the use of Scripture in the reception. This begins with the identification of which Bible verses are quoted, cited, or alluded to. For this project a database of reception in selected primary sources was constructed to facilitate analysis of the use of Scripture in natalism.[47] The various arguments were classified, and uses of bible verses were coded to the argument supported wherever that was discernible. The

---

45 A new book fills the gap in methodological literature: Robert Evans, *Reception History, Tradition and Biblical Interpretation: Gadamer and Jauss in Current Practice*. London: T&T Clark, 2014.

46 An example is David Petersen on "family values" in Genesis.

47 The method of construction and tables of detailed results are in the Appendix.

relative importance of different verses in the scheme of reception was weighed not only by frequency of citation but also by an assessment of how verses function in the major natalist arguments. Then the common features and differences between the two types of natalist (limited and unlimited) were identified. A large part of chapter 2 is devoted to these tasks.

Reception critics look at how readers' interpretations are shaped by cultural context. One aspect is the particular framework of doctrine and hermeneutics through which the readers' reception is worked out. This helps one discern the internal logic and "the integrity of the system when seen from the point of view" of the receptors (Newport 155). Another aspect is immediate historical context, including the political interests of interpreters and their sociological situation. That is peripheral to my approach and has been done for the Quiverfull type of natalist by Kathryn Joyce, who makes only brief comments on biblical usage (Joyce 8, 134). Chapter 2 briefly considers aspects of the U.S. cultural context of natalist writers.

Some reception studies investigate the historical development of a reception and explore its continuity with or divergence from earlier interpretation. An effort to trace natalism's genealogy systematically would be interesting but is not attempted here, though a brief comparison with early 20th-century natalism is offered in the next chapter. I have chosen to focus on one aspect of genealogy: the use of Luther's writings by natalists who claim him as a forerunner. Some natalists do not cite Luther, some quote Protestants from the early 20th century, and a few claim no historic root apart from Scripture. However, reception theory as developed by Gadamer suggests that influential past interpreters do shape subsequent reception even if the reader has no direct knowledge of those past writings, because they all stand in the stream of Christian reception. This applies to natalists, their audiences, and their critics. Chapter 3 will investigate to what extent Luther was a forerunner of Protestant natalism.

Evaluation of reception

Many studies of popular reception stop after analysis without adding exegetical evaluation. This raises the question of why evaluation might be considered inappropriate, and there are two different answers coming from opposite perspectives. One is based on a strong distinction between scholarly interpretation and popular reception. For example, historian Kenneth Newport judges that "eisegesis is more or less endemic" in "contemporary non-critical biblical studies" (Newport 23). From this viewpoint, popular interpretation that differs from the modern scholarly consensus is simply in error, and if its implausibility is sufficiently obvious, or if existing works of biblical scholarship address the exegetical issues raised, then it does not warrant an additional labour of evaluation. For example, Newport points his readers toward particular commentaries on Revelation where they can discover why Adventist reception is eisegesis.[48] In the case of natalism, however, its core interpretations are not obviously implausible,[49] and the brief attention given to modern application in Old Testament commentaries is divided between critics and supporters of natalism.

The other argument against evaluation arises from post-modern approaches that level readers by refusing to privilege academic over popular interpreters. Fernando Segovia argues that "informed readings can no longer be perceived as hermeneutically privileged" (Segovia, 1995: 15). Daniel Patte recommends that "different readings proposed by ordinary readers should be welcomed and affirmed as legitimate" (Patte, 1995: 11). This could be taken as a reason why evaluation of interpretation should not be attempted. I suggest, however, that equal respect for "ordinary readers" should not exempt their readings from evaluation. If it is worthy of analysis, then it is also worthy of critique. Stefan Klint is not averse to evaluative critique in principle, for although he claims that reception criticism is primarily a "descriptive task, rather than a normative one," he speculates that it may optionally "also include some kind of theological evaluation and application for the modern situation" (91).

The problem is establishing a method to evaluate popular biblical reception. There are various models for doing this. For example, Anglican tradition suggests a triad of Scripture, tradition, and reason. Richard Bauckham argues that to evaluate modern uses of Scripture (in politics) requires parallel awareness of multiple contexts. "If a biblical text is not to mean whatever we want it to mean, we must pay disciplined attention to its original and canonical contexts. But if it is to mean something for us, we must pay equally disciplined attention to the contemporary context" (*Politics* 16). While this does not provide a ready-made method, it suggests that evaluation should be multifaceted and multidisciplinary.

---

48 Elsewhere in his book, however, Newport does include his own exegetical critique of the Adventist use of type and anti-type.

49 Many instances in the details of natalist exegesis are implausible, but the core idea that human fecundity is esteemed in the Old Testament is plausible.

Walter Moberly in a chapter opposing Christian Zionist interpretation of Genesis 12:3 offers a valuable practical example of how to combine analysis and evaluation of popular reception (Moberly 162-78). He brings together five components to accomplish this: description of the popular reception through quotations from a representative sample of Zionists; analysis of its roots in past Dispensationalism; comparison with the "plain sense" of the verse in its original context; comparison with New Testament reception of the same verse; and the contemporary context of U.S. and Middle East politics.[50] These five correspond methodologically to the five remaining chapters of this book: description of natalist reception; roots in Luther; the Old Testament in its context; Augustine and his Christ-centred understanding of fruitfulness; and the contemporary context of ecological crisis.[51] The first two help toward understanding the popular reception, while the latter three enable a robust evaluation of reception as none is sufficient alone.

Ancient Near East

In the task of evaluating popular applications of Bible verses, historical-critical exegesis by biblical scholars has a foundational role. Ideally it should describe and delimit the range of meanings that a text could plausibly have had for its writers and original readers. Knowledge about many aspects of the ancient Near East, such as agriculture, demography, economics, religion, and politics, has advanced in recent decades, mostly owing to archaeology. To determine the "plain sense" of a text, scholars deploy various critical techniques (Barton 7), including consideration of a verse's canonical relation to its book and the rest of the Old Testament and its theologies. That serves as a baseline, for without it a text might mean anything anyone wants it to mean (Thiselton 1). Biblical scholarship is, however, insufficient in two ways.

For some biblical texts, though biblical scholars do narrow down the number of plausible meanings to a few, they do not achieve consensus and cannot arbitrate between the remaining options. For example, when scholars have criticized natalist reception of "be fruitful and multiply," the most common argument is that it is not a command but (only) a blessing (Van

---

50 Moberly notes that, given the limits of treatment within a single chapter, he lacks space to consider the second and fifth items.

51 Consideration of New Testament reception of Genesis 12:3 functions in Moberly's work as an instance of early Christian reception of the Old Testament, and dispensationalism provides the historical genealogy of Christian Zionism.

Leeuwen; Tucker). This claim, however, is not agreed by all scholars: many do identify it as a command. This is discussed in detail in chapter 4. More broadly, ideas about the meaning of the fruitful verses can still vary widely: they can be construed as cultural pragmatism, or as an accommodation to a prosperity cult, or as ethnocentric and competitive xenophobia, depending on differing views about the emphases of Old Testament theology.

A more fundamental problem is that the "original meaning" of an Old Testament verse (even if it were accessible and agreed) is not a suitable guide for Christian behaviour. Sawyer writes about other instances of objectionable popular reception that often "their crimes are not against the original meaning of the text, indeed, the interpretation may on occasion come very near it" (Sawyer, 2006: 4). This is a dispensational problem: the "raw" meaning of an Old Testament verse should not prescribe Christian application. However, this does not detract from the preliminary importance of historical studies. Gadamer uses the example of legal hermeneutics, in which the jurist works to "mediate between the original application and the present application" (Gadamer 325), and he argues that anyone "seeking to understand the correct meaning of a law [today] must first know the original one ... but here historical understanding serves merely as a means to an end" (326). While the capability of modern biblical scholarship to fulfil even this limited role is debatable, it surely offers the nearest approach one can make towards a discernment of the "original meaning" of Old Testament texts. As such it is the first step toward evaluation of popular biblical application.

Christian tradition

The second step is to draw on classic Christian reception of the same verses. This is helpful in a number of ways. Dale Allison makes the minimal claim that "sometimes the [modern] exegetical tradition has forgotten what it should have remembered" (237), so past interpretation is a deposit of wisdom that is profitable to consult. Sawyer identifies a more general utility because "awareness of the many meanings that a text has when read ... down the centuries, has great heuristic value in the process of establishing and evaluating a meaning" (Sawyer, 2004). When we face disputes between modern Christians about conflicting interpretations, argues John Lee Thompson (221), it is not only helpful but necessary to converse with earlier Christians, though we should not assume there was a patristic consensus or "paleo-orthodoxy" that can be used to decide between conflicting modern receptions (Tanner and Hall). Since we face the dispensational problem of deriving moral guidance from the Old Testament, it would be foolish to neglect patristic Christian wisdom gained from long wrestling with precisely this problem. Their "spiritual" exegesis developed christological and other methods for transforming the often unedifying acts, words, and attitudes of the Israelite patriarchs into lessons suitable for the church. Attention to historical reception, as featured in this book, helps provide some continuity with classic Christian thought.

Richard Fagley and Susan Power Bratton, in their researches on Christian ideas about human fertility and population, do consider the Early Church Fathers briefly, but without much expectation of finding helpful insights. Instead they are portrayed as being part of the problem. "Augustine's condemnation of both contraceptive method and contraceptive intent leaves little room for any kind of family limitation in his doctrine" (Fagley 174). Bratton considers that "the Western church chose a generally pronatalist stance" for married people and sent a "mixed message on procreation" (Bratton 76-77). Both critics treat anti-contraceptive ideas as if they were natalist, and they accept the stereotype of Christian asceticism as a two-tier system whose ideal was a small celibate elite shepherding a flock of married people who were expected to breed prolifically. That picture may have been true of 19th-century European nationalist versions of Catholicism, but it has been unfairly projected back on to Augustine and the patristic period.

This part of my method puts questions arising from contemporary issues to historical Christian writings, trusting that they can offer insights unavailable elsewhere. Gadamer confesses that: "I must allow tradition's claim to validity, not in the sense of simply acknowledging the past in its otherness, but in such a way that it has something to say to me" (Gadamer, 2004: 361). A similar approach called *ressourcement* (literally "return to the sources") was pioneered in the 20th century by Cardinal Henri de Lubac as a way of engaging contemporary issues with patristic thought. In recent years the appreciation of patristic exegesis among Protestants has risen (Williams, 2005: 15), as indicated, for example, by the book series published by Baker entitled *Evangelical Ressourcement: Ancient Sources for the Church's Future*.

A practical problem for this method is the volume of past Christian reception. Some previous research in my field does consider tradition but takes a broad survey approach. For example, Richard Fagley sweeps through the whole of church history in sixty pages. David Yegerlehner considers nineteen Fathers of East and West from the 2nd through 5th centuries, as well as Aquinas, Hugh of St Victor, Luther, and Calvin. Jeremy Cohen, who focuses only on Genesis 1:28, covers Jewish and Christian reception from the earliest records up to 1500. These broad approaches result in brief summaries with minimal historical context. However, for my purpose, a narrow and deep approach is preferable.

This raises the question of criteria for the selection of past exegetes. Parris points to Hans Jauss's helpful metaphor which he describes variously as "der Gipfeldialog der Autoren" (summit dialogue) and as "der Höhenkamm der Autoren" (Parris, *Reception Theory* 216). The imagery is a high ridge of a mountain range where a few peaks define the basic shape of the skyline even though much irregular detail exists between them.[52] The idea is that typically a very small number of historical interpreters have been decisively significant in shaping and redirecting a text's reception (Parris, *Reading the Bible with Giants* 118, 202). My priority is to include one Early Church Father, as they have a special status in shaping distinctively Christian exegesis, and one of the 16th century Reformers, as many Protestants consider them formative, and even normative, for Christian exegesis. That the InterVarsity Press is publishing two book series on *Reformation Commentary* and *Ancient Christian Commentary* testifies to the special status of Reformers and Fathers for Protestant *ressourcement*.

The patristic representative chosen here is Augustine of Hippo. In a magisterial survey of ancient and medieval reception of the text "be fruitful and multiply," Jeremy Cohen judged that Augustine made the "single most extensive and influential contribution to the Christian career of Gen. 1:28," and that later writers up to 1500 added little that was novel to the interpretation of that verse (Cohen 21). The representative I chose from the 16th century Reformation is Martin Luther, who already features in this book as part of the effort to understand natalist reception and its roots; chapter 3 thus has a dual function. These two interpreters sit well together because Luther considered Augustine to be the best of the Church Fathers. Augustine is also the Father most respected by Evangelicals, the potential future audience of natalist preaching.

Contemporary context

The third step in evaluating reception is to consider the contemporary issues that provide criteria for evaluation and signposts for construction of alternative interpretation. Christopher Rowland advises that for "liberation theologians … the test for truth is the effect it has on people's lives" (Rowland and Corner

---

52 I find the phrase "summit dialogue" unhelpful as my initial impression from the phrase was of key interpreters meeting on a mountain-top, whereas Jauss' idea is a trajectory across history represented by an Alpine skyline that includes multiple summits.

42). Any of the various contextual approaches to biblical interpretation that have emerged recently might offer particular critiques of natalism, and I chose an ecological approach. A contextual interpretation must be grounded in Scripture and the Christian tradition before venturing beyond them. David Horrell advises that "to be potentially persuasive ... an ecological reading of the Bible would need to demonstrate that it offers an authentic appropriation of the Christian tradition" (Horrell, "Ecological Challenge" 168). He also suggests that while it will necessarily be "innovative," ecological exegesis should be "coherent (and in dialogue) with a scripturally shaped Christian orthodoxy" and must "learn critically from the history of interpretation" (Horrell, "Introduction" 9). In the final chapter of this book, my constructive ecological interpretation will draw on parts of the Bible beyond the fruitful verses, and further *ressourcement* from classic (mostly patristic) Christian writings. Horrell argues that "ethical appropriation is necessarily a constructive endeavour, informed by the present context (including science, etc.) as well as by the traditions" (8), and that final chapter will also reflect on how modern science offers wisdom for reception of the fruitful verses, drawing on insights from demography, ecology, and recent calculations of the human ecological footprint and its impact on biodiversity, human welfare, and economic sustainability.

In summary, the next chapter will provide an analysis of U.S. Protestant natalism since 1985. It looks at the context of wider modern natalism, and modern U.S. Evangelicalism. The bulk of the chapter is a detailed survey of biblical reception, and natalist arguments, in the primary sources. Chapter 3 will investigate the possibility that natalism has real roots in one strand of Protestantism, through a study of Martin Luther's writings in their 16th century context. After that analysis of natalism and its historical roots, the book moves on to three chapters which are three steps leading to an evaluation of natalism. Chapter 4 considers two dimensions of the context of Old Testament fruitful verses: first, the ancient Near Eastern historical setting with its agrarian, demographic, and political aspects; second, the canonical and theological context of the verses as part of a wider divine project for creating a holy nation. Chapter 5 sets Augustine's thoughts on reproduction and the fruitful verses in the context of 4th- and early 5th-century controversies, and then in *ressourcement* uses them to challenge natalist arguments. Chapter 6 constructively applies an ecological hermeneutic to the verses, bringing together Christian tradition and contemporary demographic and ecological awareness.

2. Protestant Natalism in the U.S.

History can be divided into periods before and after the decline of premature death, and especially the collapse of infant mortality. In the pre-modern period a community's survival required on average at least five successful births from each woman (Livi Bacci 156). Given that some experienced infertility, and that many mothers died prematurely (often as a result of childbirth), the remainder had to bear rather more. I will treat separately the attitudes toward fertility of three stakeholders: parents, national rulers, and religious leaders. For parents, especially fathers, the benefit of numerous offspring was obvious: for agricultural labour, domestic service, and support in old age. Cultural norms operated to encourage fertility, and a natalist ideology was only likely to be articulated in situations where the level of fecundity desired by other stakeholders diverged significantly.

Rulers had wider horizons than parents: they perceived rivalry between nations and a struggle for political existence or dominance. David Daube has shown that fecundity was often advocated by civic leaders, and occasionally promoted by laws. For example, Spartan rulers imposed financial penalties and disgrace on bachelors, and fathers of four sons or more were exempted from tax (Daube 13). The state wanted a surplus of sons for its army: Rome in 403 BC imposed a fine on unmarried men and Plutarch ascribed this to a need for children to replenish military losses (18). During the Roman Republic two Censors were responsible for updating the census, and in 102 BC one of them spoke "On the Need for Matrimony" to preserve the state (27). A century later, emperor Augustus "penalized childless men, whether married or not, and rewarded the prolific with tax exemptions," supposedly to save Rome from invasion (31). There was a particular worry about perpetuating the aristocracy, whose members often did not see much benefit in large families, and much of the Roman natalist legislation, which used inheritance penalties, was aimed at them. In societies with a dominant class, or ethnic

http://dx.doi.org/10.11647/OBP.0048.02

divides, state natalism was often aimed at a favoured group, and its flip side was a desire to limit numbers of another group, as reflected in the story of Pharaoh killing Israelite male babies (Exodus 1).

Pre-modern religions usually included elements of natalist ideology. For example, Sampradayas Hinduism allowed men to divorce infertile wives (Coward 140), and a verse in the Quran commends "women who are loving and very prolific for I shall outnumber the peoples through you" (Kaufmann 122). Partly this reflected the surrounding culture, and many texts promise fertility as one of the rewards for religious loyalty. In retrospect we can see ways in which some religious rules had demographic effects, but it is unsafe to assume the motive was demographic. Where contemporary explanation (the best guide available) survives, it usually points to cultic or moral reasons. For example, many religions forbade contraception and abortion but the reasons given were the sanctity of life (including seed), a father's rights, and concern about promiscuity. Demographic effects can be incidental to rules with other motives. One also finds religious rules whose effect is to reduce fertility. For example, to disallow divorce when one spouse is infertile reduces births because the fertile partner might otherwise remarry and reproduce. Similarly when young widows were encouraged not to remarry (as in early Christianity), or immolated at their husbands' funerals (according to the custom of *Sati* within early Hinduism), that curtailed the possibility of further reproduction during a second marriage. So though religions did sometimes reflect the familial and national desire for fecundity, other concerns were often more important.

Modern natalism

After the unprecedented modern decline in mortality rates,[1] combined with urbanization and longer schooling which made offspring less profitable, parents had less incentive to aspire to having a large number of children. There was now a larger gap between the goals of parents and rulers. Industrial barons' desires for plentiful and cheap labor should not be overlooked, but the stronger impetus came from rulers when they felt threatened by other nations, or when imperial ambition was ascendant. Episodes of natalism in France were stimulated by the humiliation of the Franco-Prussian war in 1870

---

1   For example, in England before 1740 the mortality of infants (under one year old) was 187 per thousand, whereas by 1780-1820 it had fallen to 122 per thousand (Malanima 39).

and the peril of the Great War (Camiscioli; Barusse). Later natalism in Italy was driven by nationalism. Benito Mussolini, the Fascist leader, lamented that "1929 marks the demographic collapse of the nation" (Ipsen, 1996: 173), and in 1937 his Grand Council claimed that Italy's most serious challenge was the "demographic problem ... as without life there is neither youth nor military strength nor economic expansion" (178).[2] Mussolini's 1928 essay *Numero come forza* (Strength in Numbers) argued:

> The birth rate is not simply an index of the progressive power of the nation ...
> it is also that which will distinguish the Fascist people from the other peoples
> of Europe as an index of vitality and the will to pass on this vitality over the
> centuries. (Ipsen 66-67)

Italy's new penal code in 1930 defined the sale of contraceptives as a "crime against the race" (74), and Fascist policies to reward mothers and provide maternal health care were financed by a special tax on bachelors (73). While speaking to "summarize Mussolini's population policy," a deputy of the Fascist government called for the "condemnation of bachelorhood" and also for the "condemnation of barren and low fertility marriages" (87).

In the U.S., the birth rate began falling around 1800 (Haines and Steckel 679) as a result of Christian people's decisions about marriage and parenting, and despite denominational rules against contraception. A gap between the reproductive ideals of people and rulers had appeared but leaders ignored it for some decades. Eventually fear prompted a natalist reaction because in some ethnic and religious groups fertility decrease had begun earlier or advanced faster, resulting in relative differences in rates of population growth. U.S. President Theodore Roosevelt warned old-stock Americans against "race suicide" due to low fertility. Their dominance within a growing U.S. population was demographically eroding due to higher fertility among recent immigrants (May 61). Roosevelt in 1907 claimed that in history "the wealthier classes tend to die out precisely because of the low birth-rate" and judged that those who "refuse to have children sufficient in number ... are criminals."[3] He affirmed that "the type to be standardized is not the family from one to three, but the family of four to six." In a 1905 speech, Roosevelt

---

2 In fact, though Italy's birth rate declined in the 1920s and earlier (Ipsen 183), its total population continued growing steadily because the death rate was falling faster. Presumably this growth was not fast enough for the nationalists.

3 Theodore Roosevelt, Letter to *American Monthly Review of Reviews*, 3 April 1907.

deemed the "man or woman who deliberately forego these blessings" to be as contemptible as the "soldier who runs away in battle."[4]

U.S. Protestant natalism in the early decades of the 20th century reflected the nationalist, racist, nativist, and eugenic ideas that many held at that time. For example, in 1905 *Lutheran Witness*, the journal of the Lutheran Church Missouri Synod (LCMS), approvingly reprinted Roosevelt's speech (Graebner, 1969: 309). Such ideas were not uniquely American: in England a report on contraception by the 1908 Lambeth Conference, the international assembly of Anglicans (Episcopalians), lamented "a decline in the birth-rate ... most marked among the English-speaking people, once the most fertile of races." They observed that in a typical U.S. city with immigrants from southern and eastern Europe, "two-thirds of the families belong to the native stock and one-third to foreign stocks; but of the children born two-thirds belong to the foreign stocks and only one-third to the native stock" (Davidson, *Lambeth Conferences* 399-400). These Anglicans warned of a "danger of deterioration whenever the race is recruited from the inferior and not from the superior stocks. There is the world-danger that the great English-speaking peoples, diminished in number ... should commit the crowning infamy of race-suicide, and so fail to fulfil that high destiny to which in the Providence of God they have been manifestly called" (Davidson, *Lambeth Conferences* 402). Natalism driven by eugenic concerns about nation, race, and religion was a mainstream idea among Protestants in the early 20th century.

For some, natalism coincided with anti-contraception, but these were separate ideologies. Most of the Protestant criticism of contraception in the late 19th century focused on the danger of sexual immorality and did not feature natalism. Anthony Comstock, the architect of U.S. laws (including a federal law in 1873) banning the distribution of contraceptives, was motivated to protect young people from vice and obscenity (Carlson, *Godly Seed* 27): many people were anti-contraceptive without being natalist. Conversely, a leader of the Evangelical Alliance, Josiah Strong, came to accept family planning as a eugenic necessity for poor people in the "Appalachian South," while maintaining a natalist ambition for civilized Protestants such as the "New England stock" to increase their reproduction to advance the Christianization of the world (cited in Carlson, *Godly Seed* 73). In moving away from anti-contraception, he was a forerunner of the modern natalists who permit family planning.

---

4   Theodore Roosevelt, "On American Motherhood," 13 March 1905.

Hiatus and renaissance

In the mid-20th century anti-contraceptive ideology and natalism both went into recession, and a consensus emerged that it was acceptable for parents to plan small families. At the level of denominational policy this change was pioneered by the worldwide Anglican Communion at the Lambeth conference in 1930. Eventually all the major denominations accepted the use of family planning by married couples (Goodson 355-56), including the Methodists by 1939 (in the UK, and by 1956 in the U.S.), the Church of Scotland in 1944, and the Dutch Reformed Church in 1952 (Spitzer and Saylor 459). Pius XII in 1951 permitted family planning for Catholics on condition that specific methods were used. The most conservative groups, such as the Lutheran Church Missouri Synod,[5] were slower. According to a 1953 survey, a quarter of LCMS laity were either unsure about or definitely opposed spacing children or limiting family size by any means, even by abstinence. However, by the mid 1960s most LCMS members accepted family planning (Graebner 327).

By the 1960s most Evangelical leaders also accepted family planning. At a symposium in 1968 sponsored by *Christianity Today* and the Christian Medical Society, 25 scholars produced a "Protestant Affirmation on the Control of Human Reproduction," which is an Evangelical consensus statement. It affirmed that "partners in marriage should have the privilege of determining the number of children they wish to have" (Spitzer and Saylor xxviii). Another section, entitled "The Christian in an Over-Populated World," stated that: "control of human reproduction demands the attention of Christians from the standpoint of the desperate needs not only of individuals and families but also of nations and people. This Affirmation acknowledges the need for the discriminating involvement of Christian people in programs of population control at home and abroad" (xxxi). The reference to human numbers and to overpopulation indicates that this was not only a change in attitudes to contraception, but also a shift away from natalism toward acceptance of smaller family sizes.

From the 1950s to the early 1980s, advocacy of large family size by Protestant writers was rare. In 1966 John Warwick Montgomery (a Lutheran), while arguing in favour of allowing family planning, also indirectly used the New Testament text Hebrews 2:10 in support of his natalist ideas:

---

5 Despite its name, the LCMS is not confined to Missouri, but is a confederacy of Southern Lutherans. It is the ninth largest U.S. denomination.

The burden of proof rests, then, on the couple who wish to restrict the size of their family; to the extent possible and desirable, all Christian couples should seek to 'bring many sons unto glory.' After all, as Charles Galton Darwin informs us, those who restrict their birth rate will ultimately be engulfed by those who do not: '*homo contracipiens* would become extinct and would be replaced by the variety *homo progenitivus*.' The Christian application of this principle is obvious. (Montgomery 582)

Natalist ideas derived from Old Testament verses featured in *Christianity Today* as late as 1960, with E.P. Schulze arguing that since the "command, 'Be fruitful and multiply' has not yet been repealed ... let the omniscient Father of us all determine the size of our families" (Carlson, *Godly Seed* 126). After that, one has to venture into Reconstructionism, a fringe movement seeking enforcement of Old Testament laws, to find natalist statements by its leaders Rousas Rushdoony in 1974 and Gary North in 1982. Charles Provan observed about this period that "some theologians spoke out against the limiting of children by Christians until fairly recent times. And now, opposition to birth control is almost dead" (Provan 3).

Then in the late 1980s the near-consensus among Evangelicals was breached. One natalist rejoiced in 1989 that "more articles and books are coming out agreeing with the teachings of Scripture on large families" (Morecraft 9-10). Tracing this development, Patricia Goodson identifies Pride and Provan as significant advocates who gained a hearing among conservative Evangelicals. She points to an issue of *Christianity Today* in 1991 which carried articles for and against family planning, as the breakthrough into the mainstream (Goodson 357).

Chapter 1 listed my primary sources, publications in English since 1985 in which natalism is a major theme and is supported with biblical citation and exegesis. It is appropriate to treat these as distinct from early 20th-century Protestant natalism, since they represent a renaissance after a long hiatus, among people whose parents had small families and accepted that as the modern norm. Sproul, the son of an influential Calvinist, confesses that "I began, like most modern evangelicals, believing that God had blessed the church with the gift of birth control ... to limit the size of our families so we can be about His work" (Sproul 42). There are qualitative differences: most of the old ideas and biblical citations are rehearsed, but new arguments and more Scriptures are now added to the natalist arsenal. Back then natalism could be found among Protestants in many European countries, but now it is distinctively North American.

Some critics find in today's U.S. natalism a revival of the nativist natalism of the early 20th century. For example, Miguel de la Torre observes Albert Mohler's lament that "we are barely replenishing ourselves" and argues logically that since the U.S. has had large annual natural increase in population (almost twice as many births as deaths back when Mohler made that claim), Mohler's "we" must be referring to whites and is "white supremacy code language" (Torre 103-05). I do not think so: Mohler's odd claim was probably based on his mistaken assumption that a Total Fertility Rate around 2.1 is equivalent to "barely replenishing." Monica Duffy Toft claims that in Quiverfull the "specter of 'race suicide' ... while rarely stated explicitly, infuses the rhetoric of the movement" (Goldstone, Kaufmann, and Toft 220). But in my view this characterisation misunderstands the new natalists. They dislike racism, and even nationalism is less prominent than it used to be. The natalist Allan Carlson judges these features of old Protestant natalism's character as "problems which a pronatalist policy must avoid" in future. He regrets that Missouri Synod Lutherans supported the race suicide scare in 1905, and that "churches have also fallen back at times on the nationalist temptation" (Carlson, "Be Fruitful" 28). Carlson considers that for Christianity (and for the other Abrahamic religions) these "nationalist and racial arguments contradict their universalist claims," and so "pronatalism is legitimate only as a consequence of their theologies: as a response to God's command in Genesis" (29). That is the new reformed natalism in a pure form.

Why did Protestant natalism revive?

Explanations of the natalist renaissance among U.S. Evangelicals, the timing of its rebirth, and why it flourishes in the 21st century can only be speculative. Natalism may be a reaction to the common questioning of traditional expectations about lifestyle. Watters suggests that until recent decades Protestant couples simply reproduced "on autopilot" (26) because they took for granted that marriage included rearing children. The proportion of married couples choosing not to have children has increased in the churches as well as outside. So the implicit and cultural methods of promoting fecundity among members have had to be reinforced by the articulation of explicit arguments for (higher) reproduction.

The competitive aspect of natalism is linked to perceptions of a culture war reflected in the rise of the religious right during Reagan's presidency (1981-89). Concerns persist about shifts in the relative sizes of different religious groups in the U.S., where in 1776 over 95% of the population was Protestant. Now it is about 50% and will probably fall to 37% by 2043. The change in recent decades has been due to rises in the categories labelled Secular and Latino Catholic (Skirbekk, Kaufmann, and Goujon 303). Immigration to the U.S. since 1980 has been at its highest level since the early 20th century, which coincidentally was the era of the old wave of natalism. More recently (since 2001), a different perception of Islam as a serious competitor to Evangelicalism, and a worry that the national characters of America's allies will be changed by relatively higher Muslim fertility (the "Eurabia" scare), have exacerbated the competitive mindset of some Evangelicals.

Perception of the efficacy of endogenous growth compared to evangelism may provoke natalism. Akin and Mohler confess that studying Baptist membership data stimulated their thinking on family size (Wax). Houghton cites the *World Christian Encyclopedia* (Houghton 77), in which church growth data is tabulated under two headings: "Conversion" and "Natural" (Barrett, Kurian, and Johnson). For the period from 1990 to 2000, global annual Christian increase is estimated as 2.5 million by conversion, and 22.7 million by natural means. The editors assume that natural increase is a factor "over which religious bodies have relatively little or no control" and that "rarely are they aware of it as a cause of their growth" (475). To the contrary, natalist writers are well aware of this factor, and they believe it can and should be influenced.

Particularly with regard to the anti-contraceptive ideology held by unlimited natalists, one event which contributed was the emergence of abortion as a moral issue for Protestants in the 1970s. Narratives by some women indicate there has been a conveyor from pro-life movements into the Quiverfull movement (Garrison; Joyce 140). Pride argues that the past acceptance of "limiting family size" was implicitly "refusing to consider children an unmitigated blessing" and led inexorably to the legalizing of abortion (Pride 75-77). French suggests that campaigning against abortion while permitting family planning is incoherent because both are anti-life practices that stem from "love of self" (French 51, 53), and predicts that anti-abortion campaigns will not succeed until they also embrace anti-contraceptive teachings.

So any attempt to explain the timing of the renaissance of U.S. Protestant natalist teaching should consider a combination of long-term trends affecting both church leaders and the married couples who are expected to deliver the babies. For the latter, average U.S. fertility had fallen in the 1970s to its lowest level, so the gap between the wider culture and church expectations was exacerbated at a time when church women were also delaying childbirth and finding new career opportunities. Meanwhile the leaders and visionaries became more concerned because of trends such as the culture wars, the polarizing of politics, and Protestantism's loss of demographic dominance within the U.S. population.

Reception of Christian Scriptures

Since the "primary object of the reception critic will be to study how the Bible actually has been understood" (Klint 91), I will give detailed attention to biblical citations in the primary natalist sources. To go beyond an impressionistic approach, every quotation and citation of biblical texts in support of a natalist argument was systematically catalogued in a database. The most popular text is "be fruitful and multiply," with 23 references to Genesis 1:28, a feature in all my sources.[6] The next most popular is Psalm 127:3-5, with 18 references. It is cited by seven of the sources. I also observe that brief online presentations of natalism which cite only one or two Bible texts usually choose one or both of these.

Some natalists limit themselves to a few verses, probably due to style and academic caution. Mohler frequently alludes to the Bible but makes few direct citations. For example, his article on "Deliberate Childlessness" mentions "His mandate revealed in the Bible" and asserts that "The church should insist that the biblical formula calls for adulthood to mean marriage and marriage to mean children." Most likely those are allusions to Genesis 1:28. The same short article has one biblical citation, of Psalm 127. R. C. Sproul devotes a chapter to Psalm 127 and also refers to Genesis 1:28. Allan Carlson, in three articles presenting Protestant tradition as natalist, eight times either quotes "be fruitful and multiply" or cites it, and alludes once to Psalm 127, commending "those who have opened their lives to bringing a full quiver of children into the world" (Carlson, "Freedom" 196; "Be Fruitful" 18, 21, 26; "Children" 21, 24, 25). Dan Akin asserts that "we do have a culture mandate to be fruitful and multiply" (Wax). In his "Axioms" sermon (Akin 15), Akin

---

6 There are also ten citations of its repetition at Genesis 9:1, 7 which natalists prize as an indication that the "Fall" did not nullify the imperative.

rebukes the idea that "less is better" and cites Psalms 128 and 127, as well as Deuteronomy 6:1-9 with regard to children's education.

Other natalists range widely across the Bible. The number of distinct Old Testament texts cited by each remaining writer is: 10 by Owen, 14 by Houghton, 18 by Provan, 23 by Pride, 29 by Watters, 34 by Heine, and 104 by Campbell. These sources between them refer to 157 distinct Old Testament texts.[7] Psalm 128, with its imagery of material prosperity, marital fecundity, and long life, is cited 9 times in five natalist sources.

> You will eat the fruit of your labor; blessings and prosperity will be yours. Your wife will be like a fruitful vine within your house; your children will be like olive shoots around your table. ... May the LORD bless you from Zion; may you see the prosperity of Jerusalem all the days of your life. May you live to see your children's children – peace be on Israel. (Psalm 128, NIV)

Deuteronomy 28:4-11, which includes fecundity among the blessings Israel will receive if they are faithful to God's commandments, is cited 7 times. "Blessed shall be the fruit of your womb and the fruit of your ground and the fruit of your cattle, the increase of your herds and the young of your flock" (Deuteronomy 28:4, ESV). Genesis 35:1-12, the Onan narrative, is cited 6 times but only by unlimited natalists.

There are four texts which appear four times each. Deuteronomy 7:13-14 promises a blessing similar to chapter 28, but adds: "You shall be blessed above all peoples. There shall not be male or female barren among you or among your livestock" (ESV); Jeremiah 29:4-6 urges those exiled in Babylon (perceived as relevant to Christians living in a secular country) to marry and increase; Psalm 112:2 is favoured by those linking fecundity and prosperity; and Malachi 2:15 is cited by those who want Christians to multiply. Five texts appear three times: a blessing of Abraham (Genesis 17:2); the blessing of Rebekah (24:60); a promise that "none shall miscarry or be barren" (Exodus 23:26, ESV); a prophecy of "more children" (Isaiah 54:1, NLT); and the value to kings of a large population (Proverbs 14:28). Of the remainder, 29 texts feature twice, and 109 texts only once.

Counting all citations in contexts of natalist argument across the catalogued sources, Old Testament references are four times more frequent than New Testament references. When compared to the relative sizes of the two Testaments, a ratio of 3.7 to 1, this suggests a usage which is nearly proportionate. That

---

7   As explained in the Appendix, citations of overlapped verse-ranges, for example 3-5 and 4-5, are merged for the purpose of counting distinct texts, and only count once.

was a surprising result for me, as after an initial reading of the sources I had judged that natalism was mostly based on the Old Testament, except perhaps for 1 Timothy 2:15 and 5:14. It shows the methodological value of systematic data analysis, which indicates that 42 distinct verse-ranges are cited from thirteen New Testament books. It is, however, beyond the scope of this book to consider natalist use of the New Testament, except where it is cited to justify their use of the Old Testament.[8]

Natalists defend their application of Old Testament verses to Christianity. Provan is aware that "some may think that we quote the Old Testament too much," and in response he observes the New Testament has "1600 references" to the Old, and that "Paul gets his rules on sexual matters right out of the Mosaic Law" (Provan 3). Sproul, in support of his claim that Old Testament ordinances are not abolished for Christians (Sproul 8), cites Matthew 5:18: "not an iota, not a dot, will pass from the Law until all is accomplished" (ESV). The dispensational distance between the Old Testament and Christianity is discussed by the writers, and some minimize this. Campbell argues that in general the "truths ... in Genesis are never altered throughout the rest of the Bible, only enlarged upon," because we do not have "a God who changes His mind halfway through His written word" (Campbell 22, 116). Though most admit that some details of instructions in the Old Testament are inappropriate for Christian application, they claim that paradigmatic biblical principles are unchanging and that marital fruitfulness is one of those principles.

Some natalists admit the New Testament presents a new spiritual conception of fruitfulness, children, and family. Watters acknowledges the New Testament shift in emphasis, as the "focus on physical children and physical fruitfulness prior to the coming of Christ gives way to spiritual fruitfulness," but also argues that "Christ's coming" did not "undo the marital design for physical children" or "nullify the call to be fruitful and multiply" (Watters 40). The imperative to biological fruitfulness therefore continues in parallel with spiritual fruitfulness. On Jesus saying "go and bear fruit" (John 15: 16), Campbell comments that "God longs for fruitfulness and increase in the natural and in the spiritual sense" (Campbell 33, 48). This principle of physical fruitfulness continuing alongside, rather than being superseded

---

8   Much natalist exegesis of the New Testament depends on ideas derived originally from the Old Testament. For example, identifying refusal to reproduce as an aspect of the lifestyles encompassed by Romans 1:26, where "females exchanged the natural function for that which is against nature," depends on arguments from Genesis 1-3 about the natural order of creation demanding reproductive performance.

by, a New Testament spiritual understanding enables natalists to make use of many New Testament verses, but it is dependent on the foundation of their Old Testament reception.

All the natalist writers affirm that the Bible is inerrant as a guide for conduct. The scripture is "profitable for life" (Sproul 7), and it "tells us how to live" and so "we must follow His instructions" (Owen 29). Chronological and cultural distance between ancient and modern worlds is acknowledged but they all conclude that marital fecundity is an enduring principle. Andrews disagrees with "those who say the Bible was written long ago to ancient agrarian people in a patriarchal society … [and] cannot be applied literally today" (Andrews 361). He allows that applications may vary but insists that the "moral standards are timeless" (362). Heine sees enduring relevance in the "Hebrew family model" (Heine 83). Most natalists admit that in pre-modern cultures rearing children was more economically profitable than it is in U.S. cities today, though Campbell resists this contrast by pointing to God's parallel promises in Deuteronomy (28: 2-4) of fertility "in the city" as well as "in the field" (44; also in Houghton 35). Heine explicitly bridges the gap between ancient and modern, urging that "Christian couples should treasure their Old Testament heritage … that prizes fertility for the perpetuation of family name" (Heine 84).

Old Testament scholars are quoted within discussions of modern application. For example, the comments by Johannes Pedersen on Psalm 127, reflecting on the Israelites' affirmation of "the satisfaction and permanence of building a posterity" and their belief that "to fail to have children, therefore, is the destruction of the house" so that "he who has no progeny labours in vain," are quoted by Heine (72).

Appeals to tradition

Natalist appeals to authority are mostly to the Bible, but also to tradition. When the interpretation of Scripture is disputed, Protestant tradition becomes important. The historical Christian writer most often cited in support of their arguments is Martin Luther, and chapter 3 will focus on natalist appropriation of Luther as a case study of their use of tradition. Elsewhere in Protestant tradition, natalists find support for the argument that (home) economics should not constrain family size. Campbell quotes Matthew Henry (1662-1714), who assured his readers that "He that sends mouths will send meat" (Campbell 136). Hess quotes Adam Clarke, a Puritan theologian (1760-1832), who reasoned that since "God gives children," therefore also "he will feed them … supporting them by a chain of miraculous providences" (Hess 82). Pride quotes John Kitto (1804-54), an Anglican missionary, who rebuked those who do "not trust God to pay us well for the board and lodging of all the little ones He has committed to our charge" (Pride 36).[9] However, the historic emphasis was on admonishing parents to refrain from worry about money, rather than a call to increase reproduction. For example, in context Matthew Henry observes "they are continually full of care, which makes … their lives a burden. All this is to get money" (on Psalm 127).

Quotations from other historic Protestants are largely confined merely to arguments against contraception, which is peripheral to natalism. In this connection, Campbell quotes two early 20th-century Lutherans: Walter Maier and F.H. Knubel, a past President of the United Lutheran Church (Campbell 157). Provan also quotes from many Protestants, though except for two Lutherans most are concerned with immorality rather than demographics. One is John Fritz (1874-1953), the Dean of Concordia Seminary, who in his 1934 work *Pastoral Theology* judges that "the one-, two-, or three-children family system is contrary to the Scriptures; for man has no right arbitrarily or definitely to limit the number of his offspring … Gen.1:28; Ps.127: 3-6; Ps.128: 3-4" (Provan 71). The other is Theodore Laetsch (1877-1962), who offers as an argument against family planning that "it undermines the State. It is race suicide" and therefore "at least four children to a family" are required from Protestant marriages (78-79).

Early and medieval Christian writers are cited far less than the Protestants. Augustine of Hippo features (Houghton, 2007: 55), as does Clement of Alexandria (French 32), but only for the topic of anti-contraception. More generally, Pride assumes that "through all ages of the church … believers … were happily having as many children as God gave them" (59). Campbell points to "traditional wedding vows" according to which marriage is "ordained for the increase of mankind" (13), and Watters cites an Anglican liturgy which states that marriage "was ordained for the procreation of children" in support of arguments about the order of creation (38).

---

9 The suggestion that Christian families will always be guaranteed sufficient resources is challenged starkly by historical famines affecting Christian people, for example in Ethiopia in 1984. The benefits of family planning in contexts of global poverty is affirmed by international ministries, as reported by the umbrella group Christian Connections for International Health (www.ccih.org). In the U.S., a coalition of progressive Evangelicals similarly affirmed in 2012 that "Family planning protects the health of women and children" (New Evangelical Partnership for the Common Good).

Secular tradition also is occasionally cited. Watters, arguing that marriage's purpose is reproductive, cites the derivation of the Latin word *matrimonium* from motherhood (38). In support of the idea of "natural function," Campbell claims that the word woman derives from "womb-man" (105).[10] This confidence that etymology is relevant implies a belief that pre-modern people (even non-Christians) understood divinely-created human nature better than modern liberal Americans. Heine notes approvingly that "history records many examples of pro-natalist government policies" (Heine 220). Owen observes that "until recently the world was for the most part pro-fertility," and he cites ancient Persia, China, and the Celts as examples (Owen 16). He suggests that in the modern era, secular humanism and a "control mentality" led to low fertility (16-17). The perceived pedigree of family planning is significant: Heine suggests it "was pioneered by humanists" (111). Provan claims that family planning did not begin in churches but among "pagans like Margaret Sanger" (39). Historically, this is incorrect because Margaret Sanger began campaigning in 1914, whereas smaller family sizes had already become common in the U.S. decades earlier, within a largely Christian population.

Contours of Protestant natalism

In the first chapter I distinguished between ordinary natalists who accept the use of family planning and the hybrid anti-contraceptive natalists who do not. This corresponds to the distinction suggested by Doriani between unlimited and large-but-limited views about family size.[11] I categorize my primary sources accordingly, and one issue investigated in this chapter is the differences and similarities between the two types of natalist, in their biblical reception and arguments. Natalists who allow family planning distance themselves from those who do not. For example, Mohler in a 2004 article on "Birth Control" advises that: "Christian couples are not ordered by Scripture to maximize the largest number of children that could be conceived."

---

10 He is wrong: woman derives from the Anglo-Saxon *wifman*.

11 Doriani places his own view in the large-but-limited camp, though he goes no further than urging "at least two, if possible" and "as many as the fabric of our life allows" (Doriani 33) so he is a mild natalist. The primary motive of his article is pastoral criticism of the unlimited ideology.

Large or unlimited, but not maximized

A theoretical maximum fertility can be derived from the typical duration of childbearing potential, around thirty years, and the time between pregnancies. After infertility and miscarriages are deducted, a population's maximum average fertility has been calculated at 15.3 (Bongaarts and Potter 92). By contrast, the highest fertility recorded in a people group is 8.9 among Hutterites in North America around 1950. To achieve maximum fertility would require the removal of all moral and physical constraints. None of the natalist writers advocates maximal fertility. For example, none requires a spouse with an infertile partner to divorce and remarry (unlike in early Judaism). None condemns breastfeeding (which suppresses fertility), and some commend it. None calls for the legal minimum age at marriage to be lowered, and some suggest a higher minimum.[12] None prohibits lifelong singleness. Many reject IVF and other fertility treatments. Some favor home births, and a few disdain interventions by gynaecologists (Joyce 164), which may slightly increase natal mortality and so reduce the birth rate. None advises that a foetus predicted to be unlikely to survive should be aborted quickly to make room for a fresh pregnancy (143). Clearly other agendas also move these writers, and while some ideas complement natalism others constrain fecundity. These impinging issues include affirmation of lifelong monogamy, the rights of unborn babies, agrarianism, a preference for whatever is natural, and even the acceptance of some romantic and individualistic ideals about choosing a partner.

Advocates of unlimited fertility use the slogan "let God plan your family" and reject the labels unlimited and unplanned, since they argue that God plans and limits their family sizes by direct intervention. The labels should be taken to mean that they oppose human planning by parents. French replaces the label Quiverfull with the term Quiver$x$ based on the use of x in algebra for unknown quantities because "we don't know how many children we will have" (French xi). That may be true when "we" refers to one couple, but in aggregate the number of children born to each woman practising unlimited fertility is statistically distributed, and the birth rate is predictable. There

---

12 For example, in a 2008 episode of the reality TV series *17 Kids and Counting*, the Keller family decide that a daughter must be aged 20 before marriage (Mesaros-Winckles, 2010: 13).

have been no demographic studies confined to U.S. unlimited natalists. The many studies of pre-modern examples approximating to "natural fertility" come from various cultures. Amish and Hutterite data from the early 20th century is nearest to our case,[13] as their fertility was unlimited by contraception but constrained by Christian norms for marriage and morality, and their maternal and prenatal mortality was closer to modern than to pre-modern levels. Amish women born in the first quarter of the 20th century had a TFR of 7.7 (Greksa 195).

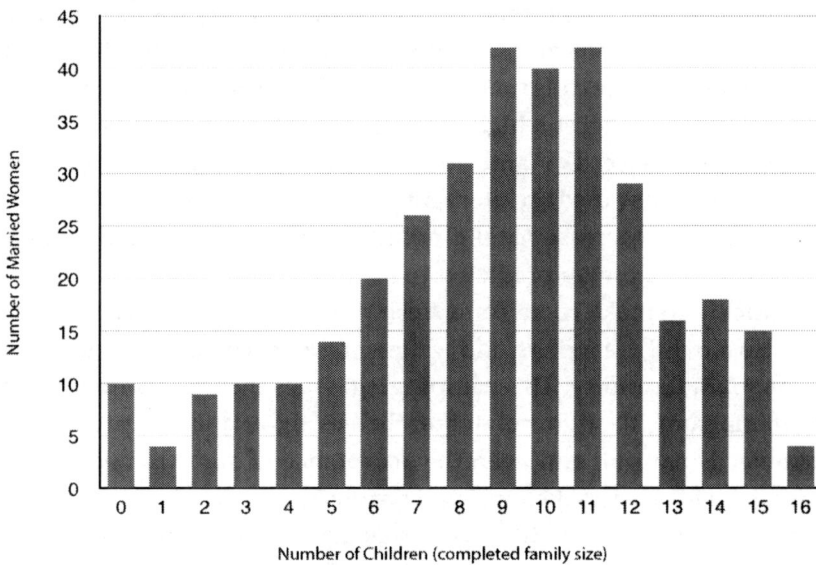

Figure 5. Children ever born to Hutterite married women aged 45 or older in 1950. Data from a 1950 survey by Eaton and Mayer.

This graph of a 1950 survey by Eaton and Mayer of Hutterite women aged 45 or older (and therefore showing completed family size) indicates that bearing eight to eleven offspring was common (Lang and Gohlen 395).

More recent Hutterite data, after they had begun reducing their fertility, indicates that family sizes of five, six, and seven are the most common. Many have eight or nine, and significant numbers have any sizes up to thirteen, but

---

13 By the mid-20th century Hutterites and Amish began slightly reducing their fertility, so later data is not quite as useful a guide to Quiverfull outcomes (K. White, 2002).

few have more than that. Very few only had two children, and only children are vanishingly rare (Kosova, Abney, and Ober).

The fecundity of adherents of the unlimited approach arguably does not prove a natalist motive. French argues that "the goal is not to have large families, though we acknowledge that a large family can often be the result" (French, 2006: 16). They claim to have turned all decision-making over to God, although to be sexually active (without using contraception) is in itself a decision, and the results are predictable within a population group. More tellingly, those claiming to be neutral with regard to family size deploy explicitly natalist arguments in favour of large numbers of children elsewhere in their writings, as will be evident later in this chapter.

How many children?

The advocacy of increased or unlimited reproduction is natalist regardless of whether or not any particular number or range of numbers is specified as an ideal family size. Among the sources surveyed, Pride, Owen, and Watters never mention numbers. French takes care to advise readers that having nine children is not "more sanctified" than having one child and "no family size is better than any other" on condition that parents are letting God plan their family (16). In other writers one can discern varying expectations about family size. Some are ambivalent, in one place distancing themselves from numerical advocacy, but elsewhere mentioning a range of family sizes which they clearly regard as desirable.

A small family size with just one or two children is disapproved of by some natalist writers. Charles Provan discerns that "God views childlessness or less children than possible as a negative occurrence, something which he uses as a punishment" (Provan 9). Houghton considers that because it has a Total Fertility Rate (TFR) of 1.5 Canada is "being unfruitful and subtracting" (28).[14] Campbell reads that God "makes families increase like flocks of sheep"

---

14 In fact, despite having a TFR below 2, Canada has more births than deaths each year. For example, in 2006/7 there were 360,900 births and 233,800 deaths (Statistics Canada), which *contra* Houghton is not "subtracting" but adding to the population. This illustrates a common misuse or misunderstanding of TFR. Replacement TFR refers to "generational" replacement: from each woman, one daughter surviving to adulthood. If lifespan (and other factors) stayed constant that would be the same as population replacement; but when lifespan extends, the number of generations alive simultaneously fractionally increases.

(Psalm 107:41, NEB)[15] and derives the argument that "one or two sheep is not a flock. God wants our families to be like a flock" (Campbell 41). She laments that "many have stopped at two or three children" (83): that extension to three of the range of family size deemed too small goes further than most natalist writers. At the grassroots level, perceptions of what is too few extend higher: the anthropologist Kathryn Joyce heard from a Quiverfull woman who had witnessed "meetings where she's seen mothers to a paltry quiver of three or four children weep and plead God to give them more" (Joyce 161).

Many advocates of unlimited reproduction do commend a large family size, and some favourably mention particular numbers. Hess rebukes those who "will not trust God. They may opt to be moderately fruitful and add instead of multiply" (123). Campbell quotes Jesus' words "bear much fruit" (John 15:8) that refer to spiritual fruit, but she argues "this is God's desire for the natural and the spiritual. 1 Corinthians 15:46 tells us that the natural comes first and then the spiritual" (Campbell 48). So it applies to the fruit of the womb as well as the fruit of the spirit: "When we are fruitful in our marriage, we are revealing a true picture of Christ" (49). With this dual application in mind, Campbell perceives a progression in chapter 15 of John's epistle from "fruit" to "more fruit," and then "still that is not enough," so Jesus calls us to "bear much fruit." She interprets this as a message that "God is not satisfied with average fruitfulness" (Campbell 48). In the multi-generational extrapolations of future growth which some writers present, the numbers chosen as a typical family size to use in the calculations are six (Pride 80; Hess 170), seven (Sproul 51), and eight (Hess 175). These numbers are realistic: they are roughly the median numbers of children to be expected with early marriage, unlimited fertility, and modern low infant mortality. These unplanned natalists are well aware of the range of family size normally expected.

The family sizes of Old Testament characters are also esteemed as models. Under a heading "the more the better," Provan points to the fourteen sons and three daughters of Heman (1 Chronicles 25:4). He also notes the eight sons of Obed-Edom (1 Chronicles 26:4-5) and the biblical remark that "God blessed him" (Provan 7). Houghton refers to those verses and also to 1

---

15 The context is about people who are hungry and poor gaining a place to settle (Psalm 107:36) and prospering. In verse 38, the verb *rbh* (to increase) conveys prosperity in general, which would include a large family. Verse 41 also includes the transition from poverty to prosperity: "he raises up the needy out of affliction and makes their families like flocks" (ESV).

Samuel 1:8, which he suggests indicates that "ten sons is a standard of great blessing" (Houghton 33, 32).

Unlimited natalists combat an oral tradition among (other) Evangelicals that ancient quivers held only a few arrows. Provan (8) opposes those who deem "three or five" a quiverfull. This idea apparently derives from ancient art, and Hess argues (correctly I think) that the artists simplified reality, and points to archaeological evidence for 12-15 arrows in a quiver, in order to refute the "mythical six-child maximum" (Hess 31). Though this might aim at demolishing an arbitrary limit rather than commending larger numbers, elsewhere the sources go further. Campbell argues that "we are in a war today and God needs arrows for His army ... When a warrior went out to war how many arrows would he want in his quiver? ... He'd want to squeeze in as many as he could" (79). These arguments seem to be aimed at other Christians (perhaps limited natalists) who read Psalm 127 in a similar way but seek to justify ceasing from reproduction after a certain number. In addition, the popularity in the unlimited camp of the label Quiverfull, with its numerical connotation, is suggestive of natalism being present alongside other values.

Advocates of limited (or ordinary) natalism rarely specify particular numbers but do present ideals about family size, and occasionally mention a typical number or desirable range. Calvin Beisner judges it "difficult to reconcile the present preference for small families – usually not more than two children per couple – with this Biblical view of children" as blessings (Beisner, *Where Garden Meets Wilderness* 182). Daniel Akin laments that "we have bought into the mindset of the modern world in that we think that less children is ... better," and he urges "pastors" to "point out that Psalm 128 talks about the beautiful gift ... God blesses the one who has a large number of them." He suggests "if you have one child as opposed to four, five or six, then you have a much smaller initial mission field" (Wax). They accept the number will and should vary depending on individual circumstances, but nevertheless they do recommend that couples aim for larger families than the contemporary U.S. average.

There has been criticism of natalist exaltation of numbers. A Baptist historian considers that Mohler's teaching "sounds like thinly-veiled Mormon theology, in which large families are a sign of godliness and ... part of the salvation equation" (Gourley). Also, narratives in Joyce testify to negative emotions among adherents who fail to achieve high fecundity (Joyce 180, 207). This highlights a problem in natalist practice, but natalist writers rarely claim that high fecundity is evidence of divine approval, though Nancy Campbell suggests that "God shows respect to us by multiplying us" (Campbell 35). Houghton warns his over-enthusiastic readers that we cannot "ascertain the degree to which God has blessed a family by simply counting the number of children" (84). Sproul similarly makes clear that "this does not mean that one can measure the level of favor one has with God by the number" of children (Sproul 49). Natalist practice may have this tendency if, by analogy with a crude version of the Protestant work ethic, children are evidence of one's character and election. Natalists, however, can reasonably respond that these are merely abuses which are inevitable among fallible human adherents.

Universal or ecclesiastical?

Who is called to high fecundity: is it particularly Christians or also people of other religions? Natalists do not speak with one voice on this question. One writer, Allan Carlson, consistently advocates universal application. Though his arguments mostly concern social welfare, economics, and demography, he also includes exegesis of texts from Genesis 1-11 and points out that the "admonition" to multiply "occurred well before" anyone began to "call on the name of the Lord" (4:26) and that Genesis "shows the family as pre-existing the church" (Carlson and Mero 86). This blessing is Adamic and he claims it was not lost or superseded by the Abrahamic blessing or any later covenant. I call this "universal" natalism.

For some writers the blessings are not oriented to reproduction by unbelievers, but are only for Christians bearing godly offspring. The clearest advocate of what can be labelled "particular" or "sectarian" natalism is Mary Pride who asserts: "Scripture draws a fundamental distinction between the children of the righteous (of whom there are never enough) and the children of the wicked (of whom there are always too many)" (Pride 63). Heine similarly asks rhetorically, "is it the church or the Hindus who have inherited God's promises to Adam and Abraham to be fruitful and multiply and subdue the earth?" His answer is the church, and he claims for Christianity both the Adamic and Abrahamic blessings. Heine warns about Muslim fertility, writing that "Christianity's biggest competitors have no qualms about bedroom-based growth programs" (Heine 9). For these writers it is appropriate that exhortations to high fecundity are aimed only at Bible-believing Christians.

Many of the writers do not explicitly confine the scope of natalist exhortation to Christians. I turn to implicit evidence. For example, Provan qualifies his slogan "the more children the better" in another place as "the more children a believing couple has, the better" (Provan 8). Others address Christians and refer only to Christian fecundity: a useful test would be to ask them whether they want higher Muslim fecundity. Daniel Akin worries about the relative difference in birth rates between diverse groups in Europe and warns that "Muslims will simply, by a natural process, outnumber the white Europeans" (Wax). Leaving aside Akin's confusion of religion and ethnicity, this suggests that his natalism is not of the universal type. In most of the natalist sources the focus is on reproduction by Christians.

A sectarian motive is implied where one argument for natalism is competitive advantage. Hess quotes Psalm 105:24 where God "caused His people to be very fruitful, and made them stronger than their adversaries," portraying fecundity as a path for Christianity to gain political power in the U.S. (177). Pride estimates the number of genuine Christians and then calculates that if every such family in the U.S. had six children while other families had only one, the nation would soon become predominantly Christian (Pride 80). The imagined Other in the U.S. are secular liberals, but globally there are different others to compete with demographically. Campbell claims that Muslims are "the fastest growing religion in the world through their birth rate" and urges readers to gain a "vision to invade the earth with mighty sons and daughters" (197). French anticipates that by having bigger families "we will be able to overwhelm the enemy by sheer numbers" (56). All such hopes depend on Christian fecundity being persistently greater than others' fecundity, which suggests their natalism is of the "particular" or sectarian type.

Survey of natalist arguments

Religious natalist arguments can be placed in two categories that I label extrinsic and intrinsic, and which might function as "carrots" and "sticks." The latter are claims about duty and obligation deriving either from God's commands, or from a wish to conform to God's purposes as revealed in the Bible and the order of created nature. However it is not all duty: the extrinsic arguments purport to show the various ways in which additional offspring are beneficial to parents, siblings, the church, and their nation. Sproul claims that additional offspring are real benefits for the recipients: "We do not begrudgingly leave the size of our family in God's hand because he says children are a reward and it would be insulting ... to say 'No thank you.' Rather ... they are actual blessings" (Sproul 48).

More blessings

The most common natalist argument is that parents should welcome additional blessings. Writing in the *Journal of Biblical Manhood and Womanhood*, Presbyterian pastor Tim Bayly argues that since "Christians are to seek God's gifts and blessings, our fundamental attitude toward the gift of babies should be to pursue – not reject – them." Limited and unlimited natalists develop this in different directions. Heine, while affirming that "In a general sense ... the more children, the bigger the blessing" (30), accepts some "valid reasons" why parents want smaller families than in the past, including "extended education" (25). Unlimited natalists, however, push the blessing further: Doug Philips asks rhetorically whether "children cease to be a blessing after a certain number" (Houghton: xv). Charles Provan has a clear answer, that "children are a blessing from God: the more the better" (7).

The general principle that additional quantity equates to greater blessing is defective. Even the Old Testament has a concept of surfeit which, though never applied to human fertility, suggests that excess of one kind of blessing can be detrimental to other blessings. Sleep is a blessing (Psalms 127:2), but an excess causes poverty (Proverbs 6:10-11; 24:33). Conversely, wealth is a blessing, but "the abundance of a rich man permits him no sleep" (Ecclesiastes 5:12, NIV). In the life of each individual and each community different kinds of blessing should be in balance. Acquisition of too many "blessings" may damage long-term interests, may even lead one to ignore God who is the source of all blessing. Israel is warned to "beware that you do not forget the LORD ... when your herds and flocks multiply ... and all that you have multiplies" (Deuteronomy 8:11-14, NASB).

The meaning of blessing is transformed in Christian tradition. In the New Testament, the word translated as blessing refers to salvation, as in 1 Peter 3:9 where "inherit blessing" has an eschatological referent. Westermann surveys the wider semantic field of blessing and argues that a few New Testament verses retain the Old Testament material references (*Blessing* 79, 85, 90). For example, blessing still applies to the maturing and health of the child Jesus (Luke 2:52). Blessing in the New Testament, however, is never applied to marriage or childbearing. In any case, Westermann agrees that the primary reference of blessing is now spiritual. Insofar as material prosperity persists as an aspect of blessing, it is transferred from the genetic kin group to the church as spiritual family. Now its "recipient was the community assembled for worship" (Westermann, *Blessing* 47). This speaks against a universalist type of natalism. For the church, it suggests that the emphasis should be placed on blessings and prosperity which are spiritual. Peter Cotterell warns that in prosperity theology "promises appropriate to one covenant are imported inappropriately into the second" (20). Natalist interpretation deserves a similar rebuke.

Blessing to families

Natalists claim that large families help siblings, parents, the church, and the nation. Children benefit in moral development, natalists argue, from having many siblings. They have "many more opportunities to learn to share" (French 91). Tim Bayly praises "the unique ability of large families to pass on some of the greatest of human virtues: sharing, helping, listening, being patient, giving up one's individualism for the sake of the group" (Bayly 15). The extreme case is a family in which parents have just one child. Bayly wonders "what effect will such a drastic decrease in the size of our families have on the moral development of our children?" (15). Nancy Campbell quotes Psalm 68:6, "God sets the solitary in families" (NKJV),[16] and argues that one meaning of the text is that "He will bless an only child by giving them family" (Campbell 41). The implication is that it is ungodly for parents to deprive an only child of a sibling by deliberately limiting their reproduction.

This amounts to a religious version of a widespread cultural prejudice, drawing upon a modern Western myth of the maladjusted only child. That stereotype is challenged by Bill McKibben in his book *Maybe One?* The myth began in the U.S. in the 1890s, and has persisted despite research findings that only children are not less sociable or more selfish than children with siblings (20-45). And whereas there is no systematic difference in terms of moral and social development, Judith Blake found that on measures of achievement children do better the fewer siblings they have (Blake, 1989: 73). From data that included families with seven or more children, she concluded that "contrary to any romantic notions ... about life in large families, the outcome measures we have used do not recommend family groups of this size as childrearing units" (6).

---

16 The last word, *bayit*, can refer to a house or dwelling and is taken that way in some translations of this verse, for example: "God settles the solitary in a home" (ESV), and "God gives the desolate a home to dwell in" (RSV). The word translated as "solitary" could refer to an only child, an orphan, a childless woman, or the homeless. In context, it probably refers to wandering Israelites or scattered exiles becoming settled in a homeland.

Material benefit from the labor of additional offspring is claimed by a few natalists. Craig Houghton observes that "older children in the family can be of great assistance in the functioning of the home ... in a variety of chores" (Houghton 80). Nancy Campbell quotes "my children have gone from me, and they are not; there is no one to spread my tent again and to set up my curtains" (Jeremiah 10:20), and suggests that "the more children we have the more help we have around the home." She mentions a mother who lives near her and has nineteen children, with ten still at home: "she trained them well and confesses that she now lives like a Queen" (Campbell 74). But domestic work alone does not offset the cost of children to U.S. parents, and even if agrarian or workshop tasks are available, the time required for compulsory education makes it difficult for parents to profit. USDA, the Department of Agriculture, estimates direct spending per child up to age seventeen to be above $150,000 even for low-income families (Lino, 2012: 14). If the opportunity cost of lost wages is added, the total is nearer a million dollars (Longman, 2004: 73). In the ancient agrarian context, a child that survived to adulthood yielded a net economic gain for parents, a material blessing, but in the U.S. today that is unlikely.

Elderly parents benefit from having many supportive children. Max Heine cites a verse in which "the women" rejoice with Naomi that her newborn grandson will be the "nourisher of your old age" (Ruth 4:15), and he claims that "grown-up children ... still can be today the best insurance available" because they "provide housing, food, fellowship and basic care" for elderly parents (Heine 232). Al Mohler warns people with few or no children that they are likely to suffer when they become old ("The Real Population Threat"). The underlying assumption is that elderly people will be cared for by their biological offspring – and because some children may fail to live up to that obligation, it is safer for parents to have a larger number.

Contrary to natalism, the idea that each person needs their own children to care for them in old age has never been generally applicable, not least because in the pre-modern era between 5% and 8% of marriages were infertile (Eijkemans 1307), while in medieval Europe more than 10% of women never married. So spreading responsibility among a wider kin or social group has always been essential for the care of the elderly. The New Testament affirms a wider vision: for example, Jesus on the cross entrusts his mother's care to a disciple (John 19:26) and not to any of his relatives. Similarly, early congregations looked after widows (Acts 6:1; James 1:27) on the basis of their membership of the body of Christ and regardless of whether or not they were genetic kin. The modern welfare state universalized and secularized the pattern of caring for all the elderly as a national responsibility.

Ancestral lineage and dynasty

Continuity of lineage is presented as another benefit, which can be divided between concern for long-range lineage and desire for grandchildren (which is qualitatively different because the grandparents are alive and interacting with living children). Campbell claims that Psalm 128:6 teaches that parents have a duty not to "deprive our parents of their reward and glory in their old age ... grandchildren" (202). Heine observes that "grandchildren are the crown of the aged" (Proverbs 17:6), and he urges parents to try hard to provide them (230). This chimes with the wider culture as most people who have adult children do want to engage with grandchildren while they live, but have less concern for lineage.

Natalists argue for perpetuation of family name, which implies a requirement for male descendants. Heine claims that a "family name can signify a personalized embodiment of God's physical and spiritual blessings," and he points to the biblical custom of marrying a dead brother's widow to save his lineage (Deuteronomy 25:6). Heine does not suggest anyone follow that custom, but he uses it paradigmatically to show the importance of perpetuating a man's name (76-79). Campbell cites Isaiah 66:22 to support her claim that "it is important to have children to carry on the family name" because it "guarantees the future" and the "family lineage" (Campbell 93). She observes that "it is not as easy as you would think ... it took fifteen grandchildren before we got one to carry on the family name!" (97).[17] It is true that ancient Israelites were concerned about family name: it was part of a set of ideas, to be explored in chapter 4, that valued past lineage and venerated ancestors. The question is whether Christians should imitate this.

A duty to one's parents and forefathers to continue their lineage was normal in pre-modern cultures, but was challenged by early Christianity. Saint Basil the Great (one of the Cappadocian Fathers, and a key developer of the Nicene Creed) identified the social instinct to build one's dynasty as a bad habit which Christians must break (Brown 291). Roman fathers arranged marriages to safeguard their lineage, but Ambrose, bishop of Milan, celebrated

---

17 Campbell's experience illustrates why a concern for family name, in effect a son preference, has large demographic consequences.

those young people who resisted parental pressure to marry. He urged their peers to "conquer family loyalty first" (Brown 344). An early hagiography, the *Life of Thecla,* portrayed pagans opposing preachers of resurrection with the riposte that "true resurrection" is simply "the succession of children born from us, by which the image of those who begot them is renewed," for these replicas "move among the living, as if risen from the dead" (Brown 7; ANF 8.488). Two different visions of how to achieve immortality were clashing.

Tertullian, aiming primarily at childless widowers who wanted to remarry, rebuked those "who go in quest of offspring!" He was appalled "that Christians should be concerned about posterity ... Is a servant of God to hope for heirs, when he has disinherited himself from the world?" He and other Church Fathers quoted the biblical promise that "a childless man has an everlasting name" (Isaiah 55:5). Tertullian asked disapprovingly if a man seeks offspring "to perform the last rites over his grave!" (ANF 4.57). A major purpose of raising descendants was to ensure burial and memorial (Brichto 4), but Jesus told a potential disciple to "leave the dead to bury their own dead" (Matthew 8:21, ESV). The New Testament supports obligations for the welfare of living parents, but there is no duty to provide grandchildren, nor to perpetuate ancestors' genes. Ancient and modern visions of immortality through descendants are incompatible with belief in a personal resurrection.

A step beyond perpetuation of name is aggrandizement of the lineage. Women "built up the house" (Ruth 4:11) or dynasty by reproducing (Campbell 91). Philip Lancaster, editor of *Patriarch* magazine, urges that "each man should aim to be the founder of a dynasty for God" (93). Doug Phillips, the pastor of Boerne church and leader of *Vision Forum,* led five hundred participants with Geoff Botkin at a conference entitled "The 200 Year Plan: A Practicum on Multi-Generational Faithfulness" in 2008. Phillips predicted that those "men who father many ... will preside over a dynasty of thousands in four generations" (Kaufmann 95). That hubris preceded Phillips' fall in 2013.[18] Botkin forecasted that a man could become the "patriarch of 186,000 male descendants within two centuries" and, in an echo of Rebekah's blessing (Genesis 24:60), he reports praying over his newborn daughter that she will be the "future mother of tens of millions" (Joyce 217, 229). If the following generations accept their role (which is uncertain),[19] then such dynastic visions could have significant demographic consequences.

---

18 Doug Phillips led *Vision Forum* (www.visionforum.org) which closed in 2013.

19 http://kbotkin.com/2014/01/16/alone-yet-not-alone-in-a-sea-of-dominionism/

Building the church

Adult members of a denomination can be categorized by their origin: whether they are children of members or not. Some statisticians of religion make a distinction between two modes of recruitment: retention of those reared inside the church (also called endogenous or natural growth), and conversion of those reared outside (Johnson and Grim 114). Growth by conversion is implicitly discounted by natalists. "If the Christian birth rate matches that of secular society, every year the numerical gap between believers and unbelievers will increase. Every year our influence will dwindle," lament Rick and Jan Hess (166). That statement assumes a long-term negative rate of conversion, with the number of Christians' offspring choosing to leave the church greater than the number of converts coming in. Campbell observes that "some Christian couples ... do not want children" and warns that if all of them "took this attitude, Christianity would be wiped from the earth. It is our children who carry on God's word" (Campbell 37). That assumes a complete and persistent absence of any conversions from among the children born to non-Christian parents, and is symptomatic of the loss of confidence in evangelism evident among some natalists.

Others claim the evangelistic mode depends on the endogenous mode. The "most obvious way to raise more missionaries is to raise more godly children" (Hess 173), and so "by having more children" we are "contributing to world evangelism" (169). Again a mechanistic assumption lies behind this idea: that a constant percentage of offspring will become missionaries. A more radical natalist argument is that parenthood is in itself evangelism. Pride draws a comparison between two methods: "Missionaries go to foreign countries to beget new Christians; mothers get pregnant to beget new Christians" (Pride 57). She describes the latter mode as "maternal missionary work" and rebukes women with few children for "giving up our God-given role as the greatest evangelists" (81). Rick and Jan Hess imagine attending a missionary meeting where "you may hear" the classic threefold call: "you can pray; you can give; you can go!" They suggest that one might "stand up and boldly say 'And you can reproduce!'" (174). In churches whose teachings or culture do not encourage women to be evangelists or apostles (which are highly esteemed vocations), this portrayal of biological fecundity as "evangelism" presents motherhood as an accessible alternative religious vocation for women.

A related claim is that fecundity raises the probability of producing a special epoch-changing hero of faith. "Who can tell but that one special combination of genes will produce the greatest revival preacher" (Pride 77). Heine cites the text (from Isaiah 49:1-6) that "he made me a polished arrow; in his quiver he hid me away … who formed me from the womb to be his servant … as a light for the nations" (Heine 115). Christian tradition read that as a messianic prophecy, now natalists appropriate it for their offspring. Transformed from messianic to heroic it becomes a goal for parents, and French admits that "I am expecting a lot from my children" (French 60). However this probabilistic effort to raise the chance of generating a hero suggests a strange view of the Holy Spirit, who surely can do that regardless of the quantity of births, or even transform a convert born outside the church.

Natalists emphasize the endogenous mode of church growth. Tim Bayly suggests that "bearing and raising of children, then, may well be the most neglected method of evangelism today" (15). Notice the word "evangelism" taken beyond its traditional meaning again there. Samuel Owen is ambivalent: he distances himself from others' claims that "we should have as many children as we can so as to Christianize the world" (71), which he considers a dubious motive for parenthood, but he also states that reproduction has "vital and long-range implications for the church" and "will strengthen the corporate body" (128). Some natalist writers calculate potential growth generations into the future. Rick and Jan Hess imagine a church where each couple has eight children and, allowing for one in eight being called to singleness, calculates that such a church could increase "from 40 to 12,890 in three generations" (175). If this model of church growth were adopted across America then "we would be part of a replay of Exodus 1:7" (171), a reference to the Israelites multiplying in Egypt. The plan can only work if most descendants end up Christian. "God does not promise that all of our children will be Christians, but we see Him working that way very often in families" (170).

A few natalists give the impression that the offspring of Christians have an intrinsic spiritual quality different from other babies, for example claiming that "we are able to … reproduce spiritual children biologically" (Watters 41). Mary Pride asserts that the offspring of a Christian are "sacred" (Pride 22). These ideas are variously based on the designation of offspring as "holy" (1 Corinthians 7:14), on the hereditary covenant, and on the model of circumcision. However, if we consider the case of a Christian household with two infants, one of whom is adopted, unless natalists want to claim higher spiritual status for the natural infant over the other they must concede that biological reproduction *per se* offers no advantage. A stronger rationale, and one that appears far more often in natalist literature, is that the real goal is influencing children, and that biological parenthood secures custody and power over education.[20]

Large families do not guarantee endogenous church growth: that depends on most of those children growing up to become Christians. And achievement of the long-range multi-generational plans also requires that the aspiration to large family size is accepted by each generation. Transmission of beliefs is essential. Houghton offers a forecast of multi-generational exponential growth but warns that it will only happen if "example and teaching are passed along" (76). Wilson, Doriani, Watters, and Houghton all cite the verse fragment "what was the one God seeking? Godly offspring" (Malachi 2:15, ESV) in support of this point, and Owen quotes Proverbs 22:6, "Train up a child in the way he should go" (88). The revival of Protestant natalism began inside the homeschooling movement of which Mary Pride was a founder (she also edits *Practical Homeschooling* magazine). Many other natalist writers are homeschoolers: for example, the French family schooled seven children, and Houghton nine. Not all natalists are homeschoolers, but the importance of upbringing is always a key feature of natalists' beliefs.

As we have seen, natalists claim that the best way to bring people under the influence of Christianity is for Christians to give birth to them. For example, Al Mohler maintains that "Those who do not reproduce become, by default, less influential in the society. Meanwhile, those who do reproduce have the opportunity to inculcate their own worldview within their children" (Mohler, "Of Babies and Believers"). Historically, however, Christian influence on children has extended well beyond the relation conferred by childbirth. First, legal custody can be granted by adoption. Until the 20th century in most Catholic countries, abandoned babies (called "foundlings") were often donated to the church and, after initial rearing by wet-nurses, some were brought up by religious institutions until the age of fourteen. Though many were added to the church in this way, the rearing of foundlings was a response to need rather than a tactic for church growth. Also parents could, following the example of Hannah who donated her firstborn to God's service (1 Samuel 1:28), give a child to the church's service as an oblate. However,

---

20 Cultures vary, geographically and historically, in how much control is granted exclusively to biological parents. Others with customary rights to shape children may include tribal elders (as in initiation customs), close kin, or the nation-state.

in 656 AD the Synod of Toledo set a minimum age of ten since the spiritual formation of older children by religious orders was a better use of their time.

Beyond custody, a more direct way to achieve the goal of formative education was the day-school model in which the natural parents undertake to house and feed their children while the church focuses on providing their spiritual formation. This became by far the more common approach to religious upbringing: the foundation of Christian schools around the world inducted vast numbers of people into the church during the history of missions (Lewis, 2004: 165). From 1890 onward, in Uganda and other developing countries missionaries and indigenous Christians ran village schools teaching literacy, as well as high schools and seminaries. These contributed greatly to the rise of Christianity in sub-Saharan Africa and South Asia. The day-school approach was fruitful and prolific in adding to the Church.

A radical critique would question the primacy of training. Youthful formation or its lack do not determine salvation because of the Holy Spirit's freedom (John 3:8). Conversion is the only way to enter the church, regardless of ancestry. Eusebius of Caesarea in *Demonstratio Evangelica* discusses the question, "Why a numerous offspring is not as great a concern to us as it was" for the Old Testament patriarchs. Eusebius asks: "why were they keenly concerned with marriage and reproduction, while we to some extent disregard it?" The answer was that they "wished to hand on to posterity the fiery seed of their own religion … [and] They knew they could be the teachers and guides of their families." But the reasons for "the ancient men of God begetting children cannot apply to Christians today," considers Eusebius. He admits that reproduction was how God's people grew in the old covenant era, but now celibate "preachers of the word … bring up not one or two children but a prodigious number" by spiritual birth. The new way of Jesus is more effective, as Christians now are "multiplying daily, according to the divine commandment, 'Increase and multiply and replenish the earth' which in them is fulfilled more truly and divinely" through evangelism and teaching (157).

The actors in church-building are spiritual fathers and mothers, not biological ones. Karl Barth sees God as the only true father (see Ephesians 3:15; Matthew 23:9) and humans as reflecting true parenthood insofar as they teach the Gospel. Mission and discipleship from the older (in faith) to the younger is the essence of Christian "reproduction," and natural parenthood is just one aspect of that, which Barth calls "incidental" (Barth 244). New

Testament usage of parental and kin language indicates that the spiritual connection is primary, while the blood relation is secondary (1 Timothy 1:2,18; Titus 1:4; 1 Corinthians 4:15; Philemon 10). Jesus says that the disciples are new brothers, and conversely the biological family may be enemies (Mark 3:31; 13:12; Luke 14:26). Paul calls the Corinthians his children, and Barth judges this more than a mere figure of speech (244). Basil the Great similarly refers to the example of celibate older women who inspire young women's conversion as the "holy lineage" of faith (Brown 278).

Building the nation

Natalists argue that citizens have a duty to increase their nation's population by bearing children. The most cited verse in this connection is Proverbs 14:28, "A large population is a king's glory, but without subjects a prince is ruined" (NIV). Some natalists, including Campbell, favor this paraphrase: "A growing population is a king's glory; a dwindling nation is his doom" (NLT).[21] Either way, one might think Americans would not be worried as the U.S. not only has a large population (third after China and India), but also has faster growth than other developed countries, much of it driven by a substantial surplus of births above deaths each year. However, the worry is relative size by comparison with other nations, and future change. Campbell notes that in 1950 the "industrial democracies" constituted 22% of world population, but "if trends continue … we will only be 5% by 2100," and she quotes "a dwindling nation is his doom" (Campbell, 2005: 197). So a population that is growing in absolute terms is perceived as "dwindling" in relative global rank.

The other half of that verse in Proverbs 14 is also significant for natalists, "a large population is a king's glory" (NIV). This "king's glory" is interpreted in two ways. First, by democratic transfer, it becomes an attribute of the nation which gains importance through a large population. Second, it brings honor to God because outsiders will see how God blesses America. Campbell points to Isaiah 26:15 and quotes the NKJV, "you have increased the nation, O Lord … you are glorified" (44). However, that text probably refers to land, as other translations indicate: "you have enlarged the nation.

---

21 The change from "large" to "growing" is not strictly literal because the word is a noun, but the paraphrase is not too distant from the sentiment of the original.

You have gained glory for yourself; you have extended all the borders of the land" (NIV). Even the NLT, one reads that "you have made us great. You have extended our borders, and we give you the glory!"

Houghton cites the same verse to support his claim that "there needs to be a growing population, otherwise destruction looms" (Houghton, 2007: 34). The danger is from rival nations. Campbell notes that Israelites in the time of Solomon were "as many as the sand by the sea" (1 Kings 4:20-34). She observes that they "dwelt safely" in the land and points to a verse telling us Israel had 12,000 cavalry (Campbell 29), suggesting military strength through numbers. Some also worry about America's allies being less fecund than their enemies. Heine claims that those nations which "embody Western values are not replacing their own stock," which is ominous for "American strength and influence" (Heine 28) because supposedly antagonistic nations and religions are at the same time expanding their numbers.

Military language features, especially among some unlimited natalists.[22] French explains that "God gives us our children for a reason," which is to build "a righteous nation that will not falter in the face of enemy activity" (French 14). The nation here refers to the U.S. Campbell laments that "we have many enemies in the gates of our nation" and calls for more arrows (a metaphor for sons): "Where are the arrows to combat these enemies?" (Campbell 81). In context this probably refers to spiritual warfare, or to non-violent political conflict, but sometimes it is ambiguous. Heine is the only writer to explicitly find contemporary military significance in the metaphor of Psalm 127. He observes that arrows were weapons: "They killed enemies." He links them to both spiritual and literal warfare: "Is this to say we should reckon children as budding soldiers? Yes, but not merely in the military sense" because they are also spiritual warriors. Heine rejects the idea that numbers are not decisive in technological warfare by arguing that "nuclear weapons may threaten and deter, but it is warm bodies who perform the bread and butter of maintaining bases, fleets, and reserve units" (Heine 231). This is unusual: none of my other sources explicitly point to military might as a benefit of natalism. However, given their hermeneutic insistence that the material meanings of old promises remain true in the new covenant, persisting in parallel with spiritual meanings, the military interpretation is not ruled out.

---

22 Monica Duffy Toft, reflecting on Quiverfull, states that "militaristic language infuses the movement's rhetoric" (Goldstone, Kaufmann, and Toft 220).

Early Christianity did not teach any duty to perpetuate by reproduction the particular nation (or ethnic group) into which a Christian was born. The church superseded national loyalty, so now "there is not Greek and Jew ... barbarian and Scythian" (Colossians 3:11). A continuing plurality of nations is assumed in the New Testament (Revelation 21:26), but no particular nation-state is guaranteed continuity. For example, while discussing the various reasons why some childless widower men were still desperate for offspring Tertullian asked scathingly: "Is it, perchance, for the commonwealth ... for fear States fail, if no rising generations be trained up?" (ANF 4.57). He considers this an unworthy motive. However, after the modern rise of nationalist ideology, some church leaders did present the aggrandizing of their nation as a Christian duty, and natalists are heirs of that recent tradition.

Population and the economy

Alongside the role of birth rates in national survival, glory, and security, is a belief that a growing national population helps the economy. Natalists detect a link in Scripture between fecundity and national prosperity, and perceive a causal relation then and now. Campbell asserts that "a growing population is necessary for a successful economic climate," and she finds that "the Bible links these two factors together" (Campbell 30). She quotes the *Living Bible* version of Isaiah 29:23, "when they see the surging birth rate and the expanding economy, then they will fear and rejoice in my name." However, the link expressed in that paraphrase is not apparent in any reputable scholarly translation.[23] Pride claims that in the U.S., "centuries of healthy population growth have brought us a better standard of living" (Pride 60), and she cites Proverbs 14:28 again. Some argue that modern economic systems depend for their viability upon persistent population growth and that this confirms the latter is God's design. Heine claims that fecundity is a "blessing to the free market" (Heine 27). "When population growth is stagnant ... it undermines the entire economy," explains Heine, and he warns the "growth constant that has fuelled the dynamo of capitalism will be gone" if birth rates fail to rise (213).

---

23 *The Living Bible* is a paraphrase by Ken Taylor, the founder of Tyndale House Publishers. In the early 1970s, it was the best-selling book in the U.S. It was revised in 1996 as the New Living Translation, which expunges Taylor's more idiosyncratic translations, including this one.

This aspect of natalism has affinities with secular neoliberal economics. In particular, cornucopian ideology claims that population can grow indefinitely.[24] A leading theorist was Julian Simon, whose central argument was that the "ultimate resource" is human ingenuity which overcomes any constraint on material resources, and so moderate population growth assists economic growth and is sustainable.[25] Simon argued: "We now have … the technology to feed, clothe, and supply energy to an ever-growing population for the next 7 billion years" (Myers and Simon 165). One idea is that more people means more inventive genius to overcome ecological constraints. French offers this as a reason for seeking to bear additional offspring (85): "What if the Lord … gives you a future great scientist who finds a clean burning fuel that will help clear pollution?"

Calvin Beisner,[26] who was one of Julian Simon's students, provides the most systematic exposition of biblical arguments for the belief that population growth stimulates economic growth. Beisner's cornucopian idea is based on a particular construal of how human beings are images of God.[27] He observes others' concerns that population growth multiplies pollution and resource use, while discerning that the "vision of humankind that underlies these two concerns" is that "humankind is principally a consumer," whereas "the Bible gives us a very different vision of humankind" (Beisner, "Imago" 177). Beisner's first step is to identify creativity as an aspect of imaging God. His next step is to claim that this "different vision begets a different prediction: that people, because God made them in His image to be creative and productive," will create "more resources than we consume" (183). Therefore, "continued population growth will result not in the depletion but in the increased abundance of resources" (190). That, in brief, is the cornucopian fantasy.

Beisner, as a Calvinist, has to wrestle with an ancillary point: for his vision of the *imago Dei* as beneficial creativity to be economically relevant, it must be

---

24 The term cornucopia derives from the Latin for the horn of plenty owned by Amalthea, a goat-like Greek goddess who suckled the infant Zeus.

25 Simon (1932-1998) developed cornucopian theory in *The Economics of Population Growth* (Princeton: Princeton University Press, 1977); *The Ultimate Resource* (Princeton: Princeton University Press, 1981); *The Resourceful Earth* (New York: Blackwell, 1984); and with Norman Myers in *Scarcity or Abundance? A Debate on the Environment* (New York: Norton, 1994). He was Professor of Business at the University of Maryland.

26 Calvin Beisner is Associate Professor of Historical Theology and Social Ethics at Knox Theological Seminary, Fort Lauderdale, Florida. His doctorate (in Scottish history) is from the University of St Andrews.

27 The text "Let us make man in our image, after our likeness" (Genesis 1:26) is traditionally read as the creation of human beings in the "image of God."

vibrant in all people, or at least common and not limited to Christians.[28] He accepts Calvin's teaching that the image at the Fall was mostly effaced, but Beisner finds a solution by proposing that Christ has restored the *imago Dei* not only in Christians but also in other people. "Environmentalists assume that people are principally consumers and polluters; Biblical Christians assume that people are principally intelligent, well-meaning, creative producers and stewards, because that is what God made them to be and what He has been transforming them to be through the redeeming work of Christ" (Beisner, *Where Garden Meets Wilderness* 111). In a defensive footnote he clarifies that he is not teaching universalism (that everyone is saved), but instead making a distinction between salvation (for Christians) and the restoration of Christ's image (for other people). Beisner's distinction is a deviation from historic Calvinism. By contrast, Doug Wilson, another natalist Calvinist, avoids making the transformation universal, for although he repeats the cornucopian mantra he qualifies its scope: "when we are obedient to God, we produce more than we consume" (Wilson 123).

Other natalists, while not necessarily adhering to cornucopian ideology, consider that in contemporary America, in the context of a low birth rate, and an ageing population, higher Christian fecundity contributes positively to economic prosperity, and they see this as one way in which it is a real blessing. That perception is challenged in my final chapter. Moving on from the extrinsic material benefits of offspring and the duties toward family and society discussed above, the next section looks at intrinsic reasons for natalism that concern obligations toward God. However, the distinction is not absolute because obeying the divine will (as perceived by natalists) is often also presented as yielding rewards in this life.

Divine command

The imperative grammar of the phrase "be fruitful and multiply" is taken to indicate God's will for every married couple to seek to conceive offspring. Various terms are used to describe this imperative: command, instruction, order, mandate, ordinance, and call. Most authors use a selection of these terms as synonyms. Though the word "command" is more popular among unlimited natalists, it is also used by large-but-limited natalists, for example Al

---

28 Calvin Beisner affirms Calvinist doctrines. He is a "ruling elder in the Orthodox Presbyterian Church" (OPC) (www.ecalvinbeisner.com), which split from the mainstream Presbyterian church in protest at theological liberalism.

Mohler asserts that "Couples are not given the option of chosen childlessness in the biblical revelation. To the contrary, we are commanded to receive children with joy as God's gifts" (Mohler, "Deliberate Childlessness"). The word is only used by Mohler in the context of deliberately childfree couples, but others apply it more broadly, for example Tim Bayly writes that:

> God commanded Adam and Eve – and Noah as well – to be fruitful and multiply ... Throughout history Christians have acknowledged God's command "be fruitful and multiply" to be binding: for millennia bearing children has been viewed not as a matter of preference but as an act of obedience. (Bayly 15)

For ordinary natalists there is still an imperative to seek a large family, but contemporary application will vary depending on circumstances and how many children a couple already has. Owen claims that "the Fall has not eliminated God's commands. It has, however, created a tension between the ideal and its realization." Consequently, "in certain situations couples may be unable to comply" and then family limitation may be permissible (Owen 78). For them the original command conveys a paradigmatic principle, not an inflexible rule.

Unlimited natalists are less willing to allow for dispensational differences, and for them the command applies today as it did in the past. Provan argues: "Nowhere is this command done away with in the entire Bible; therefore it still remains valid for us today" (Provan 5). He points to the precedent of Exodus 36, where God commands items be brought for the tabernacle and later tells Moses they should stop bringing items as there are enough. This is interpreted as indicating that a norm that commands must be obeyed until an explicit countermand is given, for "he would let us know when the world was full" (42). Heine similarly claims the imperative has not lapsed, for "God put no expiration date on His order" (Heine 58).

Some natalists claim that a divinely spoken verbal countermand is required, but many Old Testament commands and laws have been deemed obsolete by Christians without any explicit repeal in the New Testament.[29] In any case the Church Fathers believed that clear guidance had been given about this command "be fruitful," because the choice by Jesus to not marry spoke loudly of a new dispensation. Barth proclaims that "*post Christum natum* the propagation of the race [humankind] ... has ceased to be an unconditional command" (Barth 268) and "the burden of the postulate that we should and must bear children ... is removed from us all ... Parenthood is now only to

---

29 For example, the law against garments mixing wool and linen.

be understood as a free and in some sense optional gift" (266). Reproduction is now not divinely commanded.

What and who is commanded, and when?

Early Judaism and early Christianity had a similar view of what "be fruitful" originally commanded. Given a belief that only God can "open the womb," it was not within human power to guarantee successful and prolific childbearing, so that could not be commanded. Instead it was a command to marry and fulfill conjugal obligations. An early Christian writer, Jerome, observed that "so long as that law remained, 'Increase and multiply' ... they all married" (NPNF2 6:344). It was a universal obligation. Post-biblical Judaism around AD 200 similarly interpreted "be fruitful" as a command to marry which was held to still apply: "a man is not permitted to dwell without a wife" (Cohen 134, citing Tosefta 8.4). Maimonides in the 12th century drew on earlier traditions in developing his rabbinic opinion: "When does a man become obligated by this commandment? If his 20th year has passed and he still has not married, he transgresses" (134).[30] A man sins if he evades this duty by remaining single. That idea is at least internally coherent, but it is incompatible with Christianity because Jesus "committed no sin" (1 Peter 2:22), so it cannot be a sin to follow his example of avoiding marriage beyond age twenty.

Surveys of early Christian writing (in East and West) find a consensus that the command to "be fruitful" was temporary and had been abolished (243, 37). For example, Tertullian says the new covenant "abolished the ancient command to increase and multiply" (ANF 4.40). Cyprian, a leading African bishop born around AD 200, observes that "the first decree commanded to increase and to multiply; the second enjoined continence" (ANF 5.436). Basil the Great wrote "to every one who is thinking about marriage I testify that, 'the fashion of this world passeth away' ... If he improperly quotes the charge 'Increase and multiply,' I laugh at him, for not discerning the signs of the times" (NPNF2 8:214). Jerome cites 1 Corinthians 7:29 and explains that "in accordance with the difference in time and circumstance one rule applied to the former, another to us" (NPNF2 6:344).

Natalists take a different path. For them "be fruitful" is not addressed to all humankind but only to married couples, and it is not a command to

---

30 Delay might be allowed for a Torah student, but not indefinitely.

marry but a command to reproduce. Provan calls Genesis 1:28 a "command to mankind" but immediately qualifies it as a "command to a married couple" (Provan, 1989: 5). He clarifies that it is "not an absolute command for all people, just married people" (41). Owen argues that once someone chooses to marry then the mandate begins to apply to them (Owen, 2001: 39). Natalists assume that "be fruitful" (1:28) was spoken to Adam and Eve after their marriage (2:25). "What are the first words the Bible records God speaking to Adam and Eve as a couple? Be fruitful" (Watters 38).

One problem with this idea is that Genesis chapter 1, where the words "be fruitful" appear, is apparently universal in scope: "God created mankind ... male and female he created them" (Genesis 1:27, NIV). So in the next verse when God says "be fruitful," the words address all humankind. Chapter 1 is a wide-angle view. It is in the close-up narrative in chapters 2 and 3 that the couple Adam and Eve feature. Another problem is that "be fruitful" (in chapter 1) canonically precedes the first "marriage" at the end of chapter 2. Finally, because Genesis 1:28 includes the verbs "subdue" and "have dominion" alongside "be fruitful," this interpretation has to imagine half the verse addressed only to married people, while the remainder does not exclude single people who are addressed by the cultural mandate, especially since Jesus is the paragon of subduing (waves for example) and has true dominion.

Cultural mandate

The reproductive command was not arbitrary but was an integral part of the "cultural mandate": God's plan for humankind to fill the land and subdue it. Many natalists deploy this point. The reason for "God's desire for families to be prolific" is the "Genesis mandate of filling the earth" and that purpose must still drive us today because "there is still land to be subdued" (Heine, 1989: 15, 84). Parents should "bring forth many children ... to subdue the earth" and to "manage God's creation" (Campbell 7, 14). This plan is the primary reason for marriage: "God gave Eve to Adam to be his helper. Why? Because Adam had been assigned a project ... [to] fill the earth and subdue it ... [so] the biblical reason for marriage is ... to produce children" (Pride 19). Doug Wilson links another purpose of marriage to the mandate: the reasons for marriage are first, "companionship in the labor of dominion" because the "cultural mandate ... is still in force," and second, reproduction because man alone is helpless to fulfil that (19-20). Against the natalist concept, when Paul discusses why some Christians might choose to marry he does not mention children: the main reason is to prevent them falling into sexual immorality: "if they cannot control themselves, they should marry" (1 Corinthians 7:9, NIV).

The importance of humankind filling the world to advance God's purpose is reinforced by a vision of the fallen cursed earth as a disordered place to which humankind is commissioned to bring order. Some, including Beisner and Andrews, add a belief that corruption of the earth and nonhuman creatures by fallen angels predates the creation of Adam, and that God's intention for humankind was that they recapture fallen territory from Satan's rule (Andrews 30) by multiplying and spreading from Eden. Beisner adds that humankind was mandated to expand the Garden of Eden with a goal of "transforming all the earth into a garden" (Beisner, "Imago" 185).[31] Population growth therefore helps toward achieving the earth's "cleansing and transformation from wilderness to garden" (190). Human reproduction operates here as part of a post-millennial program to reclaim the fallen Earth.[32] Beisner's interpretation makes the nonhuman world the primary location of disorder, and humankind becomes the agent capable of restoring the fallen cursed Earth. That is a grotesque reversal of the traditional interpretation of Genesis 3 in which the locus of sin and the Fall's centre is located in the human beings whose corruption then affects other earthly creatures.

Order of created nature

Physiology shows that humans are designed for biological reproduction, and, according to natalists, this reveals God's will for people today. Steve and Candice Watters claim that "our bodies testify" by their design to "the

---

31 Beisner's vision of an expanding garden is essential to his critique of environmentalist Christians' appeals for benevolent dominion (Genesis 2:15), which he argues applies only inside the garden (i.e. domesticated spaces), whereas a subjugating dominion (Genesis 1:28) should apply to the wilderness outside the garden. Beisner teaches a spatially differentiated mandate, inside and outside the garden, but this distinction is not obvious in Genesis 1 and 2. His claim that Adam was supposed to expand the garden is also dubious because the garden has an "eastern entrance" (later guarded by kerubim), suggesting a secure perimeter was fixed when God planted the garden. Beisner's metaphor sounds more like the *moving* frontier of the American West. Finally, it is hard to see how a garden expansion metaphor works after Adam is expelled and denied access to the garden.

32 The post-millennial view is that God's kingdom will advance across future centuries to dominate the world, whereas a pre-millennial view expects decline until the intervention of the Rapture and the end of the world. Monica Duffy Toft's assessment of Quiverfull is that it is a "subset of neo-Calvinist Dominion theology ... not premillennial" (Goldstone, Kaufmann, and Toft 220).

mysteries of our purpose" because form follows function.[33] In other words, a physical capability for reproduction should determine an individual's actions. They point also to lessons from nonhuman nature, citing Job 12:7 "ask the animals, and they will teach you" (Watters 35),[34] and to Adam and Eve, for "He called them – and is still calling us … to be productive in fruitfulness … the full, abundant life that can only come through being fruitful" (34).[35] However, the biblical text that institutes marriage between the first man and first woman does not even mention reproduction: it says, "Therefore a man shall leave his father and his mother and hold fast to his wife, and they shall become one flesh" (Genesis 2:24, ESV). From the unlimited camp, Nancy Campbell asserts: "We were born to reproduce! All nature and all mankind were created for this purpose" (Campbell 49).

One problem here is natalists prioritizing observed nature above traditional Christian teaching and practice. Early Christian writers commend examples of married people who for long periods avoided reproduction. Eusebius points to Isaac, Joseph, and others as men who "had children in early life, but later on abstained and ceased from having them." Also, after the Flood Noah, "though he lived many years more, is not related to have begotten more children," and Moses and Aaron "are recorded as having had children before the appearance of God, but after the giving of the divine oracles as having begotten no more children" (Eusebius 9). In the early church many married couples had children in the early years of their marriages and then entered a state of marital continence. A few went further, only reproducing minimally as a concession to ancestral and social expectations, and they are praised by patristic writers. For example, Melania agreed to bear one son and then, aged twenty, she and Pinianus settled into continence. Similarly, Therasia and Paulinus of Nola limited themselves to one son (Brown 409). Continuous childbearing by married women is not normative for Christians.

Marriage is presented by natalists as the default norm for Christians. "While a few are called to celibacy, the whole tenor of Scripture is that wedlock is the usual course of life for the majority" (Owen 30). Parents are urged to assume that all their children will be called to marriage and train them accordingly. Campbell cites 1 Timothy 5:8 and advises that "We should teach our sons

---

33 Steve Watters was Director of Young Adults at Focus on the Family (a large Christian ministry), and Candice Watters was editor of *Boundless* magazine.

34 In context, the lesson learnt in Job 12 is about humility, not sex and reproduction.

35 This echoes John 10:10, "I am come that they might have life, and that they might have it more abundantly," but in that New Testament text, abundance is not referring to quantity of biological offspring but to other matters such as eternal life.

... that God has placed the responsibility upon them to one day provide for a family" (Campbell 39). Some natalists acknowledge the prevalence of singleness among early church leaders and the biblical commendation of "eunuchs for the Kingdom." This anomaly is dealt with by treating singleness as an exceptional state requiring a special gift and individual calling from God. A few natalists argue that commendation of singleness in 1st century Christianity was rooted in a belief that the end of the world was imminent.

However, some voices from Christian tradition indicate that marriage is not normative. Athenagoras, a Christian writer in the 2nd century, informs his readers that "you would find many among us, both men and women, growing old unmarried, in the hope of living in closer communion with God" (ANF 2.147). The new "image of God" in Christ is in its first instance a single person, unlike the original pair of humankind in Genesis. The apostle Paul commends singleness when he advises, "Are you unmarried? Do not seek a wife," and also counsels that "he who does not marry her does even better" (1 Corinthians 7:27, 38). Though one reason why singleness was a better choice in Paul's time was the "present crisis," that may not be a uniquely 1st-century problem and could refer to the troubles Christians always face (Payette-Bucci 32). Paul says "those who marry will face many troubles in this life and I want to spare you this" (7:28). New Testament scholar Larry Yarbrough argues that "Paul's silence about children and the benefits of married life was due not simply to the imminence of the end of the age, but also to the inappropriateness of most of the common arguments in favor of being married and producing children" (Yarbrough 108). Paul also advises that a single woman "is happier if she stays as she is" (1 Corinthians 7:40), and Payette-Bucci suggests that today "personal well-being and fulfillment" can be included among the reasons that adequately justify the Christian's choice not to marry (Payette-Bucci 32).

Delay in beginning reproduction is rebuked by natalists. Campbell cites the benefit of "sons born in one's youth" (Psalm 127) and judges that "God wants children to be born in our youth" (Campbell 108). Watters also cites the Psalm and urges couples to seek "children in your youth, the spring season of life" (92). Citing "a time to be born" (Ecclesiastes 3:1), Watters commends this "prime time for having babies, a window of opportunity" (85), and advocates early marriage as natural and normative. But through history, the average age at marriage has varied between cultures. In England in the early 17th century, the average age at (first) marriage was around 28 for men and 26 for women (Wrigley and Schofield 255). In general the age at marriage across

Europe has been higher than in most other pre-modern cultures around the world. That age did fall during the Industrial Revolution, as waged workers did not need to wait until they inherited a farm before marrying. Today the average age at marriage in England of around 30 for women is higher than it was in 1600, though for a fair comparison any duration of pre-marital cohabitation ought to be deducted. The context of longer lifespans should also be considered. If we look at the life expectancy of females aged 15 (to exclude the effect of change in infant mortality), adult women back in 1600 could expect to live 48.2 years, while by 1989 they could expect to live 79.2 years. So women now are on average spending many more years married.

Natalists highlight supposed health risks of contraceptives. French wrongly claims that vasectomy causes auto-immune diseases and prostate cancer (French 41, 45). Campbell falsely claims that "the root cause of many diseases men suffer is vasectomy" (Campbell 183).[36] The risk of delayed childbearing is deployed (and exaggerated) to commend a "natural" way of life. "Women who have a full pregnancy before the age of 18 have one third the breast cancer risk" of those who delay to age 30, and "women with the least breast cancer were those who had the most children" (Campbell 108). Two lines of argument are combined here: a promise that "none of these diseases" (Exodus 15:26) will afflict those obeying God (reproduction being the first commandment), and a belief that efforts to thwart the natural order of fertility are intrinsically unhealthy. While there can be problems associated with delayed childbearing, different personal costs are associated with youthful reproduction, and personal decisions weighing that balance are distorted by teaching that God expects youthful reproduction.

Discipline for parents

Some natalist writers regard parenthood as a discipline that conveys spiritual benefit. They believe that adults are shaped in Christian character by experiencing parenthood, and some regard it as the main instrument of Christian formation. Owen considers "family life ... the most comprehensive of all disciplines" (Owen 64), and Kurt Bruner asserts that "the most direct and intentional path to ... conforming our lives to the image of Christ ... [is] in a word, parenthood" (Watters 10).[37] The idea is not inherently natalist but

---

36　These claims contradict the consensus of medical advice, which is that vasectomy is safe and rarely causes any disease (Schwingl and Guess).

37　This idea differs from early Christianity's classic model of discipleship as exemplified by

can function that way. Two parameters of parental experience as a discipline are its intensity and duration. Intensity is not necessarily proportional to the number of offspring, and the labor of parenting one disadvantaged child might be lifelong. However, some claim that having numerous offspring is more powerfully formative than having a few. French claims that "With each child we have been forced to grow ... in patience, faith, wisdom, and love," and that, in general, "as we have more children, we mature more" (French 89, 91). Also if the most intense discipline is the care of infants, then not to limit that experience to a few years but to extend the total duration of infant rearing through additional births would be a stronger discipline.

Steve and Candice Watters describe some troubles of parenthood and then ask rhetorically "should we really encourage other couples to do this? This is brutal." Then they answer their doubts with the belief that suffering produces Christian character, declaring "we just didn't have many opportunities to rejoice in our sufferings before we had kids. We didn't have the benefit of being tested by a furnace of affliction" (56).[38] This reminds me of the voluntary "white martyrdom" of hair shirts embraced by some Christians after the Roman empire stopped persecuting them. For the minority among natalists who follow this idea (instead of expecting material benefits from offspring), rearing a large family functions as a new expression of religious asceticism for Americans who might otherwise have lived a comparatively easy life.

Sovereignty of God in planning families

Unlimited natalists claim that God controls fertility perfectly and therefore humans are foolish to intervene in the timing, spacing, or number of births. The first step is the assertion that "God opens and closes the womb! He alone decides when and ... if we have any more children" (Hess 23). Many texts (including Genesis 29:31; 30:2 and 1 Samuel 1:6) are cited in support of this belief. The second step is to argue from divine omniscience and benevolence that "God Himself is our birth Controller ... so perfectly that I have absolutely no reason to take over the responsibility," and this constitutes a "doctrine of divine planned parenthood" (Hess 141). God's control implies that "we cannot over-reproduce" because He would close the womb before that happened (86). This can be combined with the character-forming idea, for

---

the years Jesus spent with his twelve disciples.
38 This argument is in contrast to the idea described earlier, advanced by other natalists, that parenthood (as a real blessing) normally delivers prosperity and health.

as individuals parents need different types and amounts of discipline, but only God knows what make-up of family they need, so parents should not try to arrange this. Hess asks rhetorically "Can I trust God to do the best for me in terms of family size and spacing?" (62).

Isaac was born at the "appointed time" (Genesis 21:1), showing that God's timing is perfect, and Pride argues that He desires to "choose the best children for us," but human planning can result in sub-optimal family design. "Spacing is the attempt to usurp God's sovereignty by self-crafting one's family," and she cites Psalm 127 against those who "labor in vain ... trying to build their families themselves." We could miss a particular intended child due to bad timing in conception for "who can tell but that one special combination of genes will produce the greatest revival preacher ... or the greatest musician" (Pride 77). More often we miss those offspring simply because we limit numbers. French confesses that "I don't want to stand before the Lord and have him tell me that I would have birthed the next Beethoven or Galileo or Moody[39] or Da Vinci if only I'd allowed Him to give me one more (or two more or three more or however many more) children" (French 108).

Provan claims that family planning "eliminates future people" and argues that predestination is no excuse (Provan 24). He imagines a present real existence of these potential people, citing Levi's presence in the loins of Abram (Hebrews 13:4). No other natalist makes claims for pre-existence, but some draw on the wider concept of potential future people. Hess expands it greatly and presents lists of U.S. Presidents, musicians, famous Christians, and biblical characters, whose birth order was fourth or later (46-57). The lists include Augustine (a fourth child), Jonathan Edwards (eleventh), Dwight Moody (sixth), and John Wesley (fifteenth). Hess notes that David was an eighth son (1 Samuel 16:10) and asks "what if Jesse had stopped after seven sons." He speculates that "if Jacob had stopped after eleven sons" (Genesis 35:18), "we would be missing ... [New Testament letters] written by the Apostle Paul, a descendant of thirteenth-born Benjamin" (56).

The idea that divine sovereignty precludes human family planning features only in writings of the unlimited type, and is rejected by large-but-limited natalists. Mohler considers the idea analogous to medical non-intervention, and asks how those reasoning in this way can justify using antibiotics to thwart God's sovereignty over death (Mohler 2009). Doriani suggests that the message "don't plan" is popular because "many people like simple solutions

---

39 "Moody" refers to Dwight Moody (1837-99), an American evangelist and hymn publisher.

... [and] they like to be told what to do" (Doriani 31). However, while rejecting the sovereignty arguments at the level of individual families, at least one limited natalist, Calvin Beisner, affirms a belief that divine superintendence prevents humankind from seriously damaging the ecosphere. One implication is that whatever number of offspring are born in aggregate across a nation must be compatible with the capacity of that land, since God is allowing that number to be born.

Overall picture of natalist arguments

A count of how often types of argument appear in the sources was generated from the database. Most common, with 72 instances, was a paradigmatic idea that God wants fruitfulness, which encompasses all the arguments. Among the specific points, the counts were as follows: blessing (41),[40] church growth (22), practical help including care for elderly parents (19), the natural created order (18, including 9 about reproduction as the purpose of marriage), other spiritual benefits (18), God's command (12), and stimulating the national economy (9). This reinforces my impression that the focus by previous critics on portraying Genesis 1:28 as a blessing rather than a command only addresses a small part of the natalist argument.

So far I have looked at Evangelical natalism in the U.S. in the context of historical change in wider attitudes to fertility. Though natalism since 1985 can be regarded as a renaissance of interpretations that were common in early 20th-century Protestantism, it differs from early interpretations in significant ways. Since the new natalism has renounced racist, eugenic, or nationalist beliefs and some previous critiques were misdirected, a fresh analysis is needed. I attempted this by investigating natalist primary sources and the biblical reception and associated arguments found in them. I presented natalist ideas under key headings which underlie much of the structure of this book as a whole.

As we have seen, the arguments deployed by natalists are that high fertility is a blessing, a real benefit for parents and for their children, for the country by making society more youthful and helping the economy, and for church growth. It is also a divine command, a cultural mandate, the natural created order, and a formative discipline for parents. These arguments can be found among both types of natalist: ordinary natalists who accept family planning, and

---

40 This includes 15 counts of the inverse argument, that to be barren is a curse.

the unlimited type who combine with natalism a refusal to use contraception. While there is a divide between the two types over the issue of human planning, their arguments for large family size are similar. Previous critics have focused on the anti-contraceptive teachings of the unlimited natalists, but I argue that given the common ground shared by both groups they should be considered as parts of a wider Protestant natalist phenomenon. This is the perspective adopted in the remaining chapters of this book.

3. Martin Luther: Forerunner of Natalism?

Martin Luther is the most important figure in the 16th century change in attitudes toward marriage and childbearing in western Christianity.[1] Although he had little to say about population size, he discussed human fertility more extensively than any other early Protestant leader. Luther paved the way for modern natalism through his rhetorical exaltation of the biological family. Before him the primary models of ideal Christian leadership had been celibate Jesus with his twelve disciples, or celibate Paul with his missionary associates and the planted churches, or later a bishop with a cathedral fellowship of celibate canons. After Luther the model was a homely pastor with a large family: a model to be imitated by the congregation (Carlson, "Fruitful" 23). Esteem of celibacy had limited the influence of social natalism in Christianity since its beginning.[2] Luther provided biblical and theological arguments for changing the relative balance of esteem given to marriage and celibacy, with effects that went beyond Protestantism. For example Carlson discerned that "the shock of the Reformation" led to a shift in Catholic thought on the family and reproduction (18).

Luther's words and their reception

When modern Protestant natalists look to Christian history for support, the writer most often quoted is Martin Luther. Charles Provan in the first

---

1   An extract from an earlier version of this chapter was published as John McKeown, "Receptions of Israelite Nation-building: Modern Natalism and Martin Luther." *Dialog: A Journal of Theology* 49.2 (2010): 133-140.
2   There were of course other sources for the rise of "family values," including a new Renaissance ideal of children and family, as well as social and economic changes.

chapter of his book *The Bible and Birth Control* deploys fourteen quotations from Luther, many of them half a page long (2-32). Allan Carlson includes seventeen quotations from Luther in a 2007 article ("Children" 20-23), and also cites Luther in an earlier article ("Freedom" 196) and a co-authored book (*Conjugal* 12), all in support of natalism. So two very different natalists (Carlson is a professional historian, Provan a popular writer) both look to the Reformer for inspiration. Luther is also cited briefly by Mohler ("Mystery"), Bayly (15), Watters (117), French (34), and Houghton (56), of whom the first three are limited natalists while the other two are unlimited natalists.

Luther's writings do contain material amenable to natalism. For example, he seems to advocate universal early marriage, and many statements on this theme can be found in his writings. The example below is from near the beginning of Luther's 1522 treatise on the *Estate of Marriage*, and is quoted by Provan (2) and Carlson ("Children" 21):

> "Be fruitful and multiply." From this passage we may be assured that man and woman should and must come together in order to multiply. Now this ordinance is just as inflexible as the first[3] ... since God gives it his blessing and does something over and above the act of creation. Hence, as it is not within my power not to be a man, so it is not my prerogative to be without a woman. Again, as it is not in your power not to be a woman, so it is not your prerogative to be without a man. For it is not a matter of free choice or decision but a natural and necessary thing, that whatever is a man must have a woman and whatever is a woman must have a man. For this word which God speaks, "Be fruitful and multiply," is not a command. It is more than a command, namely, a divine ordinance which it is not our prerogative to hinder or ignore. Rather, it is just as necessary as the fact that I am a man, and more necessary than sleeping and waking, eating and drinking, and emptying the bowels and bladder. It is a nature and disposition just as innate as the organs involved in it. Therefore, just as God does not command anyone to be a man or a woman but creates them the way they have to be, so he does not command them to multiply but creates them so that they have to multiply. And wherever men try to resist this, it remains irresistible nonetheless and goes its way through fornication, adultery, and secret sins, for this is a matter of nature and not of choice. (LW 45.18)

Luther makes a smaller number of statements praising human fertility, and these are even more amenable to natalists, especially since almost all of them shy away from teaching an imperative for single people to marry. Provan quotes the following words once in full (5-6), and again in part (28). They

---

3   Luther identified the first ordinance as the creation of gender in Genesis 1:27.

come from a sermon where Luther comments on Rachel's envy (Genesis 30:1) of her sister's reproductive success:

> Although we like and desire it in cattle, yet in the human race there are few who regard a woman's fertility as a blessing. Indeed, there are many who have an aversion for it and regard sterility as a special blessing. Surely this is also contrary to nature. Much less is it pious and saintly. For this affection has been implanted by God in man's nature, so that it desires its increase and multiplication. Accordingly, it is inhuman and godless to have a loathing for offspring. Thus someone recently called his wife a sow, since she gave birth rather often. The good-for-nothing and impure fellow! The saintly fathers[4] did not feel like this at all; for they acknowledged a fruitful wife as a special blessing of God and, on the other hand, regarded sterility as a curse. And this judgment flowed from the Word of God in Gen.1:28, where He said: "Be fruitful and multiply." (LW 5.325)

Luther's words are important because of his past and present influence on Christianity. Cyriacus Spangenberg, a Protestant pastor and theologian, claimed in 1561 that Luther's writings "may rightly be called … Paul's mouth, … Peter's key, and the Holy Spirit's sword" and should "be held in all honor next to the Holy Bible" (Kolb 48). Luther's influence extends beyond Lutherans to modern Evangelicals and others, whether consciously (Hendrix, "Future") or subliminally. In the theological disputes after his death, factions within Lutheranism took quotations from Luther and deployed his words for "authoritative pronouncement," as all sides were able to find support within his writings for contradictory systematizations of his thought (Kolb 41, 45). The size and character of Luther's corpus of writings makes it especially susceptible to conflicting receptions and uses.

Luther did not leave a systematic theology; instead his exegesis and thought is spread across a huge collection of sermons, treatises, and letters.[5] The compiler of the index to *Luther's Works*, Joel Lundeen, after reading the whole set recorded his impression that Luther "often wrote in a hurry" and

---

4   The phrase "saintly fathers" here refers to the patriarchs in Genesis, including Abraham, Isaac, and Jacob.

5   Only a third of Luther's writings, and less than a tenth of his two thousand surviving sermons, appear in the English translation of his works (LW). That is changing, with plans for a new series of twenty volumes by Concordia Publishing, but for now some of the material in the German edition of Luther's works (WA) that is not in LW has been translated in secondary sources, so those are cited here. I found especially helpful *Luther on Women: A Sourcebook* (LS), edited by Susan Karant-Nunn and Merry Wiesner, whose choice of extracts for translation prioritized material that does not appear in LW.

rarely went back to revise (Foreword LW 55.vii).[6] Much of it was occasional writing in response to events at Wittenberg or nearby. Many of his pastorally motivated works were designed to meet the needs of particular audiences (Hendrix, "Future" 128), so their retrieval today for use in contemporary debates requires close attention to their immediate historical context. Finally, since Luther's thought continued developing up to the end of his life, self-contradiction is likely.

Luther's comments on the fruitful verses[7] and his thoughts about human fecundity are scattered across many of his writings. The most significant are his references to "be fruitful and multiply," which appear in commentaries on Genesis, Deuteronomy, Psalms, Isaiah, Hosea, and Zechariah; in sermons on marriage from 1519 and 1531; in the treatises *Monastic Vows* (1521), *Estate of Marriage* (1522), and *Exhortation to the Knights of the Teutonic Order* (1523); in a commentary on 1 Corinthians 7 that was written as a wedding present (1523); and within *Table Talk*.[8] Luther's commentaries are essentially sermons: they were usually preached from very brief outlines, and then published from hearers' transcripts. He preached twice weekly to trainees for the Protestant ministry as a model of homiletics (the art of preaching) suitable for their congregations (Baue 410; Nestingen, "Front" 191). From 1523 to 1524 these sermons covered Genesis and were printed under the title *Declamationes*[9] in 1527 (Mattox, *Defender* 31, 262).[10] He returned to preach on Genesis at greater length from 1535 to 1545 and these were published by 1554, some years after Luther's death, as *Enarrationes*.[11]

---

6   Exceptions to this rule are his Bible translation, Catechisms, and the *Smalcald Articles*.

7   These were identified using the Scripture Index in *Luther's Works* (LW 55).

8   *Table Talk* consists of snippets of Luther's conversations with guests at his house. It was recorded by Luther's disciples and later edited to safeguard his reputation, so it should be treated with caution as a source.

9   Most of Luther's writings are referred to in (American) Luther studies by English titles, but for these two series of sermons on Genesis (presumably to avoid confusion) the Latin titles are commonly used (as in Mattox, *Defender*).

10   *Declamationes* is entirely omitted from LW, but some sermons are translated in LS.

11   The authenticity of *Enarrationes* is debated. Luther died three months after finishing the sermons, and they were published by his disciples, especially Veit Dietrich. In 1936, Peter Meinhold claimed that *Enarrationes* was edited to support Melanchthon during theological disputes after Luther's death (Nestingen, "Front" 187-89). Consequently, until the 1990s little use was made of *Enarrationes* in Luther studies, though Jaroslav Pelikan (the editor of LW) was confident that the words are mostly Luther's (LW 1.x-xi). A rehabilitation began in the 1990s. After surveying this debate, Mickey Mattox in 2003 concluded that *Enarrationes* preserves the "authentic voice" of Luther (*Defender* 81, 263-73), and I find his argument convincing.

Little research has been done on Luther's writings with regard to the theme of human reproduction, let alone natalism in particular. David Yegerlehner's PhD thesis about the historical reception of Old Testament "fruitfulness texts" devotes a section to Luther (160-72). He refers to the commentaries but not to the treatises, and provides little historical context. Jeremy Cohen's survey of the ancient and medieval career of Genesis 1:28 stops at the year 1500, but his conclusion includes one page on Luther and claims he led a revolution in Christian interpretation of the verse (307). Surveys of Luther's thought on the topics of marriage and family by Scott Hendrix in 2000 and Janet Strohl in 2008 say little about fertility. Steven Ozment does discuss it but does not deal with biblical reception (8, 101). Susan Karant-Nunn and Merry Wiesner survey research looking at Luther's works from the perspective of gender and sexuality (7-8), but that is concerned with issues such as women's status, and the matter of fecundity is rarely addressed directly.

Luther's battle against 'works-religion' and sin

Luther's reception of "be fruitful and multiply" should be understood in the context of theological concerns that converged on the issue of celibacy. His emphasis on justification by faith, and his war with a religion of salvation by works (as he saw it), led him to attack vowed celibacy (Bultmann 425; Ozment 1). He was also deeply concerned about sin and its consequences, and one breeding ground of sin (in his view) was the compulsion of celibacy for priests which led to sexual immorality.[12]

Luther's ideas arose in the context of a unique event, the early 16th-century revolt within the elite of the Catholic church. Many of the early Protestant leaders were celibates (as monks, friars, priests, or in minor orders) before they changed allegiance (Chadwick, *Reformation* 151), and a central feature of the Reformation was the shift from a celibate to a married church leadership. This was experienced intensely by Luther, who had been an earnest monk of the Augustinian community but came to believe that he had lived a false piety that trusted in works for salvation. His vow was especially invalid in his eyes because it was against his father Hans' wishes. Luther writes, "I recall that my father despised the monks ... accordingly, when I first entered the

---

12 Luther perceived other sources and types of sin, including the ways of market traders, business, and usury. His idea of sin was not narrow in scope.

monastery ... my father bore this with the greatest reluctance" (LW 8.181).
Later he wrote to his father:

> It is now nearly sixteen years since I became a monk, against your wishes
> and without your knowledge ... Your own plan for my future was to tie me
> down with an honourable and wealthy marriage ... you said – "May it not
> prove an illusion and a deception." That word penetrated and lodged in the
> depths of my soul, as if God had spoke through your mouth; but I hardened
> my heart against you and your word as much as I could. You said something
> else ... "Have you not also heard that parents are to be obeyed?" ... my vow
> was not worth a straw, because in taking it I was withdrawing myself from
> the will and authority of my parent.[13] (LW 48.331)

Luther intervened in the debate over compulsory celibacy for priests in 1520,[14]
and in *To the Christian Nobility of the German Nation* he observed that "many
a poor priest is overburdened with wife and child, his conscience troubled"
because of the "universal commandment forbidding priests to marry," and
he advised the Pope to "leave every man free to marry or not to marry" (LW
44.175). Later, while Luther was in exile at Wartburg in November 1521 one
of the other monks at Wittenberg began urging his peers to abandon the
monastery, and this prompted Luther to turn his attention to monastic celibacy
(Lohse 141). By February 1522 the community was depleted from thirty friars
to six, and by 1523 only three diehards remained of whom one was Luther,
who kept to all his vows and wore his habit until October 1524, at a time when
in some Protestant towns anyone seen in a habit risked being thrown out of
church or pelted with mud (Chadwick, *Reformation* 153, 156). Luther believed
that outward disciplines were beneficial if done with a good conscience, but
perilous if regarded as good works to earn salvation.

Motives for the campaign

Luther's first motive for attacking vowed celibacy was his pastoral concern
for the consciences of those constrained, either by their own scruples or

---

13 Luther included this letter to his father as the dedication of his treatise *Monastic Vows* in
    November 1521. His father Hans had risen from being a peasant to a mine-owner and
    had paid to send his son to Erfurt University to become a lawyer. Martin's decision at
    age 23 to abandon this career and enter a monastery provoked his father temporarily
    to "cut me off from all further paternal grace." Erik Erikson judged Luther's relation
    with his parents significantly formative for his thought, but most historians are wary of
    psychological methods.
14 The chronology of the celibacy crisis is outlined by Bernhard Lohse (137-43).

pressure from others, to keep vows which they regretted. He was especially concerned about those who had been put inside religious houses as youths by their parents (LW 44.216), and also young adults who joined impetuously (LW 39.296). Luther's treatise *Monastic Vows* declared such vows to be invalid, and in a 1524 pamphlet, *How God Rescued an Honorable Nun*, he argued that "God wants no forced service ... They should be released because man is not created for celibacy but to multiply" (LW 43.87).

His second motive arose from his view that an idle life in a monastery often led to sin. In his job as regional supervisor of Augustinian monasteries, Luther had been informed about cases of immorality. He criticized the wealthy religious orders for economic parasitism and permitting laziness. In his later writings he recalls the stories he heard about friars' fornications, infanticide at nunneries, and "Italian marriages" (homosexuality) among supposed celibates (LW 39.241; 46:198). He is alluding to such rumours when he mentions common knowledge of the results of celibacy.

Luther's third motive was to save society from temporal disaster. He perceived a chain of consequence from the avoidance of marriage to sexual immorality which brought not only peril to souls but also temporal judgment on society.[15] His belief in the link between sin (in general) and natural disasters is clear, for he wrote: "when new sins increase, new punishments also increase. Within our own time unusual kinds of diseases and disasters have become widespread" (LW 2.136). In 1538 while preaching on the destruction of Sodom (Genesis 19), he remarked that "this year, a goodly part of the earth in the territory of Naples ... vanished because of an earthquake and an inundation – not by some chance, as the papists think, but because of the sins of the people" (LW 3.295). The contribution of sexual immorality is illustrated in his statement in 1522:

> The estate of marriage, however, redounds to the benefit not alone of the body, property, honor, and soul of an individual, but also to the benefit of whole cities and countries, in that they remain exempt from the plagues imposed by God. We know only too well that the most terrible plagues have befallen lands and people because of fornication. (LW 45.44)

His fourth motive arose from his soteriology[16] that hinged on a doctrine of justification by faith alone. Writing in *Good Works* (LW 44.24) in 1520, and in

---

15 The arrival in 1494 of syphilis, previously unknown in Europe, had provoked a debate. The emperor Maximilian (in a 1497 edict) declared it to be a punishment for blasphemy, but others linked it to sexual immorality (Cunningham and Grell 248-53).

16 Soteriology is the branch of doctrine concerning eternal salvation.

Monastic Vows (LW 44.262, 290, 301), Luther identified the vows of monks and priests as the mainspring of papal theology and the religious culture (as he saw it) of salvation by works (Pelikan 76; Wendebourg 133). He also considered that religious people who were genuinely chaste but were trusting in that for their salvation were in spiritual peril, for "all nuns and monks who lack faith, and who trust in their own chastity and in their order ... cannot boast that what they do is pleasing in God's sight" (LW 45.41). These motives moved Luther, in his roles as pastor, prophet, and theologian, to urgent and forceful exegesis of Genesis to promote marriage and child-rearing as a religious vocation to replace vowed celibacy.

Strategy of promoting marriage

The only solution to all these problems was marriage, the estate ordained in Genesis (LW 1.115). Luther deemed it the best antidote to lust and fornication, for "the married estate is for evermore a hospital to the sick, so that they do not fall into greater sin" (LS 91). So he urged early marriage. In 16th century western Europe, the average age at first marriage was around 25 for a man and 21 for a woman,[17] but Luther in *The Estate of Marriage* asserted: "A young man should marry at the age of twenty at the latest, a young woman at fifteen to eighteen" (LW 45.48). The reason he gave is significant: "A girl of eighteen is ready for marriage, for this age feels the burning of the flesh" (LS 149). Luther's concern is the age at which he considers temptation becomes too strong. His focus is the young adult's spiritual welfare, not the potential for increasing the birth rate. Luther urged parents to help every one of their children to marry:

> Parents should understand that a man is created for marriage, to beget fruit of his body (just as a tree is created to bear apples or pears), unless his nature is altered ... by supreme grace or a special miracle. Therefore, they are in duty bound to assist their children to marry, removing them from the perils of unchastity. (LW 45.390)

In 16th century Europe about 15% of adults never married (LS 7). Some of those were vowed celibates, and Luther considered that many chose that path because of the imagined spiritual superiority of celibacy. Many other people were simply unmarried, and Luther identified various reasons

---

17 A study of the elite of Württemberg found an average age at first marriage of 25.3 years for men and 21.4 for women (Ozment 38).

for that choice, including the bad reputation of marriage, worries about insufficient income, and canon law. He wanted to demolish anything that delayed or prevented marriage. Luther judged that many people remained single because marriage had been given a bad reputation (LW 45.22, 390). He complained: "The whole world still cries out about what an evil thing marriage is" (LS 24). According to one modern historian, in early 16th century Europe marriage had become a "despised, and rejected estate" (Ozment 4, 44). Luther's assessment in 1522 was similar:

> The estate of marriage has universally fallen into such awful disrepute ... Every day one encounters parents who ... deter their children from marriage but entice them into priesthood and nunnery, citing the trials and troubles of married life. Thus do they bring their own children home to the devil, as we daily observe; they provide them with ease for the body and hell for the soul. (LW 45.37)

According to Protestant historiography this popular view was the result of medieval Catholic preachers denigrating marriage.[18] Luther aimed to repair the damage. He advertised that "the most pleasant life is an average home life" (LS 149, *Table Talk*). Luther wanted to dissuade young people from entering religious orders, and persuade them to marry instead. In his 1523 commentary on 1 Corinthians 7, he wrote that "God has laid it upon me to preach about marriage and to tear the veil from the chastity which is of the devil, so that there may be less fornication and our poor youth may not be so pitiably and dangerously misled by falsely glorified chastity" (LW 28.5). In 1531 he exhorted wedding guests that "we must lift this estate even higher, praise and honor it even more" (LS 153).

Lack of economic means of subsistence should not delay marriage in Luther's view. Carlson quotes Luther's assurance to poor men: "Let God worry about how they and their children are to be fed. God makes children; he will surely also feed them" (LW 45.49). This was not based on any optimistic cornucopian ideology since Luther considered that "today and always the whole creation is hardly sufficient to feed and support the human race" (LW 1.72). But the moral risks of young people delaying marriage outweighed any financial hardships. In the special case of wealthy estates that sought to avoid a subdivision of the family inheritance between too many heirs Luther had no sympathy and wrote: "It is even more disgraceful that you

---

18 A fairer assessment might be that medieval Christians normally affirmed both celibacy and marriage but esteemed the former more highly.

find princes who allow themselves to be forced not to marry, for fear that the members of their house would increase beyond a definite limit" (LW 1.118).

Another obstacle to marriages was the "impediments" in canon law. These rules included a ban on polygamy, prohibition based on affinity that extended to a wide range of relatives and even to godparents and their relatives, strict control of divorce (with a requirement for annulment by church authority), and the ban on marriages between an adherent of another religion and a Christian. Luther called for abolition of all such impediments, except the ban on polygamy and the degrees of relatedness that were explicitly forbidden in Leviticus chapters 18 and 20. He wrote in *Estate of Marriage*, "let us now consider which persons may enter into marriage with one another" (LW 45.22), and proceeded to attack those canon laws one by one, including the impediment of faith:

> The fifth impediment is unbelief; that is, I may not marry a Turk, a Jew, or a heretic [… but] marriage is an outward, bodily thing, like any other worldly undertaking. Just as I may eat, drink, sleep, walk, ride with, buy from, speak to, and deal with a heathen, Jew, Turk, or heretic, so I may also marry and continue in wedlock with him. Pay no attention to the precepts of those fools who forbid it. You will find plenty of Christians – and indeed the greater part of them – who are worse in their secret unbelief than any Jew, heathen, Turk, or heretic. A heathen is just as much a man or a woman – God's good creation, as St. Peter, St. Paul, and St. Lucy. (LW 45.25)

Luther's view that, for example, it is appropriate for a Muslim to marry a Christian indicates how far he was from any motive of sectarian natalism because that is incompatible with mixed-faith marriages. Luther's motive in wanting to remove these impediments was to help people escape the temptations that he thought were afflicting the unmarried. For the same reason he attacked Jerome for his "shameful book against Jovinian about widows who transgress against their first troth and fidelity, just as though it were improper for them to remarry" (LS 130). Luther wanted to encourage widows to remarry quickly. Removal of the impediments would, by increasing the possibilities for marriage, also increase the birth rate, but that was not Luther's motive.

Child-rearing as penitential discipline

Weddings might prevent fornication, but to remedy the sins of idleness and greed a further medicine was needed: the responsibilities of parenthood. Luther critiqued the lifestyle of monks and friars not only for producing fornication but also for its dependence on endowments and begging (by friars), which he suspected led to idleness and sloth. His vision for marriage transferred to the marital condition what he regarded as the better features of Augustinian penitential discipline (LS 13). In the new marriage service liturgy, written by Luther for Wittenberg in 1524, the minister was to declare marriage "a penitential institution in which the wife freely accepts the pain of childbirth … and the husband the pain of daily labor and worry over his family's well-being" (Ozment 8).

Commenting on Genesis 3 in *Declamationes*, Luther stated that God's response to humankind's fall was not the deserved penalty of immediate extinction, but instead curses that are designed to help the soul by hurting the body. Aside from death, the curses on woman and man only become fully operational in parenthood, since they relate to childbearing (for the woman), economically supporting the family (for the man), and the rearing of children (for both spouses). Those who avoid family life by staying unmarried were missing out on these means of grace and were likely to end up being punished spiritually instead:

> He gives the woman her torment, but … absolves her of spiritual misery, and lays the penalty upon her body … God turns eternal punishment into a temporal and physical one … upon all those who shall become the daughters of Eve. It is not said to her alone. It is said as though they should all become pregnant … This is a gentle, gracious punishment … [but] the land is full of whores and knaves … everybody shies away from marriage because they might have grief with the bearing of children, that pertains to the woman, or the man because he has to provide for and nourish his wife and child … Nobody wants to bear this burden, but it must be borne. If you do not take a wife and eat your bread in the sweat of your brow, God will take his punishment from your body and lay it upon your soul. This is not a good exchange. He wants to be gracious to the soul and helpful, but He rightly wants to torment the body. On that account, where people stand in faith, they … bear this burden gladly – they take wives, labor, and let their lives be painful … where one finds a marriage in which the wife has no misfortune with children and in which the husband is not bitter, something is not right. The world is so crazy and foolish, contrary to God, that it is of the opinion that one can be married … only to have good days and live well. But God wants exactly the opposite. (LS 23)

In 1535, preaching on Rachel's desire for a son, Luther found the same fault in those who, although they marry, contrive to be childless:

> For most married people do not desire offspring. Indeed, they turn away from it and consider it better to live without children, because they are poor and do not have the means with which to support a household. But this is especially true of those who are devoted to idleness and laziness and shun the sweat and the toil of marriage. But the purpose of marriage is not to have

pleasure and to be idle but to reproduce and bring up children, to support a household. This of course is a huge burden full of great cares and toils. But you have been created by God to be a husband or wife and that you may learn to bear these troubles. (LW 5.363)

Parenthood was construed by Luther as a religious vocation, and he hoped family households would be places of penance and discipline turned from self-oriented to other-oriented works of piety (Mattox, *Defender* 252). Luther's reasons for wanting people to marry and rear children were primarily moral and spiritual rather than a natalist desire to increase the number of births.

Commands, and orders of creation

The nine arguments against birth control devised by Charles Provan include his claims that "multiply, and fill the earth" is a command to be obeyed today (5), that creation reveals child-bearing as "the natural function of women" (27), that "children are a blessing ... the more the better" (7), and that choosing to beget "less children than possible" is a sin (9). Provan quotes Luther's words in support of each of these ideas.[19]

Provan portrays Genesis 1:28 as "the first command to a married couple." This sits uneasily with his earlier quotation from Luther (which appears above on the first page of this chapter) that it is "not a command" but rather a "nature," for God "does not command them to multiply but creates them so that they have to multiply" (4). There is a difference. Provan implies it is a command addressed only to married couples. By contrast, the scope of a law of nature must be the whole species, implying a necessity for all to marry. But that logic leads to a condemnation of those who choose singleness and that is incompatible with Christian history. The only exception to this logic could be cases in which the Creator miraculously alters an individual person's physical nature.

Singleness against the law of nature?

Whereas the early Church Fathers believed God had established the estate of celibacy alongside marriage, Luther seems to claim that the Bible, created nature, physiology, and medical wisdom all indicate that everyone is made

---

19 With regard to contraception, Christian tradition condemned this for reasons that were not natalist (as discussed in chapter 1), and Luther followed that tradition with little comment.

to reproduce. *Table Talk* observes: "Marriage exists in all nature, for among all creatures there is the male and the female. Even trees are married" (LS 122). Luther also says,

> God presents to our eyes the marital estate in all creatures, ... among the birds, ... animals, ... fishes ... male and female are to be found among trees, such as apples and pears ... If one plants them beside one another, they grow and develop better near each other than otherwise. The man stretches out his branches toward the woman ... The sky is the man and the earth the woman; for the earth is made fruitful by the sky. (LS 124)

Luther asserted that "man is created ... to eat, drink, produce fruit of his body, sleep, and respond to other calls of nature. It is not within the power of any man to alter this" (LW 45.391). He suggested that a celibate is "like a man who resolved not to urinate" and who, in Luther's anecdote, "held off for four days and became very sick" (LW 28.29). According to this rhetoric, celibacy or even continence prolonged for more than a few days is against nature and unhealthy for the human body. Luther writes in *Estate of Marriage*:

> God's word does not admit of restraint; neither does it lie when it says, "Be fruitful and multiply." You can neither escape nor restrain yourself from being fruitful and multiplying; it is God's ordinance and takes its course. Physicians are not amiss when they say: if this natural function is forcibly restrained it necessarily strikes into the flesh and blood and becomes a poison ... That which should have issued in fruitfulness and propagation has to be absorbed within the body. Unless there is terrific hunger [20] or immense labor or supreme grace, the body cannot take it; it necessarily becomes unhealthy and sickly. Hence we see how weak and sickly barren women are. Those who are fruitful, however, are healthier, cleanlier, and happier. And even if they bear themselves weary – or ultimately bear themselves out – that does not hurt. Let them bear themselves out.[21] This is the purpose for which they exist. It is better to have a brief life with good health than a long life in ill health. (LW 45.45-46)

Although this would raise birth rates in practice, Luther's focus here is on the adult, and specifically her physical health, rather than quantity of offspring. However in *Declamationes*, his early Genesis sermons, he does seem to portray reproduction as the main purpose of life. Eve had been created alongside Adam

---

20 Luther is referring to fasting (hunger) and physical work, both monastic disciplines.
21 The phrase "bear themselves out" refers to the premature death of women either during pregnancy or labor, or later as a result of its effects. Luther suggests that infertile women are sickly *because* they have not reproduced, rather than the reverse possibility of their being infertile because they are sickly or malnourished.

to help him to give birth in accordance with God's word, "Be fruitful and multiply." … Women are not created for any other purpose than to serve man and to be his assistant in producing children. (LS 17)

Luther affirmed that celibacy may be received as a gift, which could hardly be denied as the apostle Paul and most of the Early Fathers were celibate, but in the 1520s he portrayed celibacy as a theoretical possibility, rather than a live option, by arguing that it cannot be chosen. He also suggested that the gift of celibacy had become rarer after the early church era and vanishingly rare in his own time, which may be linked to his belief that the moral quality of humankind had continued to decline after the apostolic era (LW 2.7). An open letter in 1523 on *Why Virgins Are Allowed to Leave the Convent in a Godly Way* explains that nuns may and should leave because

> it is impossible that the gift of chastity is as common as the convent. A woman is not created to be a virgin, but to bear children. In Genesis 1, God was not speaking just to Adam, but also to Eve when He said, "Be fruitful and multiply," as the female organs of a woman's body, which God has created for this reason, prove. And this was not just said to one or two women, but to all of them, with no exceptions. God establishes this not through our oaths or our free will, but through His own powerful means and will. Whenever He has not done this, a woman should remain a woman, and bear children, for God has created her for that. (LS 140)

In a letter of 1524 to three nuns, Luther went further in that he attempted to persuade contented nuns that their way of life must be false because the gift of celibacy had become very rare in his time:

> Scripture and experience teach that among many thousands there is not one to whom God gives the grace to maintain pure chastity. A woman does not have the power herself. God created her body to be with a man, bear children and raise them, as Scripture makes clear in Genesis 1. Her bodily members, ordained by God for this, also demonstrate this. This is as natural as eating and drinking, sleeping and waking up. It is created by God and He also wants what is natural, that is men and women being together in marriage. (LS 141)

Rhetorical use of "be fruitful and multiply"

In general, Luther's method of argument was "to take everything to its logical limit, to drive matters to extremes," and to set up paradoxes (Matheson, *Rhetoric* 174), and his approach to theology tends toward sharp polarities. Also, his expressive style tends to hyperbole in polemic and "extreme formulation" in exegesis (Pelikan 19). Sometimes he was deliberately offensive to stir up his readers.[22] I contend that Luther's portrayal of "be fruitful and multiply" as a law of nature compelling all to marry, and making it impossible to abstain from conjugal relations, is an example of this style and should not be taken at face value. His meaning was easily mistaken even by contemporaries: in 1528 Johann Lansburg of Cologne wrote that Luther's idea of chastity as "beyond human nature" was an insult to courtiers, merchants, and all who had to be away from home for days on end, since it implied that they and their wives were inevitably guilty of adultery (Ozment 24).

Evidence for the presence of hyperbole comes where Luther makes apparently contradictory statements within one piece of writing. In his 1521 treatise on *Monastic Vows*[23] he urges that "all monks be absolved from their vows" (LW 44.283) and that any monk who finds lust irresistible should be free to marry (LW 44.337).[24] Luther imagines their colleagues saying to monks in that frame of mind, "You must pray to God for grace," and Luther responds to those counsellors that

> you are trying to compel God to revoke his word, that divine commandment of nature by which he created all things, "Increase and multiply." All this is absurd and puerile. Each one is left to see from his own experience whether this law, or rather, privilege of increasing and multiplying, is quite settled and established, or whether he has the power to change things. (LW 44.339)

The claim seems to be that Genesis 1:28 testifies to an unalterable created order that makes celibacy impossible. But a few pages later Luther writes: "We do not advocate marriage as an easy way out ... We want it to be permitted, to be a matter of option, so that the man who is able may be continent for as long as he wants" (LW 44.395). The central idea of the treatise was after all that "lifelong poverty, obedience, and chastity may be observed, but cannot be vowed" (LW 44.315).

Less than a year later *Estate of Marriage* includes what seems to be a strong assertion (quoted above) that an immutable law of nature compels marriage for everyone. Later in the treatise he states that celibacy is impossible,

---

22 As in the carnivalesque *Against Hans Wurst* (1541) and *Against the Papacy at Rome* (1545), for which Luther commissioned a set of cartoons with a defecation theme to illustrate his text (Matheson, *Rhetoric* 212).

23 Written in November 1521 and published in February 1522.

24 Near the end of this treatise Luther recognizes that his case against vows could be turned against marriage vows, and his attempt to distinguish between vows in the two circumstances is unconvincing.

because "he who refuses to marry must fall into immorality. How could it be otherwise, since God has created man and woman to produce seed and to multiply?" (LW 45.45). However a few pages further on Luther qualifies what he has just written:

> In saying this, I do not wish to disparage virginity, or entice anyone away from virginity into marriage. Let each one act as he is able, and as he feels it has been given to him by God. I simply wanted to check those scandal-mongers who place marriage so far beneath virginity. (LW 45.47)

Admittedly during this period Luther became increasingly antagonistic to celibacy. In 1520 he made a few critical remarks with balancing statements; in 1521 there are many apparently absolute statements disallowing celibacy but also some balancing remarks; but in 1522 he heaps up hyperbole against singleness with only one qualifying statement at the end. Despite the imbalance in his rhetoric, Luther did not really believe that nature compelled everyone to marry.

Marriage and reproduction is not commanded

Luther in the early 1520s was torn between a wish to allow voluntary celibacy and a worry that the mere existence of religious houses sent the wrong message to people: that life in the world is spiritually inferior (Chadwick, *Reformation* 152). His treatise *Monastic Vows* rejects permanent vows and condemns the idea that works justify, but allows voluntary monastic life with temporary vows as a legitimate path for Christians (Wendebourg 141), for "if you live with men of like mind … without your thinking thereby that you are better than he who takes a wife or takes up farming, then in that case you are neither wrong to take vows nor wrong to live in this way" (LW 44.304). This exception was temporarily submerged by waves of Reformation hostility to monasticism, but in later years it resurfaced.

Further evidence that Luther did not make marriage a law of nature appeared in the case of Oldenstadt Abbey. Duke Ernst of Luneberg disendowed that Benedictine house, and Abbot Gottschalk (who accepted Protestant theology) wrote to Luther asking if they could stay on there as monks under a modified Rule. Luther replied affirmatively in February 1528, and added on a personal note that if monasticism had been practised in this manner earlier he would have stayed as a monk "because by virtue of this spirit of freedom it brings them joy." Luther also wrote to Duke Ernst advising that monks "in the freedom of the Spirit" could "with great benefit remain in the monastery," and in general defending those monasteries and convents which had re-ordered their houses in a Protestant manner (Wendebourg 142; Chadwick, *Reformation* 168).

Luther intervened in other cases. The best documented is Herford, where local pastors and the Town Council wanted to close both houses (Brothers and Sisters) of the Brethren of the Common Life, who obeyed a Rule of celibacy without permanent vows (Brecht 30; Chadwick, *Reformation* 166). Luther wrote to the Council in 1533 that "such communities are extraordinarily pleasing to me," and he also wrote to the Brethren: "Your habit and your customs which you have so laudably preserved are in no way contrary to the Gospel but help its progress against the fanatics who want to pull everything down" (Chadwick, *Reformation* 167). To the Sisters he wrote: "Your way of life, since you teach and live according to the Gospel, pleases me no end … If only there had been, and were, more convents like yours" (Wendebourg 143). The Town Council relented, but instead proposed to stop new novices joining. Melancthon complained: "What is this new doctrine which forbids people to stay unmarried?" Luther agreed and described the Town Council in October 1534 as the "new Pharisees" (Chadwick, *Reformation* 167). Luther knew that celibacy was not made impossible by any law of nature, and that singleness was an option which an individual could choose.

In *Table Talk* for September 1538, discussing a letter from some nuns, Luther said, "One should allow such nuns to stay," adding that he felt similarly about all well-ordered houses: "Nor have I proposed anything else from the beginning" (LW 54.312). Luther portrayed pious husbands in midlife renouncing marital relations: Jacob after Bilhah's adultery "lived as a celibate to the end of his life," as did David after Absalom's betrayal (Mattox 251, citing LW 6.255; 6.278). One of the prompts to Luther's early battles against vowed celibacy had been his concern for young people. After the antagonism of the early 1520s he expressed a positive appreciation of voluntary celibacy in the 1530s, and preached in 1539 about "young people" that "if some have the gift of continence and are able to live chastely without marriage, let them by all means have the benefit of continence and do without a wife" (LW 3.210).[25] Contrary to his 1520s rhetoric, he affirms that even young people are not compelled by any law of nature to marry and reproduce.

---

25 The date is sometime before March 1539 according to Pelikan.

Saved through childbirth: then and now

The polemical concerns discussed in the previous section were not the only influences on Luther's exegesis and he was not simply mining Genesis in support of his Reformation agenda. The hermeneutic for Christian application of the Old Testament that he inherited and developed governed his interpretation, especially for the long series of sermons in which he worked through Genesis systematically.

Examples of God's people exercising faith in God's promises attract Luther's interest and comment when he preaches on Genesis, because of his theological emphasis on justification by faith alone. Some major characters in Genesis receive divine promises of numerous descendants: notably Abraham (at 13:16 and other verses), Sarah (17:16), Isaac (26:4), and Jacob (28:12; 35:11). Luther finds them exercising a faith oriented toward hopes for childbirth. That alone would guarantee strong links in Luther's commentaries between salvation and reproduction, but it goes deeper because of his idea about the saving faith of Adam and Eve.

Perhaps when we imagine exemplars of faith those two are not first in line, and we may wonder what was the divine promise by which they exercised faith? God's curse upon the snake in Eden – "I will put enmity between you and the woman, and between your seed and her seed; he shall bruise your head, and you shall bruise his heel" (Genesis 3:15) – was understood by ancient tradition, which Luther followed, as the first prophecy of Jesus' birth, the *protoevangelion* (the first gospel).[26] Luther also believed that when Adam and Eve heard God speak these words they understood the prophecy: "Adam and Eve were encouraged by this promise. Wholeheartedly they grasped the hope of their restoration … When Eve had given birth to her first-born son, she hoped that she already had that Crusher" (LW 1.193). They were justified by faith in this promise, in their hope for a baby that would save them, for the prophecy "contains the word of life by which they came back to life" (Mattox, *Defender* 61 citing *Declamationes*). Luther, linking Genesis 1:28 and 3:15-17, discerned many divine purposes converging on childbirth:

> [Adam] understood that he was to produce offspring, especially since the blessing, "Increase and multiply," had not been withdrawn, but had been reaffirmed in the promise of the Seed who would crush the serpent's head.

---

26 Seed is the old translation for offspring, used in quotations from Luther in LW. When he uses a capital "S" for the word "Seed," it always denotes the one unique child, the foretold Messiah.

> Accordingly, in our judgment Adam did not know Eve simply as a result
> of the passion of his flesh; but the need of achieving salvation through the
> blessed Seed impelled him too. (LW 4.237)

Luther portrays Adam as a model (especially for the original audience
of his sermons: ministerial candidates) in another way, as the first gospel
preacher, who passed on the promise of the coming birth of the Savior to
his descendants, who each in turn transmitted it across the generations:

> This Light shone on the patriarchs before the Flood. They had the promise
> of the woman's Seed, who was to crush the serpent's head (Gen. 3:15). He
> was their Life and Light too. He illumined them to life eternal. With this
> promise they comforted themselves and bolstered their faith. Of Him they
> preached wherever they dwelt and thus passed this on to their progeny.
> (Mattox, *Defender* 24)

The lineage passed on the word until it reached Abraham for whom, Luther
thought, it was reinforced by direct communication from God. Therefore
all the patriarchs and their wives (the matriarchs) knew this promise and
labored to bring it to fruition. But they did not know when the Savior's birth
would happen, so they were eagerly anticipating it in each birth.

Luther suggested that Eve mistakenly assumed that her firstborn son
would be the promised Savior. Eve "had something greater in mind about
him, as though Cain would be the man who would crush the head of the
serpent" (LW 1.242). Baue notes that Luther based this idea on a fresh Latin
translation of Genesis 4:1 which says (rendered in English), "Eve said, I
have acquired the man of the Lord," and suggests that this "goes a long
way toward explaining the anxiety of Sarah and other barren women in the
Bible. Someday *one* mother in Israel would be the mother of God" (Baue
410). Each woman descended from Eve heard the promise and wondered
if she would be the one favored to bear the Christ child (Nestingen, "Front"
190, citing LW 1.191; 6.227). Those women, in Luther's reading, were aware
of that special extra reason to marry and bear children.

Luther links the *protoevangelion* with God's later promises that Abraham
would have many descendants (Mattox, *Defender* 61, 62, 95). Commenting
on the promise "count the stars ... so shall your offspring be" at Genesis 15:5,
he claims that "Moses implies in a hidden fashion that this passage includes
the promise about the spiritual and heavenly Seed, while previously he is
speaking solely of physical descendants" (LW 3.18). Luther also links another
theophany, in which God says that all nations will be blessed through

Abraham, to the messianic birth: "Thus it is an outstanding distinction that God bestows on Abraham when He speaks with him and gives him the promise concerning the Seed who was to bless all nations" (LW 2.236). From Luther's perspective, all the promises of descendants, in addition to their undoubted thematic significance for the founding and building of the Israelite nation, also carry this association with messianic hope.

The saints of Genesis are saved by faith in these promises. Abraham and Sarah were elderly and infertile, but (eventually) they put their faith in God's promise of a son, and in "things not yet seen" (LW 3.17). Commenting on the episode in which Sarah hears a promise by three mysterious visitors that she will bear a child in her old age and laughs in disbelief (Genesis 18:9-15), Luther draws a parallel with Christian faith awakening in one of his congregation: "it is necessary for Sarah to hear a word by which she, as though brought back to life, may rise again to the hope of fruitfulness; for the word is truly a voice that raises from death" (LW 3.211). So infertility is associated with spiritual death and fertility with spiritual life, but it is a metaphor: Luther wants his audience, like Sarah, to exercise faith, but the object of faith now is the Gospel, not biological fecundity.

Imitating the faith of patriarchs and matriarchs

One medieval approach to exegesis presented edifying literal exegeses of Genesis' narratives. Luther followed this tradition and refers to "the four righteous women, Sarah, Rebecca, Leah and Rachel" (LS 37). He read Israel's patriarchs and matriarchs as exemplars of virtue (Hendrix, "Background" 235, 238). Some stories about them are paradigms of repentance in which the hero strays into sin but God gracefully speaks, restores, and renews the promise. But in other stories they are exemplars of a good life, and Luther labors to explain that actions which seem morally dubious actually spring from faith (Mattox, *Defender* 8, 21). For example, "Lot ... is a saintly and guiltless man; he is beyond reproach" (LW 3.280). This contrasts with Calvin who usually finds fault with the characters of Genesis, whereas "Luther seems to find faith and faithfulness, along with nobility tempered by suffering, wherever he turns" (Thompson, "Hagar" 224).

The story of the rivalry of Leah and Rachel, the two wives of Jacob, to bear sons for him runs from Genesis 29:16 to 30:24. Leah, the wife less favored by Jacob strives to win appreciation through reproductive success. "Leah became pregnant and gave birth to a son. ... Surely my husband will love me now" (29:32). It seems that bearing the first son did not achieve all she hoped for, but additional sons subsequently improve her status. "Now at last my husband will become attached to me, because I have borne him three sons" (29:34). The other wife, Rachel, now becomes distressed and fights back by using her maidservant as a surrogate child-bearer (30:3). Faced with this narrative of polygamy, favoritism (29:31), aphrodisiac drugs (30:14), and payment for conjugal relations (30:16), many earlier commentators had turned to allegory. Luther, however, strove to practice literal exegesis (Forde 244; Meyer 435). The repentance motif was not an option here, for at the low point (29:31) Rachel is oppressed and God has pity on her distress; then the story advances to successive triumphs (for both wives), and there is no divine word against the competition or its methods. The only exegetical option for Luther is that Rachel is a hero of faith and an edifying model for his student-pastors' wives.

The lesson for Luther's hearers is faith in God's word, not the specific goals for which Sarah or Rachel exercised faith. Throughout the Genesis narratives, the Old Testament saints have faith in God and His provision of things for which they hope: descendants, later the promised land (though Luther makes less of that), deliverance from enemies, and prosperity. Luther did not collapse the distance between ancient Israel and the New Testament, and noted that "the external promises are like a shell; but the essential part of the nut ... is Christ and eternal life" (LW 3.149). Back then, it was "enclosed in this shell ... of the material blessing concerning ... the descendants of Abraham." But "this temporal blessing is now at an end. For the shell has been opened and broken" (LW 3.150, see also 3.148). Luther agrees with the Early Fathers that the promise to Abraham must be spiritualized, because "the promise concerns the spiritual seed, that is, the believers, more than it does the physical descendants" (LW 3.152). The object of faith now would be Jesus' cross, not Israelite nation-building, or a second messianic birth, but this is only occasionally explained by Luther, whereas his praise of the exemplary faith and life of the patriarchs and matriarchs extends across his commentaries. Contemporary natalist retrieval often quotes Luther without appreciating this.

Birth a sign of grace, barrenness a sign of wrath

One of Provan's claims is that to limit one's offspring is a negation of blessing, as "God views childlessness or less children than possible as a negative occurrence, something which he uses as a punishment" (9). Provan argues that since infertility is "a bad and undesirable thing," it follows that voluntary infertility (birth control) must be contrary to God's purposes:

> Luther had this to say about sterility, "… saintly women have always regarded childbirth as a great sign of grace. Rachel is rude and exceedingly irksome to her husband when she says: Give me children or I die! She makes it clear that she will die of grief because she sees that barrenness is a sign of wrath. And in Ps.127:3 there is a glorious eulogy of offspring: "Lo, sons are a heritage from the Lord, the fruit of the womb a reward." Surely it is a magnificent name that children are the gift of God. Therefore Hannah laments so pitiably, and John's aged mother Elizabeth leaps for joy and exults: "The Lord has taken away my reproach." Thus when the world was still in a better state, barrenness was considered a sign of wrath; but childbirth was considered a sign of grace. (Provan 10, quoting LW 3.134)

However, immediately preceding Provan's extract is the word "Consequently," and the previous sentences give Luther's reason why these women regarded childbirth as a "sign of grace" and infertility as a "sign of wrath." Provan ignores them and also misses the significance of the context of this quotation, which is in the middle of Luther's comments on the divine command to circumcise boys (Genesis 17:10-11), where God

> applies the law of circumcision to this so-called lewd member, which has to do with … the propagation of all flesh … God selects this member because he wants to point to original sin … Yet this is not actually a condemnation; it is rather a threat and a display of wrath. (LW 3.136)

Luther identifies circumcision as a "sign of wrath" through its bodily location in the "lewd member" which he linked to original sin. Similarly, the curse on childbearing in Genesis 3:15 is a mitigation of divine wrath, for "The woman's members were condemned to punishment, but they were not condemned to sterility" (LW 3.135; Meyer 433). Luther considers:

> if God had merely wanted to be angry and to punish and not also to forgive and have compassion, He would have said: "You shall remain barren." … Eve gained the sure hope of salvation, inasmuch as both a holy Seed had been promised and the blessing of giving birth and of multiplying had remained, which God did not take away. (LW 3.134)

Luther does not exclude the mundane reasons for desiring offspring, but these are not his focus. First, the "holy Seed" refers to the birth of Jesus, for which Eve hopes. Second, the word of blessing (1:28) had given her fertility, and since God warned that sin would be punished by death, she expected complete loss of blessing. God mitigates his punishment and does not take away his blessing, so conception and birth are a sign of grace for Eve. Each future generation similarly looks anxiously for childbirth as evidence that God's blessing is still with them. Luther comments on the text "Isaac prayed to the LORD for his wife, because she was barren" (Genesis 25:21) that the saints of Genesis were afflicted by

> fear and worry about perpetual barrenness, which they considered to be a curse. For the fathers laid very great stress on this statement (Gen.1:28): "Be fruitful and multiply." They felt that a special blessing of God rested on this statement; and because they did not multiply, they supposed that they were cursed and under God's wrath. (LW 4.337)

Third, the covenant that God makes with Abraham includes a promise that his descendants will be numerous, a great nation. So from then onward, that is another reason why his descendants and their wives (including Rachel)[27] hope anxiously for births. Often their bad behavior gave them reason to fear that God might remove the covenant blessing, at least from some family branches (2 Kings 17:18). Each birth is a sign that God continues to be faithful to His covenant promise.[28] Provan continues by discussing Deuteronomy 7:12 and complains:

> Yet in our culture, barrenness is "no big deal" and people are always attempting to tell sterile couples that "everything is all right." But everything is not all right! Listen to what Martin Luther had to say, commenting upon Rachel's great desire to have children: "... from this it is clear that the very saintly women were not lustful but were desirous of offspring and the blessing. For this was the cause of envy in Rachel, who, if she had been like other women whom our age has produced in large numbers, would have said: 'What is it to me whether I bear children or not? Provided that I remain the mother of the household and have an abundance of all other things, I have enough.' But Rachel demands offspring so much that she prefers death to remaining sterile ... Therefore she is an example of a very pious and continent woman whose only zeal and burning desire is for offspring, even if it means death ... . this feeling is decidedly praiseworthy. 'If I do not have children, I shall die' says Rachel. 'I prefer being without life to being without children.' ... [X] Consequently, she determines either to bear children or die. Thus later she dies in childbirth. This desire and feeling of the godly woman is good and saintly." (Provan 10-11, citing LW 5.328)

---

27 Especially the wives (Sarah, Rebekah, Leah, Rachel, Tamar, and others), because in the pre-modern world infertility would normally be blamed on the wife.

28 A point obvious to Luther and confirmed by him elsewhere is that in the new covenant Christians should look to a different sign of forgiveness: the Cross of Christ.

This use of Luther's comment on Genesis 30:2 is defective. The worst problem is the ellipsis by Provan which I have marked [X].[29] The missing text is as follows:

> There was no small reason for this desire, for Jacob undoubtedly proclaimed to both that he had the promise that the Blessed Seed would be born from him, and because of this proclamation the desire for acquiring offspring was kindled, especially in Rachel. (LW 5.328)

"Blessed Seed" refers to Jesus, and by omitting this reason, Provan loses the gospel message that Luther found in the story and which is central to his exegesis of it. Luther wanted to clarify what Rachel's motive for conceiving offspring was, and also what it was not (lust). The messianic motive is repeated in Luther's text immediately after Provan's quotation ends:

> For they did not look at the shameful and wretched pleasure of the flesh in marriage. No, they looked at the blessing of offspring for the sake of the Promised Seed. (LW 5.328)

Provan mistakenly focuses on the temporary objects of faith, and also too readily commends imitation of the culture, lifestyle, and actions of the patriarchs of Genesis and their wives. Obviously natalism was not a phenomenon in his time, but Luther was in general wary of imitation of Biblical characters' behavior, and with regard to issues such as polygamy and armed resistance he urged contemporary Christians against copying them. He warned that the Israelite patriarchs "have an extraordinary call and impulse. You do not. Therefore when such accounts are presented, you must remember not to lay stress on the examples or deeds" (LW 3.292; see also Mattox, *Defender* 178). Christians should only be like the patriarchs in having faith in God's word, not in imitating their behavior.

Luther's apocalyptic eschatology

I will now move beyond Provan's appropriation of Luther's words to consider other natalist arguments and assess whether Luther was a pioneer of natalism. The possibility of cornucopian or sectarian natalist ideas finding support in Luther are affected by his eschatology. He expected an

---

29 In general, and especially for an author as verbose as Luther, the use of ellipses in quotations is helpful. Many of the ellipses Provan makes are harmless, but in this case he removes a section essential for comprehension of the surrounding text.

imminent apocalypse: the Second Coming of Jesus, the resurrection of the dead, and the Last Judgement. Modern historians debate many details, such as whether Luther was more apocalyptic than other early Reformers and whether his anticipation of the end increased in his later years,[30] but that Luther's future horizon was short is a consensus (Parsons 628). Nestingen claims that "apocalypticism was the controlling factor in Luther's response to the challenges of his day" ("End" 257). Oberman and Barnes consider that eschatology was central to Luther's theology. Lohse disagrees, but affirms its presence (333) and admits that expectation of the end of the world was "more intense" among Europeans in the early 16th century than in earlier or later periods (33). Others have traced the rise of apocalypticism in the late 15th century (Reid 56; Nestingen, "End" 204). Apocalyptic language can sometimes be merely conventional (Lohse 332-34), and when Luther refers to a "last day" it may simply always be existentially close (Parsons 644). However, even if one grants that his phrases such as "the last hour has come" (LW 44.241), "the day of the Lord is drawing near" (LW 2.24), and "now at the end of the world" (LW 2.13) represent language of that type, there is other specific evidence for the imminence of Luther's expectation of the end.

The first evidence is Luther's "self-understanding as an end-time prophet" (Matheson, *Imaginative* 83), and also his later belief that the Papacy was the ultimate Antichrist (Cunningham and Grell 4), the persecutor of the true church in the last days. In a letter in 1545, Luther declared: "I believe that we are the last trumpet which prepares for and precedes the advent of Christ" (Gritsch 276). Luther saw himself as a second Noah, and his lifetime as being like the last days before the Flood (Parsons 644). All this suggests his expectation of an imminent end.

His statements about world chronology are the second pointer. Luther never predicted a specific year for end-times events, but he followed the tradition of dividing history into six millennia preceding Christ's second advent, and he asserted: "The world is six thousand years old and thereafter it will break apart" (Parsons 644). Luther's chronological treatise, *Supputatio annorum mundi*, published in 1541, identified the sixth millennium as an era of papal power after the spiritual decline and fall of the church (Gritsch 275). Luther was unsure of exactly when the church had begun falling, but he came to focus on the rise of the papacy and especially on Pope Gregory I, who began his reign in AD 590 (Reid 56). Given a millennial scheme, that

---

30 For the historiography in Reformation studies of the terms apocalyptic, millenarian, chiliasm, and eschatology, see Darrell Reid (55).

might point to 1590 as a significant date, though he admitted an earlier or later date for the end was possible.

The third piece of evidence is his view that prophecies from the Bible (and Saxon folklore) were being fulfilled, and that signs of the end were appearing. Luther wrote in 1541 that "the last day must be at hand. For almost all the signs have now appeared" (Lohse 33).

> The last day is at hand. My calendar has run out. I know nothing more in my Scriptures. All the firmaments and the course of the heavens are slowing down and approaching the end. For a whole year the [river] Elbe has remained at the same level and this too is a portent. (LW 54.134)

Commenting on Genesis, he discerned the "extreme old age of this world" (LW 6.188). Luther wrote in a letter in December 1544 to Jacob Propst: "It looks to me as if the world, too,[31] has come to the hour of its passing, and has become an old wornout coat ... Nothing good can be expected, therefore, except that the day of glory ... may be revealed" (LW 50.245). These words suggest his expectation for an imminent end of the world.

Luther's view on the proximity of the end seems to have fluctuated as his theology developed, and was also temporarily affected by personal circumstances and events such as the Peasants' War in 1525 (Oberman, *Luther* 278). However his persistent belief, in common with many of his contemporaries, was that the horizon of the world's future was a few years rather than decades or centuries (Headley; Oberman, *Luther* 12). Sectarian natalism requires a long-range vision of a secular future, at least several generations, time for the advantage of a higher birth rate to accumulate. If only for that reason, sectarian natalism would be alien to Luther.

Luther would find cornucopian belief even stranger. He believed that humankind's abilities and dominion had collapsed after the Fall, and that since the Flood there had been progressive and irreversible decline both in the Earth and in humankind: "We may assume that the closer the world was to Adam's Fall, the better it was; but it has deteriorated from day to day until our times, in which live the dregs and, as it were, the ultimate dung of the human race" (LW 2.7; Barnes 32). Luther's comment on the collapse of Adam's dominion (cited earlier) is not amenable to a cornucopian view: "By contrast, today and always the whole creation is hardly sufficient to feed and support the human race. Therefore what this dominion consisted of we cannot even imagine" (LW 1.172). Luther, unlike the Hussites, did

---

31 Luther is here drawing an analogy between his own old age and the world's decrepitude.

not expect the end of the age to bring earthly renewal, but rather the end of the world (Oberman, *Roots* 27). He believed that their Gospel proclamation would provoke a backlash from Satan that might hasten the last battle, and predicted that "the entire world will slide into obedience to the Antichrist … It is not our job to hold it back" (Oberman, *Roots* 43, 33).

Preserving the human species and society

Luther was determined to reform churches and to amend the nation, in spite of the imminent end of the world. Oberman calls this an "interim ethic" of preserving society (*Roots* 35, 36). It allowed room in his thought for a worldly pragmatism desiring sufficient reproduction for the survival of humankind and the nation. Anyone born into the pre-modern situation of high premature mortality would, if concerned for society's welfare, advocate high fecundity. Social natalists go a step further and claim that the necessity of preventing population decline should have priority over individual preferences. It would be fair to identify Luther as a social natalist of this type, though it did not much occupy his attention.

Luther's praise of human fecundity must be set in its demographic context. In the 16th century, over a third of infants died before the age of five (Ozment, 101), and, indeed, there was significant mortality among older children, young adults, and at all ages. Before and during Luther's formative early years, the population of Europe was lower than it had been two hundred years earlier. Numbers had begun falling around 1300, probably due to agricultural over-extension and small climate changes (Livi Bacci 38), even before the Black Death struck Europe around 1350. A slow decrease in population had continued into the 1400s, followed by stability until 1475, when it began increasing (Cunningham and Grell, 14-15). That was the demographic situation into which Luther was born in 1483, and the context for his praise of high fertility. Abandoned farmland was still abundant and being reclaimed in his lifetime (Livi Bacci 42, 88), evidence of the late medieval decline in the German population. This meant that any small increases in population which Luther might have anticipated could easily be accommodated. If he considered the longer-term future, which is unlikely, Luther was also aware of contemporary discoveries of new territory overseas, writing that "of late, many islands and lands have been discovered" (Lohse 16), so there would have been no reason for concern about overcrowding.

Luther identifies the temporal maintenance of humankind as one benefit of marriage. In his sermon at the wedding of Sigmund von Lindenau in 1545, he observed: "The human race would go out of existence" were it not for marriage (LS 98). He says in *Table Talk*: "When we look backward and think about the past, marriage is not so bad, for by means of it the future and the world are maintained. For our parents ... lived out their faith inasmuch as they obeyed God's command to raise children" (LS 125). Though he used this as an additional argument in favor of marriage in *Table Talk* and wedding sermons, he does not deploy it in his treatises against vows of celibacy, perhaps regarding temporal maintenance as a weaker argument than moral reasons. He does, however, turn to this point to explain, though not excuse, why Lot's daughters (Genesis 19:30-38) resorted to incest (as with other stories, Luther looks for ways to present the behavior of the men and women of Genesis as models of faith whenever possible):

> Thus they devise this plan ... because of their extraordinary compassion for the entire human race ... Lot's daughters thought: "God does not want to destroy the human race; He wants to preserve it. But now there is nobody left besides our father" ... Thus it is nothing but genuine concern for preserving the human race that troubles the saintly girls. (LW 3.280, 310)

The verbs (in English translation) that appear in Luther's comments on birth and population are "preserve," "maintain," "increase," and "multiply." He commented on a law in Deuteronomy (24:5): "It is fair that a bridegroom be granted a year with his bride ... that the commonwealth may increase through progeny and families" (LW 9.241). To modern ears the words "increase" and "multiply" likely bring to mind the rapid increase in total population experienced in the 20th century, but that is alien to medieval demographic experience and was not the concept in Luther's mind. In a sermon in January 1525, when he preached that the purpose of childbirth is "so that the human race is maintained" (LS 95), he explicitly stated that reproduction has the same purpose for humankind as for all species, and therefore "the body of a Christian must fructify and multiply just like that of other human beings, birds, and all the animals" (LW 28.26). Luther did not imagine that God intended all species to increase *absolutely* in successive generations: it was commonly known that wild animal populations did not continuously rise decade after decade. Rather, the word "multiply" refers to reproductive efforts replacing the regular losses to death. Luther believed that reproduction is part of all life in order to ensure the survival of species: "For when God once said (Gen.1:28): Be fruitful, that Word is effective to this day and preserves nature in a miraculous way" (LW 4.4). In another text, Luther treats the words "preserve" and "increase" as amounting to the same thing:

> When God says: "It is not good that man should be alone" ... God is speaking of the common good or that of the species, not of personal good ... he was not yet in possession of the common good which the rest of the living beings who propagated their kind through procreation had. For so far Adam was alone; he still had no partner for that magnificent work of begetting and preserving his kind. Therefore "good" in this passage denotes the increase of the human race. (LW 1.115-16)

Luther shared in the common cultural desire to maintain the paternal lineage and family name. Around the time of his marriage in June 1525, he mentioned the various reasons why he was taking this step. Writing to his friend Nicholas von Amsdorf, he referred to "my father's wish for progeny, which he so often expressed" (LW 49.117). Writing to John Ruhel, he wrote that "I cannot deny my father the hope of progeny" (Bainton 290). In a letter to his father that is prefixed to *Monastic Vows*, Luther mentions his duty to provide grandchildren as one reason invalidating his vow of celibacy (LW 48.331). However, he does not deploy this argument in the main work, nor in any of his treatises. Perhaps he did not consider it a sufficiently weighty theological argument for reproduction.

Nursery of the church

Marriage and reproduction have the potential to benefit not only civil society, but also the church. Luther pleaded that "marriage should be treated with honor; from it we all originate, because it is a nursery not only for the state but also for the church and the kingdom of Christ until the end of the world" (LW 1.240). He points out that bishops, the Pope, and the Early Fathers all owe their existence to marriage. But neither state nor church is blessed by mere biological increase unless the offspring are well brought up. Luther preached in 1519 in a sermon on marriage: "It is not enough, however, merely for children to be born ... Heathens, too, bear offspring," but parents must "raise children to the service, honor and praise of God and seek nothing else out of it, which unfortunately seldom happens" (LW 44.12). From this we may draw the implication that rearing a few children disciplined as good citizens and educated in Scripture is a better practice of parenthood than bearing many children but neglecting their discipline and education.

The assumption that faith is likely to be inherited by children from parents is severely qualified in Luther's writings. Parents and children hang between heaven and hell. For the parents, "bringing up their children properly is their shortest road to heaven. In fact, heaven itself could not be made nearer or achieved more easily than by doing this work" (LW 44.12). But Luther continues:

> By the same token, hell is no more easily earned ... than [by] spoiling children ... False natural love blinds parents so that they have more regard for the bodies of their children than they have for their souls ... "If you beat him with the rod you will save his life from hell" ... O what a truly noble, important, and blessed condition the estate of marriage is if it is properly regarded! O what a truly pitiable, horrible, and dangerous condition it is if it is not properly regarded! (LW 44.13)

In 1520 Luther repeated his warning to parents who fail to train children properly: "O how perilous it is to be a father or mother ... parents cannot earn hell more easily ... If they had not had children, perhaps they might have been saved" (LW 44.83, 86). This might prompt some to think twice before embarking on marriage and childbearing. But even if the parents do well there is no automatic progression for their offspring from infant baptism to salvation, for each one must believe.

> The flesh has its gifts, but nothing is owed them except bread and water. Eternal life does not come to the children of the flesh; it comes to the children of the promises, that is, to those who believe ... God added a blessing for married people when He said: "Increase and multiply." But this is a physical blessing and is restricted to the filling of the earth. No matter how saintly a father and a mother are, this is nevertheless of no advantage to the children born to them. Nor are the children saved on this account. If they are to be saved, they must become children of the promise, and they themselves must believe the promise. (LW 4.52)

On the *protoevangelion*, the messianic prophecy perceived in Genesis 3:15, Luther comments that "without this promise procreation would indeed continue to go on among people, as well as among the other living beings, but it would be nothing else than a procreation to death" (LW 1.195).

Though there is material in Luther's writings amenable to natalism, much of it arose from other motivations. The history of early Lutheranism shows that his writings have always been susceptible to conflicting types of reception. Similarly, in recent debates on gender "there is plenty of ammunition in Luther's words for both sides" (LS 8). Provan's use of Luther often misleads because he ignores the historical, theological, and hermeneutical context. Carlson, by contrast, shows awareness of context and his presentation is fair, though he sometimes mistakes Luther's rhetoric, for example on the impossibility of celibacy ("Children" 20). Despite intemperate words in the

1520s, Luther did not believe that natural law prevented celibacy. Also, the later doctrines of Lutheran theologians on the "orders of creation" should not be read back into Luther's occasional polemics. Luther confronted a Catholic culture that regarded celibacy as a work meriting righteousness. As a counterweight, he elevated marriage and childbearing. We can imagine that if he encountered people holding the opposite view, and regarding childrearing as a "good work," he would equally have resisted that as a distractor from justification by faith.

Luther's eschatology and secular pessimism put him far from cornucopian ideology, and his short temporal horizon left no time for sectarian natalism. Insofar as Luther had any interest in demography (the topic is not prominent in his thought), it was a common secular pragmatism desiring the perpetuation of the human species and one's family name, though even that was tempered by his eschatology. Luther is amenable to the idea that obligation to perpetuate the nation through reproduction outweighs personal goals such as the wish for a retired life of prayer and study. Very few earlier Christian writers would accept that view (though it was common among Stoics and other early non-Christian writers), so it is fair to regard Luther as a forerunner of social natalism.

4. The Old Testament Context

I begin this exploration of the Old Testament context by looking at the ancient Near Eastern background in its agricultural, demographic, economic, political, and religious dimensions. I will then focus on the canonical and theological contexts of the verses most commonly used by natalists (Genesis 1:28 and Psalm 127) to identify a range of plausible original meanings. This analysis leads to a comparison of the arguments advanced by modern natalists with features of Old Testament exegesis and theology from which significant differences emerge. In the first place, Old Testament blessings contribute materially to prosperity, and were regarded as a reward for loyalty to God: when modern natalists rebuke those supposedly refusing additional blessings, they lose sight of this original meaning. Secondly, distinctive features of the original text are ignored by natalists as inconvenient, for example the gender preference for sons. Finally, I will examine some recent attempts by biblical scholars at contemporary application (for their Christian readers) of significant fruitful verses.

The modern natalist sources that I analyzed make 264 references to the Old Testament, and these cover 27 out of the 39 canonical books.[1] Just over half (139) of the citations are to the Pentateuch,[2] including 84 to Genesis. "Be fruitful and multiply" (Genesis 1:28) is the most popular text, but the patriarchal narratives from Abraham onward account for over half (46) of the references to Genesis, and there are 35 references spread across Deuteronomy. Psalm 127:3-5 is the second most popular text, but spread

---

1 The only Old Testament books never cited in my catalogued sources are Esther, Song of Songs, Daniel, and nine of the minor prophets. Nine other books attract only one citation each: Numbers, Joshua, Judges, 2 Samuel, 1 Kings, 2 Kings, 2 Chronicles, Nehemiah, and Lamentations.

2 The five books (Genesis, Exodus, Leviticus, Numbers, and Deuteronomy) written by Moses, according to tradition, are collectively called the "Pentateuch" and have in Judaism a higher status than the other books of the Old Testament.

http://dx.doi.org/10.11647/OBP.0048.04

across the books outside the Pentateuch are 75 other verses that receive 109 mentions. Natalists refer to verses from different parts of the Old Testament, so the historical context is broad.

The background

The various parts of the Old Testament[3] were composed in the ancient Near East.[4] Their dates are generally uncertain and controversial. According to tradition the Pentateuch was wholly authored by the prophet Moses in the wilderness before 1200 BC. Few academic scholars accept that, but many think early narratives and laws were incorporated by later redactors (Ska 192) and that some parts date from various early periods including the time of Judges, the early monarchy from the 10th century BC, later in the First Temple period, after the Babylonian invasion and the fall of Jerusalem in 586 BC, and after the return of Jewish exiles. However, most of my points about context are not sensitive to particular dating because the features of the demographic, agricultural, economic, social, cultural, and (popular) religious context that are relevant to family size changed little across the range of possible dates. Even the political context, which did change, had an element of continuity in that one or another nearby empire was always a prominent feature.

Demographic context

A rough chronology derived from archaeology finds proto-Israelite farmers settling during the 13th or 12th century BC in the hill-country or highlands of modern Israel (Dever, "Who" 196). The highland region where the early Israelites[5] lived was sparsely populated. Other peoples already occupied the coast and lowlands, so the Israelites had settled in the central hill-country which had fewer occupants. The area was even less populated than it had been a few centuries earlier. The population of the Near East during the late Bronze Age, from the 15th through 13th centuries BC, had declined by half

---

3 "Old Testament" is the Christian name for a canonical collection of books that roughly corresponds to the Jewish *Tanakh*. Academics often call it the Hebrew Bible.

4 "Near East" is the term used in archaeology and biblical studies to label the region that outside those disciplines is usually called the Middle East (http://stylemanual.ngs.org/home/M/middle-east-west-asia).

5 In the centuries before the foundation of the monarchy and the states of Israel and Judah (in the 10th century BC), proto-Israelites can be identified archaeologically by their house design and the absence of pig bones (Dever, "What" 105, 113).

(Liverani 328, 381). Finkelstein estimates that numbers in the highlands had shrunk to only a third of the Bronze Age peak (Dever, "Who" 156). When the Israelites arrived in the 13th or 12th century, the highlands were less populated than they had been, and so through the early formative centuries of Israelite history there was "more land than people" (Liverani 22).

In the ancient Near East, high rates of premature mortality made numerous births necessary just to maintain a population. Death stalked all age cohorts but especially infants, as more than a third died before the age of five (Meyers, "Family" 19). A typical family unit had between two and four surviving children (Blenkinsopp 51), and this produced a slow increase. Between the 13th and 12th centuries, inward migration by Israelite settlers in the highlands was the main cause of population growth, but in later centuries the slower growth of a "long-resident population" is observed. Archaeologists offer various estimates for the number of Israelites living in the highlands. William Dever suggests 12,000 in the 13th century, 55,000 in the 12th century, and 75,000 in the 11th century ("What" 110). So the average annual percentage rate of natural increase was around 0.3% for the latter century. By the 7th century BC, the highland population was 150,000 ("Who" 196), giving an average rate of less than 0.2%, which probably masks fluctuations during those centuries. Either rate is typical for the ancient world, and much lower than some developing countries today which exceed 3% annual increase.

Child survival, health, and strength were more important than maximizing the number of births. Spacing between births was desirable not only for the mother's health, but also for the child's robustness. After a birth there is normally a time of natural infertility (postpartum infecundability) that includes suppression of the menstrual cycle. With on-demand breastfeeding as the only sustenance, natural low fertility (lactational amenorrhea) can persist up to 18 months, and this was common in pre-modern societies (Gruber 62). Beyond that, in some (especially polygamous) cultures, husbands avoid sex with lactating wives. Among ancient Israelites breastfeeding usually lasted three years (King and Stager 41). Hannah waited until weaning Samuel before delivering him to the Temple (1 Samuel 1:22), and the specification of his substitute offering as a three-year-old bull is indicative of his age (Blenkinsopp 98). A later text includes the saying: "I carried you in my womb for nine months and I nursed you for three years" (2 Maccabees 7:27). This often resulted in a helpful spacing between births.[6]

---

6 Some neighboring cultures followed a similar pattern: a surviving contract formula for Assyrian wet-nurses specified a three-year term (Gruber 76).

For ancient Israelites the demand for reproduction came very close to home. About 80% of people lived in clan-based rural settlements of less than 100 people (Meyers, "Family" 12). Each of those communities depended for its perpetuation on a small number of women of childbearing age. Given the likelihood of some being infertile and other women dying prematurely (especially as a result of childbirth), and the randomness of demographic events, such a small scale community would occasionally encounter crises in which reproduction temporarily threatened to be insufficient for local viability. In those circumstances it would be unthinkable for a woman to choose to opt out of reproduction.

Old Testament writers had some awareness of demography. At a popular level, farmers breeding livestock (Genesis 30:31-41) knew about demographic patterns. Casual observation of birds and other wild animals would reveal a pattern of many births with many dying young. The degree of excess varied greatly: some species' numbers periodically soar and crash, for example locusts and frogs (Exodus 8:13; 10:15). Other species seem fairly stable over many generations. Though it is easier to perceive demographic patterns in creatures with a short lifespan, they also knew about human demography: for example, that women bore many babies who died in their first year or as children. They might see an extended family living on the same land as they had for generations and deduce that numbers had not much risen. Scribes and rulers shared that popular knowledge, but they also knew tax records and perhaps old censuses. Old Testament texts include genealogies, enumeration of clans, and they mention royal efforts to count people with a view to taxation, labor (1 Kings 5:13), and military recruitment.

Cultural context

The writers of the Old Testament were scribes and priests. Though they were part of a religious elite with wider concerns than farming, around 95% of ancient Israelites were farmers (Blenkinsopp 54), and the writers would have been aware of agricultural concerns. It is helpful to consider the contribution of material culture to Old Testament ideas about fertility. In brief, ancient farmers would normally esteem prolific human fecundity, and that was accentuated in early Israel due to their circumstances.

Archaeology suggests that the early Israelites grew cereals, grapes, and olives, and kept livestock (Meyers, "Family" 3). The land was hilly with small intermontane valleys. Much was scrub woodland which was, however, deficient in valuable timber trees. The land was rocky with poor soil. The highlands demanded more labor than lowlands to clear the scrub (Joshua 17:18) and remove stones. The farmed land was mostly sloping with rare flat areas, so farmers had to do the "very laborious" work of building and maintaining terraces (Dever, "Who" 113). The effect of these conditions was an "extraordinary intensification" of the demand for labor, and since the early Israelites did not have many slaves there was a need for "large families" (Meyers, "Procreation" 581), beyond even the normal pre-modern desire for offspring.

As in other pre-modern agricultural societies, parents benefited practically from having numerous offspring.[7] Though the period of infancy was an economic loss due to the time spent caring and feeding, ethnographic studies of modern subsistence cultures suggest that from age five a child of subsistence farmers would help in tasks such as food preparation, gardening, water-carrying, wood-gathering, and guarding livestock from predators. As a child grew, the range of tasks and the hours worked would increase to the point at which production exceeds consumption (Meyers, "Family" 27). Research in the context of Bangladeshi farmers in 1977 found this crossover at age nine for boys (Sullivan 34): after that, a child was profitable. In the ancient Near East, children who survived infancy were economic assets for their parents,[8] and for their clan.

Daughters were typically as economically valuable as sons while they were children, but when they reached teenage years almost all daughters married and consequently moved to another man's household where they worked. The bride-price (Exodus 22:16) was compensation for the father and would vary according to status. Laban's daughter was exchanged for seven years' labor from Jacob (Genesis 29:20). One legal text which requires a rapist to pay the father the bride-price specifies fifty shekels, which is around five years' wages (Deuteronomy 22:28-29). Sons were even more valuable. After marriage, they continued to be affiliated to the *bêt 'ab* (literally "father's house," but materially a small cluster of dwellings around the patriarch's house) and owed obedience. In the nearby Ugaritic culture, a list of an adult son's duties to his father includes roof-patching and clothes-washing (Blenkinsopp 71). Adult sons could also support their father in disputes,

---

7 Though mothers only benefited if they survived childbirth. For each birth, the maternal mortality rate was around 2.5%.

8 Meyers suggests this may be reflected in Leviticus 27, where a lower compensation value is assigned to people aged under five ("Procreation" 585).

which some commentators identify as the background of Psalm 127:4,[9] discussed in detail below.

Parents expected that when (and if) they reached old age, their children would help them (Proverbs 23:22). That is reflected in the textual link between filial duty and long life (as well as secure possession of the land) in one of the Ten Commandments: "honour your father and mother so that you may live long in the land" (Exodus 20:12). Edesio Sánchez claims that the fifth commandment was aimed at adult children and constitutes a "requirement to take care of elderly parents" (40). Given that most daughters would be married, perhaps living in another settlement and certainly with duties redirected toward a husband and his kin, it was usually the sons (and their wives) who would be responsible for elderly parents.

Perhaps even more important, sons provide continuity in the lineage of male descendants, important for the inheritance of family land and, through memory, for conferring proxy immortality on the father (Brichto 21). They perpetuate the father's name (which might be recited in genealogies): "bless the boys and in them let my name be carried on" (Genesis 48:16).[10] The importance of this is shown by the custom that if a man died without an heir, then his eldest brother had a duty to marry the widow and to count the first of any offspring as belonging to the dead brother, so resurrecting his name. Long-term preservation of a male lineage was not easy: to reach the third generation, given pre-modern rates of premature mortality, a man would need at least three sons born to secure a high probability of one surviving to produce a grandson.[11]

Burial and the afterlife were additional reasons why ancient Israelites wanted offspring. Sons had a duty to bury their father (Petersen 14). When Isaac died, "his sons Esau and Jacob buried him" (Genesis 35:29). These people wanted to be buried with their ancestors; for example, the dying "Jacob called to his sons" and his last words were "I am to be gathered

---

9   That Psalm "deals ... exclusively with the sons" (Kraus 455). Though in some texts referring to infants as *bānîm* can be gender-neutral, in Psalm 127 the common male referent is appropriate (Davidson 419; Fleming 441; Dahood 224). Among translations, the RSV and NIV agree on "sons," but others including the ASV and ESV put "children," guided perhaps by a desire to make the text palatable to modern readers.

10   In the case of Zelophehad (Numbers 36:2-12), who dies with no son and only daughters, there is an emergency provision that the daughters may inherit his land on condition that they marry within their father's clan.

11   This can be illustrated from the story of Judah who has three adult sons (and probably other sons who died in infancy), two of whom die without progeny (Genesis 38). Only the third son lives to produce grandsons for Judah (1 Chronicles 4:21).

to my people: bury me with my fathers in the cave ... There they buried Abraham and Sarah his wife; there they buried Isaac and Rebekah his wife; and there I buried Leah" (Genesis 49:1, 29, 31). Family had a duty to ensure burial at the ancestral site (Genesis 30), or at least a decent interment: to go unburied was a dreadful prospect (Jeremiah 16:4).

In the ancient Near East, regular memorial rituals for dead ancestors were a duty performed by their descendants, ideally at the burial site on inherited family land: so it was important to have heirs to keep the ownership of that place in the family (Stavrakopoulou 4). This was done to honor the memory of the ancestors, but it was linked to beliefs about the afterlife and fellowship across the generations. Rituals might include food offerings to the ancestors. Occasional critiques of such customs (e.g. Deuteronomy 26:14), alongside archaeology, suggest that similar practices were common in ancient Israel. In that worldview, to be childless was to fail to maintain the line of descendants and cut off the forefathers.

Political context

The political context of the writers varies depending on the dating, but in any case there are common features. Moses would look forward to the nation living in the land; while those writing after the exile look back to a golden age when they were not subject to any empire. Writers in exile looked forward to returning to the land, but also with an eye to their exiled community. Babylonia and other ancient empires dealt with conquered peoples by enslaving the survivors and deporting some or all of them to other locations in the empire. Consequently, exiles were scattered around the empire, and that exacerbated perceptions of their being few. They were often unable to own land, vulnerable to oppression, and lacked self-determination. One important concern of their leaders was to preserve a distinct national religious identity.

Old Testament writers shared the concept of a distinct *'am* (people) named Israel, belonging in a particular land as one of the nations. It is unlikely that Old Testament writers worried about perpetuating the human species. Its survival had not been precarious since a time far beyond any collective memory. More importantly, humankind did not exist as one united community but rather as many rival peoples. The concern of each was national survival, often under threat from other nations and empires. There was a subsidiary interest in preserving the constituent parts of Israel. Communal efforts to rescue the tribe of Benjamin from near extinction are described in Judges 21. Whatever the later reality of the tribes, the continuity of each clan was valued. A basic concern was maintaining and increasing clan numbers. Elites with a wider perspective were concerned about the national scale of this phenomenon.

The slow natural increase of population could periodically be reversed, usually due to plague or war. After the Assyrian war in 701 BC, part of Judea's population increase of previous centuries had been lost (Borowski 8). Human fertility could therefore be a symbol of national hopes (Hosea 9:11). The exiles in Babylonia were exhorted to "increase in number there; do not decrease" (Jeremiah 29:6, NIV). During the earlier captivity in Egypt the Israelites are pictured as becoming "more and mightier" (Exodus 1:9-10, KJV), which set a good example for later exiles.

Rearing sufficient offspring to offset normal mortality and replace the current generation demanded continuous effort, but political concerns were more pressing and demanded higher fertility. In the ancient Near East, rivalry between nations for political existence and dominance required fertility partly to offset deaths in war, but mainly to match or outnumber other peoples. The Canaanites as archetypal enemy are depicted as "a great horde, in number like the sand" (Joshua 11:4, ESV), and there was a perceived need for a large number of warriors to defeat them. Large sections of the Pentateuch consist of lists counting each clan's contribution to the number of "all who were able to go to war" (Numbers 1:20, ESV).

Surrounded by empires, Judea had good reason to fear the political extinction that later overtook it. Ryan Byrne argues that "social reproduction … represented a priority of state as well as family in Iron Age Judah" (145), and claims that central production of mould-made fertility statuettes in Judea should be understood in the context of the Assyrian aggression which had extinguished nearby city-states (Arpad, Hamath, and Damascus) and the northern kingdom (Samaria). Judean towns also fell, and even Jerusalem was besieged (2 Kings 18:9, 17). Archaeologists have retrieved from 8th- and 7th-century BC sites across Judea more than eight hundred statuettes of a lactating female, and Byrne judges that these "pillar figurines portray the fertile archetype, an ideal model of the dutiful Judean woman, wife, mother, the progenitress of Judeans" (143). Perhaps at times of defeat and loss there was a stronger emphasis on reproduction.

The demands of war and rivalry that could generate a pro-fertility attitude are relevant whatever the dating of the Pentateuch. Moses was pictured leading a host of landless ex-slaves to conquer and occupy Canaan. During the kingdom period the emphasis was on holding land, and training sufficient sons to defend it militarily. Writers in exile would regret the kingdom's defeat, and belonged to a minority that was sometimes competing with other minorities or dreaming of triumphs like that of Mordecai (Esther 9:16). So the uncertainty of dating is not a problem for this argument.

Beyond national interest, parts of the Old Testament may voice the specific interests of rulers. Whether and how particular texts are polemical in supporting or critiquing ruling powers is hotly debated. For example, Philip Davies identifies many texts as the voice of a ruling class mediated by scribes (21),whereas others discern anti-monarchy voices. Attitudes to the institution of monarchy, the Davidic dynasty, the northern kingdom, and post-exilic Jerusalem governors authorised by Persia are certainly part of the background for the Old Testament.

Kings had a dynastic interest in fathering many sons.[12] To continue his dynasty a king needed at least one heir, surviving and suitable. Mortality rates among royal infants were probably little better than the pre-modern average.[13] Beyond the normal attrition, princes faced other perils: some might be killed due to fraternal rivalry, like Amnon (2 Samuel 13:29), or disloyalty to the king, like Absalom (2 Samuel 15:6). Though primogeniture (the eldest son inheriting lordship) was common in the ancient Near East, it was not automatic: a king could choose from among his sons, so more sons offered more chance of a worthy successor.[14] Often the reasons for setting aside older sons are not given: some might be deemed unfit to rule due to incompetence, insanity, or physical disability.[15] Others might be politically unsuitable, if born of a wife from a broken foreign alliance or from a local family that had fallen from favor. The writers of some fruitful verses in Proverbs and Psalms (including 127) have a royal audience in mind. And their writings were not mere flattery: they hoped the king would have sons for the sake of continuity, stability, and good governance.

Ambitious kings wanted their people to increase in number because "a large population is a king's glory" (Proverbs 14:28, NIV). Also, prolific reproduction among the common people provides more young men for the

---

12 At a lower rank, similar issues of succession faced the heads of clans.

13 Lower infant mortality rates for the upper class did not emerge until the 18th century in Europe.

14 David passed over his eldest surviving and loyal son Adonias, and appointed the younger Solomon as his heir (1 Kings 1:32). Rehoboam made Abijah the heir and set aside his older brothers (2 Chronicles 11:18-22). Josiah was succeeded by a younger son named Jaochaz.

15 A grandson of King Saul named Mephibosheth was crippled and not regarded by David as a threatening rival for the crown (2 Samuel 4:4; 9:13).

king's army, more tax income, and more forced labor for royal land and for the king's building projects. The prophet Samuel had warned the people about how rulers behave:

> This is what the king who will reign over you will claim as his rights: He will take your sons and make them serve with his chariots and horses, and they will run in front of his chariots ... others to plow his ground and reap his harvest, and still others to make weapons of war and equipment for his chariots. He will take your daughters to be perfumers and cooks and bakers. (1 Samuel 8:11-13; NIV)

Solomon rejoiced that "you have made me king over a people as numerous as the dust" (2 Chronicles 1:9), and the narrator says he then conscripted 153,600 people to build his palace and a temple (2:2). Another text records that 183,300 labored at Solomon's projects in various ways (1 Kings 5:13-16). The commander Joab counted 1.3 million men owing military service to the king (2 Samuel 24:9). Archaeology suggests that these numbers are unrealistically high, but they show the aspirational ideals of kings seeking grandeur and glory.

Ideas about reproduction

The fruitful verses should be interpreted in their immediate literary context, their canonical context, and the larger framework of Old Testament theology. The canonical and theological investigation cannot be confined to Genesis 1:28 and 9:1 (the only fruitful verses addressed to humankind universally) for two reasons. First, because the natalist sources do not confine their reception to Genesis 1-11; out of 264 references to the Old Testament, only 37 are to those early chapters. All the natalist writers refer to texts outside Genesis, even if these are just the Psalms for the least prolific quoters. Second, because the primeval history (Genesis 1-11) is part of the Pentateuch and the wider canon. In this respect, Old Testament theology suggests that some verses from the primeval history are thematic for the narrative from Genesis onward, from Joshua to Kings and beyond.

The sinful and defective character of humankind is depicted in Genesis, and God's response is to create a holy nation. The chosen instrument is the man Abraham and his seed (offspring) established in a particular land. The worship of God, embodied in religious practices, will endure through the matrix of this nation. The foundations of the nation are divine promises to Abraham, repeated to Isaac, Jacob, and the Israelites. Abraham's heirs will be his genetic offspring (15:4), they will be very numerous (13:16), and will cohere as a "great nation" (12:2). They will receive a land (12:7), good pasture and fertile fields, and will spread out across it (28:13), to fill and subdue it. In all this God promises that "I will be with you" (26:3), to bless, to give prosperity, to keep secure, to deliver from oppressors, and to defeat enemies. Old Testament scholars synthesize those promises in various ways. David Clines identifies "three elements: posterity, divine-human relationship, and land" (30). Desmond Alexander identifies descendants and land as the two prerequisites of nationhood (84). The divine agenda of creating a holy nation requires a number of related elements: genetic offspring is one of them, and increase in numbers is one aspect of that. Israelite fecundity is necessary but not sufficient; it is part of a larger project.

Integrated and sequential

Land is an integral feature of the promise, since in the pre-modern world any people reliant on herds and crops would need more land if they increased absolutely in population (Numbers 26:54; 33:54), because stocking density and crop yield rates did not rise steadily. Without access to more land they would suffer. Norman Whybray observes that for ancient peoples in the Near East the "search for living space was an essential condition of the good life" (5). When the God who provides for His chosen people promised numerous descendants, that was accompanied by a promise of land (Genesis 12:7; 15:5, 7). Similarly, when Abraham is promised that his seed will be as numerous as dust, he is also promised that they will be able to *prtz* (spread out) to the west, east, north, and south (28:14). A repeated theme is that Israel will be fruitful and become many "in the land" (Genesis 41.52; 47.27; 48.4; Deuteronomy 6:3). Though Jacob's extended family grows to number seventy (Genesis 46:27), this was far short of the nation promised to Abraham. Only after they are given the land of Goshen (Genesis 47:6) do the three verbs *prh, rbh,* and *ml'* (be fruitful, increase, and fill) occur together again (Exodus 1:7), expressing fulfilment of the blessing. And the label "nation" is first applied to the people when they are on their way to a larger land in Canaan (Exodus 13:13). In the wilderness the people are sustained by manna, but it is not an enduring solution. When the promise is remembered at Mount Sinai, the verb *rbh* (increase) and the noun *'rtz* (land) are linked together: "I will multiply your seed as the stars of heaven, and all this land that I have spoken of will I give unto your seed, and they shall inherit it for ever" (Exodus 32:13, KJV). Land was a prerequisite enabling the sons of Israel to be fruitful and become a nation.

A progression, a changing balance in the relative prominence of the elements of God's nation project, can be observed across the Pentateuch. While in Genesis 12-50 the foremost element is offspring, in Exodus and Leviticus the covenant is dominant, and in Numbers and Deuteronomy the land is highlighted (Clines 30). God's promise of offspring is rehearsed only once in Exodus (32:13), and in the books of Leviticus and Numbers it never appears. Deuteronomy revisits all the earlier themes, and the offspring element reappears there alongside the elements of land and covenant. I would not expect it to disappear permanently because the normal regular losses from mortality require a continuous state of being fruitful. Maintaining a numerous people demands the addition of replacement people in each generation. To keep the land filled with the living requires persistent reproduction, and if it ever slackens the land would quickly empty. Continued references after the origin narratives do imply endless fertility, but not necessarily absolute growth. Also, the birth of Israel and the subsequent stages of its national life are an historical process, and the relative importance of the elements varies according to the situation. Joshua has the whole land to fill so the situation is like that of Adam or Noah. When he is old there remains room for growth because much land has still not been occupied by Israelites (Joshua 13:1; Exodus 23:30).

Quantity

A large quantity of descendants is part of the plan. God promises offspring as numerous as the stars, sand, or dust. All these metaphors extravagantly picture a large number. Moses at Sinai encourages Israel that God "has multiplied you ... as numerous as the stars of heaven," but he looks to a future in which they will become "a thousand times as many" (Deuteronomy 1:10-11, ESV). Rhetorically, there seems to be no upper limit in view, but when Moses speaks the Israelites are still fewer in number than their enemies. Israel may already be a "great nation" (Deuteronomy 4:6), but it seeks to subdue or drive out stronger peoples described as "greater nations" (Deuteronomy 7:17; 11:23), and that is a reason why they keep hoping for greater numbers.

Building a holy nation requires not merely a large quantity of offspring, but also qualities such as loyalty to God, unity, and corporate identity, which are all linked to divine covenant. Whenever there is a choice between quality and quantity, the former is prioritized. Abraham has many sons, and Isaac has two sons, but in each generation only one "child of promise" is needed (Bratton 84). Attempts to build a holy nation including the extra sons would not yield a greater result; rather, it would hinder the project. When at Sinai the Israelites turn to a golden idol, God's first proposal is to eliminate them all and rebuild his nation from Moses alone (Exodus 32:10). As it turns out, God relents and instead commands that only three thousand unrepentant men be slain (Exodus 32:28). In the wilderness (Numbers 16:21) and in Israel's later history, the strategy of pruning back to a few people continues to be a thinkable option. There are also incidents in which loss of numbers is portrayed as necessary to maintain national holiness. For example, two hundred and fifty dissident Israelite leaders are slain by fire, and the family encampments of Korah, Dathan, and Abiram, together with "their wives, children and little ones," are swallowed alive into *Sheol* (Numbers 16:31-33, NIV). It is better for the Israelites to be reduced in number than to compromise the covenant.

Though quantity is not the most important feature of offspring, this does not suggest any virtue in limiting fertility, because the pruning is done after birth. It is amenable to a lottery natalism that gives birth to many in hope that some will turn out to be "godly offspring." The case of Abraham is different, with a revelation before any child is born that the nation will be built only from the son promised to Sarah. Despite this Abraham, due to his unbelief, fathers Ishmael by Hagar (and later six sons by Keturah), but sends them all far away (Genesis 21:10; 25:6) because the holy nation must be built only through Isaac, the child of Sarah.

Birth or covenant?

Ancient nations were not simply extended families. Though many small rural settlements might be purely kin groups, the people of a nation were not all closely related. Genesis emphasizes this as a feature even of Abraham's household, the first *bêt 'ab* (father's house). Its members are numerous, but most are not his kin. Abraham's heir for many years is a servant named Eliezer of Damascus (15:2). Abraham obeys God's command for all: "Whether born in your household or bought with your money, they must be circumcised" (17:13, NIV). It is the sign of membership among God's chosen people, an "everlasting covenant" for his non-kin household. Later in Israel, national identity was not strictly ethnic as many Israelites were not descendants of Jacob, and that is reflected in biblical narratives which mention some Israelites having names that indicate a different ancestry, including Uriah the Hittite (2 Samuel 11:6, 11). Non-kin could be incorporated into Israel by marriage, but *gerim* (strangers and resident aliens) could also join Israel, and there was no requirement for a connection by marriage to a descendant of Jacob. "The LORD will have compassion on Jacob ... Foreigners will join them and unite with the descendants of Jacob" (Isaiah 14:1, NIV). A clan of *gerim* could join Israel. The requirement was loyalty to God and nation, not ancestry or kinship connection.

On the other hand, some Old Testament writings express the idea that ancient Israel is essentially a kin group, built and maintained through birth. Abraham's heir will come "out of your own loins" (Genesis 15:4, ESV). Often an ideal is presented in which a hierarchy of groups, *bêt 'ab* (father's house), *mišpāhā* (clan), and *šēbēt* (tribe), constitute the nation (Joshua 7:14; 1 Samuel 10:19). Though such groups include some who are not kin, they are essentially kin-based. In genealogies each clan is assigned genetic descent from Jacob/ Israel, and the whole nation is sometimes portrayed as if it consisted solely of biological descendants of people who entered the land after the Exodus. The nation is called the "sons of Israel" (e.g. Genesis 50:25). Some texts indicate a policy of endogamy (rules against marriage to foreigners) forbidding, for example, marriages between Israelites and people from Canaanite nations (Deuteronomy 7:3). The question of whether the nation was and is to be built through biological reproduction, or by chosen adherence to God's Covenant, is an unresolved tension in the Old Testament.

The nation-building promises were essentially for Israel. A few texts extend the blessing to Abraham's other descendants, notably Ishmael (Genesis 17:20). Apart from these, no particular promise of fecundity is directed toward *goyim*, the other nations. Even among the Israelites, the promise is only for keepers of the covenant. One of the prophets asked God to give the disloyal Israelites a "miscarrying womb and dry breasts" (Hosea 9:14, KJV), so their babies would not survive. The Israelites are warned through Moses that if they break the covenant their children will be killed: "if you walk contrary to me ... I will continue striking you ... I will let loose the wild beasts against you, which shall bereave you of your children ... and make you few in number, so that your roads shall be deserted" (Leviticus 26:22, ESV). Biological descent from Jacob did not guarantee loyalty to the national covenant and God is portrayed as intervening to limit the number of offspring.

Genesis 1:28

The divine blessing on humankind in Genesis 1:28 includes five imperative verbs: *prh* (be fruitful), *rbh* (be many), *ml'* (fill), *kbs* (subdue), and *rdh* (rule or have dominion). Since 1970, in response to claims that reception of the last two verbs provided a motive or an excuse for exploitation of nature, biblical scholars have devoted much attention to "subdue" and "have dominion," and far less attention has been given to the ecological implications of the first three verbs: "be fruitful and multiply, fill the earth."

The verb *prh* is associated with the ability to give birth from a fruitful womb, the opposite of the closed womb that afflicted Sarah and Rachel. The verb *rbh* means to be "many" or "much" or "great," and its usage later in the canon often refers broadly to prosperity. For example, when the "oppressors of the poor" (Proverbs 22:16) grow richer the verb *rbh* is used. Biological reproduction and large family size is part of its meaning, but the 16th-century choice to translate it as "multiply" here may wrongly convey to modern readers an impression of an exclusive interest in quantity of offspring rather than human flourishing.

The verb *ml'* (fill) in Genesis 1:28 and 9:1 denotes the spatial extension of population across the face of the land, and shares its object *'rtz* (earth or land) with the verb *kbs* (subdue). All other biblical texts combining the verb *kbs* with the object *'rtz* (Numbers 32:22, 29; Joshua 18:1; 1 Chronicles 22:18) are about Israelites defeating Canaanites and consolidating their control of the land (McKeown, "Christian Faith and the Environment" 72), and Genesis echoes that. *Ml'* also refers here to occupying land: filling is not a once-only event because though a land may be filled, after a catastrophe such as war one or more settlements might empty out as happened to some Judean towns in the 7th century. So to "fill the land" was not only a past event but also a recurring imperative: "so will the ruined cities be filled with flocks of people" (Ezekiel 36:38, NIV).

The verbs *prh*, *rbh*, and *ml'* occur together as a triplet only four times (Genesis 1:22, 28; 9:1; Exodus 1:7). The first two are at creation addressed to nonhuman species and to humankind; the third revives the blessing for Noah and his sons as they make a new beginning in an empty world. The last is a report of the fulfillment of the original blessing in the land of Goshen in Egypt, indicating that God is still true to His covenant even though the people are temporarily distant from the promised land.

The verb pair *prh* and *rbh* occurs in twelve other verses (Genesis 8:17; 9:7; 17:20; 28:3; 35:11; 47:27; 48:4; Leviticus 26:9; Jeremiah 3:16; 23:3; Ezekiel 36:11). This pattern, as with most occurrences in Genesis, indicates an emphasis on *prh* and *rbh* at the origins and formation of the nation, and its recollection as a promise of restoration after the depletion and dispossession of war and exile. It is spoken by God to the patriarchs at difficult points in their lives, as reassurance. The four instances outside Genesis offer hope of future success. The people will increase in the land if they obey God's law (Leviticus 26:9); Jeremiah pictures revival if the people turn to God (3:16; 23:3); and Ezekiel links it with "waste places rebuilt" (36:11). Here, the offer of fertility and prosperity functions as a "carrot" to encourage the people to choose loyalty to God, and to seek religious and moral reformation.

Presenting fertility as a blessing from the one creator may also be polemic against ancient Near Eastern fertility cults. Leading archaeologist William Dever emphasizes the "central role of sex and reproduction in Canaanite religion" ("Who" 199). John Hartley suggests that most people in the ancient Near East "believed that fertility rites practiced at local shrines enabled their lands, flocks and wives to produce abundantly" (49). Israelite popular folk religion was perhaps similar. Figurines of a pregnant or lactating woman have been found all over Judah from the time of the Davidic dynasty, perhaps linked to a cult of Asherah and probably connected to prayers for fertility. Victor Hamilton observes that fertility rituals were often associated with the retelling of creation stories (139). Westermann suggests that Genesis 1:28 is designed to warn its hearers that when they seek fertility (the words of the blessing may derive from a traditional marriage blessing), they should not seek help from other gods because fertility is a gift from the God of Israel, and since God gave all life the capacity to reproduce at its origin, no subsequent ritual is needed (*Genesis* 161). Genesis chapter 1 is thus "a deliberate rejection of the fertility cult" (Cohen 44).

Reproduction under God's curse

When human reproduction first appears in Genesis it is unambiguously part of God's blessings on humankind. But then comes human sin and God's curse under which all human endeavor, including reproduction, becomes ambivalent. In the second creation story (chapters 2 and 3) the first appearance of *rbh* is doubled but ironic: God says "unto the woman ... I will greatly multiply (*rbh rbh*) thy sorrow and thy conception; in sorrow thou shalt bring forth children; and thy desire shall be to thy husband, and he shall rule over thee" (3:16, KJV). Soon after, a recounting of successive generations (4:17-22), producing sons who themselves in turn are fecund, such as Jabal "the father of those who dwell in tents and have livestock" (4:20, ESV), might look like a fulfillment of the original blessing. For six generations which span hundreds of years, Cain's lineage prospers genetically with the multi-generational fecundity that *Vision Forum* and other modern natalist would-be patriarchs dream of and plan. But their fecundity is not a sign of God's favor: Cain is especially cursed (4:11), and his great lineage is doomed as generations later every one of its offspring is destroyed by God's Flood, exposing all their mothers' labors as futile.

There are two lines of descent from Adam and Eve, the lineages of Cain and Seth (5:6-27). In each generation of the Sethite genealogy (5:6-31) the eldest son is named (Noah comes from this line), but for each of the nine generations it is also recorded that "after he became the father of [the named eldest son] … he had other sons and daughters" (5:7, 10, 13, 16, 19, 22, 26, 30). These other descendants are the great bulk of this branching Sethite population which looks like it will produce the godly people that God wants, for in the second generation some "began to call on the name of the Lord" (4:26). However, in the ninth Sethite generation only one "righteous man" (6:9) survives, Noah and his household. All the other Sethites, half of humankind, are destroyed in the Flood. Most of their earlier reproductive effort that had looked so promising turned out to have been as futile as the births of the Cainites.

The first verse of the Flood story, "when men began to multiply on the face of the earth" (Genesis 6:1), includes *rbh* and recalls the divine imperative at 1:28. At first this sounds like a success story: fulfilment of the blessing. Then in verse 5 we hear that *adam* (humankind) has become "great" (the noun form of *rbh*), but ironically it is "wickedness" that has multiplied. Similarly, the first use of the root *ml'* after chapter 1 appears when God sees that the Earth has become "filled with violence" (6:11, 13). This suggests that mere numbers are not the highest priority, and there will be divine discrimination between what is acceptable and unacceptable. This is based simultaneously on God's election and on the quality of human behavior. After the Flood the sons of Noah are a hopeful fresh start for humankind and we read that:

> Kana`an became the father of Tzidon (his firstborn) and Heth, the Yevusi, the Amori, the Girgashi, the Hivvi, the `Arki, the Sini, the Arvadi, the Tzemari, and the Hamati. Afterward the families of the Kana`anim were spread abroad. (Genesis 10:15-18, HNV)

That report of human fecundity sounds like a fulfillment of the blessing, fruitful for generation upon generation, the root of many tribes. But the lineage of Kana`an (or Canaan) the son of Ham was cursed (Genesis 9:25). The story of the many progeny and tribes descending from Canaan illustrates what the reader already knows from the earlier story of Cain and his numerous descendants: being under a curse does not hinder reproduction, which continues because it is inbuilt in human nature and has not been uncreated. One implication is that the outward evidence of prolific reproduction is not a clear sign of God's favor. This cursed reproduction looks like fruitfulness, but in due course the land will vomit them out (Leviticus 18:25) and its futility will become clear.

Is disobedience of "be fruitful and increase" thematic?

Some early Jewish rabbis, and a few modern exegetes, suggested that the central recurring sin of humankind in Genesis 1-11 is disobedience of the commands "be fruitful and increase and fill the earth." In line with this idea, they interpreted all the sins of Adam and Eve (3:1-6), Cain (4:8), the obscure "sons of God" (6:4), other people before the Flood (6:5, 13), and Ham (9:21-25) as offences relating to sex and reproduction (Cohen 60). Kikawada makes a bizarre suggestion that the original sin in the Garden of Eden was that Adam and Eve refused to reproduce (3:10).

> God tried the sedentary life for man and it did not work ... what happens when Adam and Eve try to become civilised? They become ashamed of their genitals. What does this shame signify? Perhaps they no longer wanted to fulfil God's command to be fruitful and multiply ... Eve was trying to avoid reproduction. (Kikawada and Quinn 68)

Other early sins were construed as sexual acts that were non-generating or wrongly generative. For example, rabbinic midrash regarded Cain as born from a union between Eve and the serpent, therefore producing a trans-human lineage. Cohen seems to be persuaded by some "rabbinic homilies" which argued that "Noah's contemporaries incurred the punishment of the Flood because of ... their refusal to fulfil the procreative mandate" (78).

However, this effort to identify primeval sins as offences against the command to "be fruitful" is unconvincing. Even if some of the sins featured in Genesis 1-11 are sexual, they are less about failure to reproduce than about transgressions of boundaries (between the sons of God and the daughters of men in Genesis 6:4), disrespect for parents (Ham making fun of Noah's naked body), breaking of marriage, and incest. For those who seek a thematic sin in Genesis 1-11, hubris and violence are better candidates. Genesis 3 narrates a theft of godlike knowledge, and before the Fall of Babel men want to make a "name" for themselves.[16] The sins of Cain include envy and murder (4:8), and similarly the widespread sin that provokes the Flood (6:11) is clearly identified as *hamas* (violence).

Few biblical scholars agree with Kikawada that the thematic sin of the first eleven chapters of Genesis is voluntary infertility, a refusal to be fruitful and increase. However some identify a refusal to "fill the earth" as the sin of humankind on the plains of Shinar when the people say: "Come, let us build ourselves a city, with a tower that reaches to the heavens, so that we may make a name for ourselves; otherwise we will be scattered over the face of the whole earth" (Genesis 11:4). Laurence Turner argues that "in the Babel story ... the human sin was a refusal to fill the earth" (41), and their scattering (11:8) is interpreted as forcing them to fill the earth (Wenham, *Genesis* 240), but Kaminski demolishes this interpretation (31). The verb used in the Babel narrative is not *ml'* (fill) but instead *pws* (scatter), which has negative connotations and would remind readers of Jerusalem's fall and the scattering of its people into exile. For example, *pws* features in these verses: "I will divide them in Jacob and scatter them in Israel" (Genesis 49:7, ESV); and "May your enemies be scattered" (Numbers 10:35, NIV). Whereas *ml'* connotes occupation in strength, a prospect that any ambitious ancient people (like those at Babel) would welcome, *pws* instead denotes a scattering in weakness, as used in this warning: "The LORD will scatter you ... and only a few of you will survive" (Deuteronomy 4:27, NIV). The text in Genesis 10 does not identify the provocation as being a failure to fill the land; instead, the focus is on their unified language and their project of building a tower, and the reason given for divine intervention is that "nothing they plan to do will be impossible for them" (11:6, NIV). To prevent that they are disunited by a confusion of languages and then scattered across the land.

Genesis as polemic against Atrahasis?

Some commentators discern a sharp contrast in views on human fertility between biblical and ancient Near Eastern culture, and claim that Genesis includes a polemic against the 18th-century BC Babylonian epic *Atrahasis*.

---

16 "Name" or "renown" also features before the Flood (6:4).

In that writing, the lesser gods complain about their work of farming and maintaining canals, so humans are created as laborers. Men, however, multiply and become too noisy, their "uproar" disturbing the peace of the gods. The gods try to reduce human exuberance with plague, drought, and a famine, but these fail and so they unleash a flood to wipe out humankind. The gods soon regret this because they need human service and are pleased to discover that the god Enki warned a man named Atrahasis to build a boat. Enki then proposes less drastic measures to restrain human population growth in future: "Let there be among the peoples women who bear and women who do not bear. Let there be among the peoples the Pasittu-demon to snatch the baby from the lap of her who bore it" (Genesis 1:17). Ronald Hendel identifies divine strategies limiting human population: removing immortality or preventing its acquisition, reducing human lifespan, the establishment of categories of women who are not child-bearing, incidence of barren infertility, and infant mortality (24). There would still be occasional disasters of famine, plague, and war to regulate population, but the gods will not again seek to annihilate humankind.

William Moran identifies the words "be fruitful and multiply" after the Flood (Genesis 9:1) as a "conscious rejection" of *Atrahasis'* presentation of the "limitation of man's growth" as a remedy for disorder (61). Anne Kilmer similarly argues that whereas *Atrahasis* calls for man to "limit his increase … the biblical text indicates the opposite command" (174). Isaac Kikawada argues that here "God, far from punishing man for population growth, is rather ordering him 'be fruitful and multiply and fill the earth' … this command … was argumentative, almost polemical, in its original context" (38-39). This is speculative, assuming that *Atrahasis* was known to the biblical writer, but plausible given Israelite natalism.

Kikawada goes further in venturing to construct a theological principle: "Population growth is from the very beginning of the Genesis primeval history presented as an unqualified blessing … Genesis 1-11 … argues in favour of … unlimited human reproduction" (51-52). Kikawada asserts that to become fully the image of God one must reproduce biologically, because:

> the creative motion of God has as its highest product his reproduction of himself according to his own kind … Mankind, to live fully, to be the image and likeness of God, must exercise his dual capacities … reproduce and move … If he is to reproduce to his fullest, he must be willing to give up his sedentary way of life … *Atrahasis* argues that … mankind should curb its reproductive drive … The Hebrew author responds that procreation is God's greatest command to us, our greatest blessing … What about overpopulation? To this civilized question the Hebrew gives a nomadic reply. (79-80)

This is based on a contrast between nomadic and settled viewpoints, in which nomads solve overcrowding by migration and dispersion, whereas settled farming people respond either with fatalism (the gods will reduce us), by planting colonies, or by genocidal conquest. Kikawada claims that "*Atrahasis* offers population control as the solution to urban overcrowding; Genesis offers dispersion, the nomadic way of life." Jacob Milgrom, reviewing Kikawada's work, rejects his idea of a nomadic ideal in the Bible (373). And even if they had such an outlook, typically nomads also experience constraints on population. Nomads often live on marginal land because the fertile land has been occupied by settled peoples.

Tikva Frymer-Kensky argues convincingly that Genesis' main equivalent to the remedies proposed in *Atrahasis* are laws to stop violent shedding of blood polluting the land. With regard to "be fruitful and multiply" she makes two assertions: it is a "conscious rejection of the idea that the cause of the Flood was overpopulation and that overpopulation is a serious problem" (152). I agree with the first clause but not the second. Genesis certainly identifies the reason for the Flood as sin, rather than any other cause such as the gods wishing to reduce human noise and numbers. The text's aim is not to advocate unlimited fertility, but to oppose amoral explanations of disaster and insist on a theodicy of justice. It is a central theological claim of the arc of narrative from Genesis to Kings that the fall of Jerusalem and other disasters were God's judgment for sins against the covenant.

Also, the contrast between Israelite and Babylonian approaches to some issues in the stories is not absolute. *Atrahasis* offers an aetiology of human mortality, and there are traces of parallel ideas in the Old Testament (Hendel 24). Genesis includes a decree of mortality (3:19, 22) and a limiting of lifespan to 120 years (6:3). Genesis also includes a malediction on childbearing (3:16) which can encompass not only labor pains but also maternal sorrow at premature deaths (e.g. 2 Samuel 21:19) and infant mortality (e.g. 1 Kings 3:19), and the risk of maternal death itself (Genesis 35:17-18). The divine right of closing wombs (Genesis 20:18) and killing infants (2 Samuel 12:14) also features in the Old Testament. What is distinctive in the Old Testament is that the implementation of these constraints on human life is vested solely in the one true God, whereas in *Atrahasis* they are implemented by sub-divine agents.

In any case, it is unwise to characterize ancient or Mesopotamian thought on the basis of the one text, *Atrahasis*. Desire for fecundity is evident across the ancient Near East in artefacts and texts. These do not often specify human fertility, but that is partly due to genre. In mythologies full of gods and demigods, ideas about humanity are expressed through stories about divine beings. For example, the fecundity of Enlil and Enki is exalted, Asherah has seventy sons, and the Akkadian mother goddess bears seven sons and seven daughters (Yegerlehner 54). Near Eastern figurines of a pregnant woman represent goddesses, but they also express human goals. The *Instruction of Anii*, from Egypt, urges hearers "Take a wife while you're young, That she make a son for you ... Happy the man whose people are many, He is saluted on account of his progeny" (Hallo 1:111). Many rituals identify barrenness in women as a curse, and children as blessings. One Hittite prayer pleads with absent gods "come ye to ... Hatti land. Bring with you life, good health, long years, power of procreation, sons, daughters, grandchildren, great-grandchildren" (ANET 352). Sons were wanted more than daughters. In the Ugaritic *Legend of Kirta*, the god El blesses "the woman you take into your house ... [she] shall bear you seven sons" (Hallo 1:337). Ancient cultures usually valued human fecundity.

Psalm 127:3-5 as a Song of Ascent

> Sons are a heritage from the LORD, the fruit of the womb a reward. Like arrows in the hand of a warrior are the sons born in one's youth. Blessed is the man whose quiver is full of them. He shall not be put to shame when he contends with his enemies at the gate. (Psalm 127:3-5)

Many scholars consider that this Psalm was developed from a pre-existing proverb, and identify the genre of its origins as proverbial wisdom for ordinary people about "everyday life" (Kraus 453) and "the farmhouse" (Hunter 237). It was "domestic" (Gerstenberger 346), and spoke to the "universal preoccupations" of work, security, and family (Kidner 440). The notion that "the larger the family, the less vulnerable" reflects ancient culture (Mays 401). However, most scholars believe that, whatever its origins, Psalm 127 was reshaped to convey theological messages. Using an imagined domestic origin as the interpretive key is therefore problematic: for example, the everyday ways that a farmer's sons would have helped him (as detailed earlier) do not match the Psalm's specification of how these sons help – they contend with enemies at the gate (127:5). Some suggest the Psalm refers to a "law court" (Allen 181), where "perhaps having many sons present would sway judicial decisions in one's favor" (Clifford 240). Perhaps, but that would contradict the Old Testament ideal of ensuring justice for those who lack strong male advocates (Deuteronomy 10:18; Goulder 67). Alternatively, if local conflict is imagined it would present a norm of settling disputes by intimidation, as whoever can call upon more muscle (of youths) prevails, which sits uneasily with a cultural ideal that wisdom (of elders) is the essential at the gate (Proverbs 24:7). The simile of arrows may connote ambush and wounding (Psalm 64:7),[17] which at a domestic level would mean private feuding, but that would be frowned upon by any writer associated with the king or priesthood. It makes more sense to understand the imagery as depicting "national military rather than individual legal conflict," so the noun *'ōyebîm* (enemies) refers not to private enemies but "armies of enemy peoples" (Fleming 436, 442). Against those who claim that the verb *dbr* (speak, contend) indicates a non-violent setting, it can be translated as "subdue," as in "He subdued nations under us, peoples under our feet" (Psalm 47:3, NIV; also 18:47). Here the translation to "repulse" or "drive back" enemies from the gate may be suggested by ancient Near Eastern usage (Dahood 225; Crow 67).

The relation of the Psalm's two strophes is important in exegesis. I think the first gives the key message, which is the futility of human plans and effort without God's help (Davidson 418), while the second is an illustration (Clifford 241), and the wordplay between the verb *bnh* (build, verse 1) and the noun *bn* (sons) merely links the two parts. By contrast, some argue that a family theme rules the Psalm. Allen suggests that "house" (verse 1) "refers metaphorically to raising a family" (178). However, reading the Psalm in its canonical Old Testament setting raises it to national and messianic meanings. Psalm 127 is one of a set of fifteen (Psalms 120 to 134) which have the superscription *shir* (song) *hama'aloth*[18] (steps, stairs or ascents). They are collectively labelled the Songs of Ascent, and are associated with the Jerusalem temple. Elie Assis links Psalm 127 to a time when attempts to rebuild the temple had failed (Ezra 4:1-5); it is a theological explanation that God's timing for a new temple is future not present (263, 266), so "it will not be possible to construct it," and the people should instead focus on domestic life until "a more auspicious time" (268, 271). Assis suggests that Haggai 1:9 rebukes these ideas. Alternatively, with more speculative precision, Michael Goulder associates the Ascent Psalms with Nehemiah. He links Psalms 127 and 128 to Nehemiah 7:5 and 11:1, where he finds "traces of a policy to repopulate the city" with settlers (30), for the "strength of Jerusalem" will be a larger population and "their number depends in the long run on children, not imported adults" (67). These two scholars' different proposals both link the

---

17   Arrows shot by God can be punishments (Lamentations 3:13), embodied not just by war but also by sickness (Psalm 38:2), plague, and famine (Ezekiel 5:16). But these arrows are a man's.

18   Psalm 121 has a slightly different form: *lama'aloth* (121:1).

fecundity message with particular historical anxieties, making it specific to Israel's past and less amenable to natalist appropriation.

Some key words in the Ascent Psalms are associated with kingship: "David, anointed, throne" (Hunter 229). Insofar as the "house" at 127:1 is familial,[19] it may be dynastic; it echoes the story of 2 Samuel 7, in which David wishes to build a house (a temple) for the Lord, but instead God promises to build a house (a royal dynasty) for David (Clifford 239; Mitchell 123). A Psalm of Ascent recalls that God swore to David: "One of your fruit of the womb I will set on your throne" (132:11, ESV).

A further contextual feature is that Psalm 127 is one of only two in the Psalter linked by superscription to Solomon. Regardless of provenance, this can legitimately shape a canonical interpretation. The "man" like a *gibbōr* (mighty hero) whose heirs (arrows) are destined to subdue enemies (127:4-5) may be a national leader. A ruler must ensure the "continuity of his dynasty through numerous sons" (Dahood 224), and the people want sons born in his youth (127:4), so he may not die while his heir is still a child, a time of weakness inviting opportunistic enemies. If the Ascent Psalms' redaction is post-exilic, the royal motif may show an "interest in ideal kingship" (Hunter 236) and perhaps a messianic hope. The images of harvest and fertility in the Ascent Psalms may look to an eschatological *Sukkoth* (Mitchell 114), and if so, the quiver of sons is the fecund hyperbole that typically accompanies eschatological *shalom*, like the tree that bears "fruit every month" (Ezekiel 47:12). The varying scholarly interpretations of this Psalm depend on which features of context are emphasized. Any of the theological interpretations described above is preferable to the domestic interpretation.

Natalism compared with Old Testament ideas

Universal or sectarian?

Chapter 2 observed that among Evangelical natalists most focus on calling godly Christians to increase their birth rate, but a few (notably Allan Carlson) call people of all religions to higher fecundity.[20] Almost all the verses cited were addressed exclusively to Israel in their original context,[21] so their use

---

19 It is, however, more likely to signify the temple, as the parallels of house/city elsewhere (Jeremiah 26; 1 Kings 8:44; 23:27) refer to Jerusalem and the temple (Fleming 436).

20 Some natalists occasionally extend their exhortation beyond the church, calling on their fellow Americans to have bigger families.

21 There are only two among the hundreds of verses cited by natalists that were, perhaps,

to support universal natalism is dubious. There is no warrant in Christian tradition for applying the Israel-oriented promises to all (unredeemed) people without distinction. By contrast, there is an established rationale and method for applying promises to Israel to the church by extension or supersessionist transfer. However, the same tradition changes the meaning of the fruitful verses in other ways, transforming the hope from sexual to spiritual fecundity. Natalists have pulled apart the Christian tradition's approach to these verses, happily adopting its transference of addressee, but neglecting the transformation of meaning.

Blessing in the Old Testament

To have many sons is a greater blessing than to have a few, and there seems to be no upper limit. After the seven sons of Meshelemiah are enumerated, the eight sons of Obed-Edom are also listed with the remark "for God blessed him" (1 Chronicles 26:5). A list of temple servants observes: "All these were sons of Heman the king's seer. They were given to him through the promises of God to exalt him. God gave to Heman fourteen sons and three daughters" (1 Chronicles 25:5). This number comes close to the biological maximum for one wife, and the ratio of sons and daughters (14:3) may suggest a typical Israelite father's ideal hope.

Genesis 1:28 is framed as a blessing. In the ancient Near East that meant, in a word, "prosperity" (Grüneberg 102) or "success" (Wenham, *Genesis* 24), which is a gift from God. Blessing can refer to particular good things, or to a general state. The word blessing is used with reference to rain (Ezekiel 34:26), springs of water (Joshua 15:19), food (Proverbs 11:25; Malachi 3:10), wealth (Proverbs 10:22), reproduction (Genesis 49:25), and life (Psalms 133:3).[22] It is a long-term condition, and a typical picture of a blessed life might run as follows. A child matures healthily; he gains the use of land and livestock, which through his labor prosper. Each year the land yields a harvest and the livestock produce lambs and kids.[23] The man acquires a house, marries a helpful wife, and has many offspring (preferably more sons than daughters) who are also helpers. He accumulates wealth, and is kept secure from thieves and enemies. He is given good health, and as an old man is surrounded by respectful descendants. At a ripe old age he dies and rests with his ancestors,

---

originally intended to have universal scope: Genesis 1:28 and 9:1, 7.

22 Blessing in the Old Testament can also refer to a speech or act that conveys it: a gift or thanks to God.

23 These moments of blessing are intimately linked to Old Testament religion in the timing of the main religious festivals in autumn and spring.

but his heirs ensure that his name and memory endure. This is a picture of what blessing meant in the ancient world.

Such blessing was desired by men (and women) across the ancient Near East because it offered obvious and objective benefits. In the modern world a similar generic idea of prosperity is easily recognizable: health, wealth, and long life. The most significant difference now is that numerous offspring do not materially benefit a man in so many ways as they once did. When modern natalists chastise those who do not want to produce additional offspring they neglect this characteristic of blessing as a real benefit. If potential recipients prefer to avoid those additional "blessings," then they are not really blessings in the Old Testament sense. So the phrase "be fruitful and increase" is qualified and limited by being a blessing. Since the Old Testament meaning of blessing is prosperity and flourishing (Grüneberg 110), if population rises to a point at which it is detrimental to the flourishing of some human individuals or nations then it is certainly not a blessing.

Economic cornucopia?

Calvin Beisner finds in the Old Testament a lesson that people of faith should not worry about ecological limits on population. He sees in the story of "Abram and Lot ... the earliest instance recorded in the Bible of the impression that a local human population had outstripped the ability of the land to support it" ("Imago" 173).

> Abram was very rich in cattle ... Lot also, which went with Abram, had flocks, and herds, and tents. And the land was not able to bear them that they might dwell together, for their substance was great. There was a strife between the herdsmen of Abram's cattle and the herdsmen of Lot's cattle." (Genesis 13:2, 5-7a, KJV)

In an interview for *Christianity Today*, Beisner argued that Lot "feared the land would not support both of their families, whereas Abraham trusted God to provide," and he warns those worried about overpopulation that they "reflect Lot more than Abraham. They don't trust in God's ability to provide." But the text contradicts Beisner. The biblical narrator reports that "the land could not support both of them dwelling together" (Genesis 13:6, NIV). The problem was not imaginary. Both had "flocks and herds" and there was "strife between the herdsmen of Abram's livestock and the herdsmen of Lot's livestock" (13:7a, ESV), probably over water or grazing. Given the maximum feasible distance herders could go from the camp, they had to separate. And *contra* Beisner, it was Abraham (not Lot) who saw the problem and took the initiative in suggesting their separation.[24]

"Canaanites and Perizzites were also living in the land at that time" (13:7b, NIV). The potential for conflict with other tribes over resources is hinted at in the story of Abram and his nephew, and later becomes explicit. In that region the main constraint was water, scarcer than land which is useless without water. Isaac had controversies over wells with Philistines and had to move (26:15, 18). His herders dug new wells into the underground water-table, but then "the herdsmen of Gerar quarrelled with Isaac's herdsmen, saying 'The water is ours' ... Then they dug another well, and they quarrelled over that also" (26:20, ESV). When at last Isaac found an uncontested water supply at Rehoboth he exclaimed "now the LORD hath made room (*rchb*) for us, and we shall be fruitful (*prh*) in the land" (Genesis 26:22). Notice that finding water and space leads to the verb *prh*, which means here that Isaac will prosper but also echoes "be fruitful," and immediately afterward God promises to "multiply (*rbh*) your offspring" (26:24, ESV) and completes the echo of 1:28. The need for space and resources is closely tied to reproduction.

The "room" made for Isaac's group is *rchb*, meaning breadth, which here is a similar concept to *Lebensraum* or living space. When the number of people or the size of their herds increase, conflict arises. Abraham's God invites him to "walk through the length and the breadth (*rchb*) of the land, for I will give it to you" (Genesis 13:17, ESV), anticipating the future dispossession of the Canaanites to accommodate new Abrahamic seed numerous as dust. In the next generation, when Jacob and his sons move near "the city of Shechem" (33:18) and "Hamor the Hivite, the ruler of that area" (34:2, NIV) sends men to negotiate, the Hivites say "these men are at peace with us; let them dwell in the land and trade in it, for behold, the land is large enough (*rchb*) for them" (34:21, ESV). They are unaware of the land promise and naively think there is enough space (*rchb*) to accommodate Jacob's clan. Seeking integration with the Jacobites, the Hivite men agree to be circumcised but while they are incapacitated the tricky sons of Jacob kill the city's men and take the women captive (34:22-29).

---

24 An ecological reading might imagine Abraham hearing quarrels at the well, noticing the signs of overgrazing, and acting decisively to solve the environmental problem. But the Old Testament writer's main interest is the departure of Lot as Abraham's heir apparent, for the chosen people will not stem from Lot's descendants, from Moab or Ammon (Genesis 19:37), but from the descendants of Isaac.

Natalist cornucopians fantasize that population growth can be sustained by ingenuity without causing conflict, but the Old Testament is more realistic: the growth of one people requires that other peoples be displaced. The Israelites are exhorted to "cast out nations, and enlarge your borders" (Exodus 34:24). When Dan, one of the twelve tribes of Israel, "was seeking a place of their own where they might settle" (Judges 18:1, NIV), they sent five men "to spy out the land" (18:2) and, after finding Laish inhabited by a "quiet and unsuspecting" people (18:7, ESV), they reported back. "Come on, let's attack them! We have seen the land, and it is very good ... When you get there, you will find an unsuspecting people and a spacious (*rchb*) land that God has put into your hands" (18:9-10, NIV). The settlers need space and resources, so the former inhabitants must be displaced. It is "when YHWH enlarges your borders as he has promised [that] you may eat meat whenever you desire" (Deuteronomy 12:20). Similarly, the motive for Ammonite war crimes was a desire to enlarge their territory in Gilead (Amos 1:13). The cornucopian vision of conflict-free growth differs from the *realpolitik* of the ancient Israelites, who considered that an emergent nation had to struggle to take land away from other peoples.

High population density as God's will?

Some natalists read the number of Israelites in the Exodus from Egypt, and the divine superintendence of rapid population growth, as an indication that God aims for a high density of human habitation. Beisner claims that in calculating the number of Israelites who left Egypt, there is "one firm figure" ("Imago" 174): 603,550 men aged at least twenty and fit for war (Numbers 1:46). Other natalists use the same number as their starting point. However, biblical scholars find that in the Hebrew Bible "numbers have for various reasons been peculiarly susceptible to corruption" (Wenham, "Large Numbers" 3). For example, vocabulary translated as "thousand" can alternatively refer to military units that are less numerous (18), and an alternative translation of the Exodus census finds around 18,000 warriors (14). Others note hyperbolic numbers in ancient military narratives produced in Akkad, Sumer, and Assyria (Fouts 383), and regard them as grossly exaggerated.

One implication of the huge numbers that feature in many Bible translations is a high rate of Israelite population growth during the years spent in Egypt. Heine observes that "history's first population boom is recorded in the Bible, after Jacob and his clan migrated to Egypt" (190). Given his starting point of 600,000 fighting men, Heine's estimate of the total population at two million is rather low. Even so, for the original seventy in Jacob's family (Exodus 1:5) to reach that number during 430 years (Exodus 12:14) in Egypt implies an average annual growth rate of 2.4%. That would be remarkable: there is no pre-modern instance of that rate of population growth being sustained throughout a century, let alone for four centuries. Heine further claims that even after this boom, from "God's perspective they had not multiplied enough" because two promises given in Exodus 23:26 would produce more growth: "God promised them long life and no miscarriages ... conditions for a population explosion" (61). Further in Deuteronomy 1:11, Moses wishes the people were a thousand times more numerous (190).[25] Heine claims this shows that rapid population growth is a divine purpose.

Another implication is high population density. Beisner uses an estimate of family size partly based on Old Testament genealogies to suggest an "Exodus population of 3-5 million" ("Imago" 174). He calculates the "population density in Goshen" (the region of Egypt where the Israelites had been living) as between 1,200 and 3,125 per square mile, and correctly states that "very few modern countries have such high population densities" (175). It is similar to the density today in the most populous areas of the Nile delta. Beisner regards this as evidence of a general divine intention for high population density. The accounts of Israelite numbers after the settlement in Canaan are also used. Pride observes that Israel was a "very small area" but despite this, citing Deuteronomy 28:11, "God was promising them a population explosion in a limited area with limited resources" (58).

Biblical accounts of Goshen and Palestine are read as models for the lesson that apparent limitations of land and resources should not constrain fecundity. However, most archaeologists consider the high numbers unrealistic. Oded Borowski suggests a population of 20,000 in the highlands in 1200 BC (8), which is less than 1% of the population size claimed by natalist writers.

Commanded to multiply?

The most common argument used by critics of the anti-contraceptive subset among natalists is that "be fruitful" is not a command but a blessing. Beisner offers two counter-arguments: first that "the verbs are in the imperative," and second that blessing and command are not mutually exclusive, for "God

---

25 The context is Moses calling for judges to be appointed because with larger numbers, "How can I bear by myself the weight and burden of you and your strife?"

blessed mankind by giving us the command to be fruitful and multiply, and we in turn are blessed when we obey the command" (*Garden* 207).

Possible functions of the imperatives in Genesis 1:28 include command, blessing, description of nature, and a theological attack on ancient Near Eastern fertility cults. Though many imperatives in Genesis are commands or requests (23:4, 8; 34:8), others are invitations (24:18, 31, 44, 46), offers (23:15; 24:51), promises (12:2), blessings (24:60; 33:11), negotiations (23:13), suggestions (34:10), reflections (19:34; 27:27), consolations (18:5), or exclamations (39:14; 41:41). Some invite the hearer to an unprejudiced choice, as in "settle wherever you please" (20:15, NASB), or "live wherever you like" (NIV), or "bury your dead in the choicest of our tombs. None of us will refuse you his tomb" (23:6, NIV): in other words, choose whatever you like. The betrothal blessing spoken to Rebekah by her family (Genesis 24:60) is imperative in form but is not a command (Van Leeuwen 60). So grammatical imperatives are not necessarily commands; that must be decided by context.

The idea that Genesis 1:28 was a command (as well as a blessing) should not be lightly dismissed as there is no scholarly consensus. Norbert Lohfink discerns that "fruitfulness … is a blessing and not a commandment" (7). Raymond van Leeuwen similarly judges that 1:28 "is not a commandment but a blessing" (59), and Gene Tucker agrees (6). John Sailhamer confirms that "the imperatives are not to be understood as commands" (96). On the other hand, some dissent: Laurence Turner asserts that 1:28 is "both blessing and command" (22), and so does David Clines ("Eve" 53). Others, while not discussing it, refer in passing to 1:28 as a command. For example, Gordon Wenham claims that reproduction is "the first command given to humankind" ("Family" 25). Though the majority of substantial treatments are against 1:28 being originally a command, the question is unresolved.

There is further debate as to whether it makes sense to think of "be fruitful" as a command. Since a similar imperative to "be fruitful and increase and fill the waters" (Genesis 1:22) is addressed to all sea creatures, some argue that because nonhuman creatures do not hear God or respond (or at least that some kinds are too primitive to be able to do that), it cannot be an ethical command and must be something else: a description of the created order. For example, John Calvin commented on 1:22 that God "infuses into them fecundity" (24). Another argument is that fertility was not (in the ancient world) something over which human beings had control. For example, when Rachel asks Jacob to "give me children" he rebukes her and asks, "Am I in the place of God who has kept you from having children?" (Genesis 30:1-2, NIV).

Since God alone can "open" the womb (Genesis 29:31; 30:22), reproduction cannot be a command.

Created nature

Those forbidding contraception (whether from natalist or other motives) claim that Onan was punished by death for spilling his seed (Genesis 38), which is against nature. Most biblical scholars consider that Onan's offense was his failure to donate a posthumous heir for his brother Er, but opponents of contraception argue that the penalty for refusing that obligation was shame, not death (Deuteronomy 25:5). However, the offense that would incur the penalty of ritual humiliation for Onan (assuming a culture similar to that in Deuteronomy) was a public refusal of the duty, something Onan never did. Instead he agreed to his father's request which put him in a different legal (and moral) situation, since by marrying Tamar he agreed to try to provide an heir for Er. Onan secretly avoided consummation "so as not to give seed to his brother." Deceiving one's father was a more serious offence, perhaps meriting death (Deuteronomy 21:21). Further, if Onan had simply refused, then Judah could have turned to the third brother Shelah and asked him to marry the widow, but his deception forestalled that possibility and threatened to terminate his brother Er's posterity. There is also a greater issue in the background: the narrator tells us that the Davidic royal line will come from this widow, so Onan is obstructing a central divine purpose, a unique feature of the story that is not transferable to modern Christians.

Natalists advocate early marriage, for both women and men, claiming it is normal, natural, and biblical. In the ancient Near East most females were married soon after puberty (Meyers 28), but whereas girls usually married in their teens, "men waited until well into their twenties or even early thirties before marrying" (King and Stager 37). Given an average life expectancy of forty, this was rather late. Neither does early marriage for men find support in Old Testament narratives. The stories of Genesis do not portray men rushing to marry; for example (in the absence of information on marriage age), the age at which a man's first son was born in the pre-Flood genealogies (in a narrative context of multi-century life spans) ranges from 65 to 187. After the Flood, among the shorter-lived descendants of Shem (11:10-26), a man's age at the birth of his first son ranges from 29 for Nahor to 70 for Terah. Later there are some mentions of age at marriage: 40 years for Isaac (25:20) and Esau (26:34), while Jacob was even older when he married (29:20 and see 27:1).

Application of fruitful verses

Biblical scholars who are Christians and believe that the Old Testament is a resource for Christians today make a distinction between a text's original meaning, which is anchored in the ancient Near East, and its contemporary application for ethics. Further, many limit themselves to working at unearthing the original meaning and avoid venturing into the disciplines of theology and ethics. The dangers of trying to apply the Old Testament directly to the modern world are often obvious.[26] Its use in Christian ethics is complicated by the distance in time, culture, and technology, but the main difficulty is the dispensational gap between old and new covenants.

Commentaries that discuss the various fruitful verses note the distance between ancient and modern worlds, and warn that Old Testament ideas about fertility may not be appropriate for contemporary application. For example, Robert Davidson finds that Psalm 127 embodies "cultural and social assumptions that are far removed from those of the Western world … Large families are out of fashion today. Indeed, to many they are regarded as irresponsible in a world of population growth and finite resources" (420). Leslie Allen is more forthright: "The modern reader of Psalm 127 finds himself detached from its cultural setting … Living as he does in days of overpopulation" (181). Turning to Psalm 128, he warns against ideas that a literalist reader might derive from it: "Fertility … is the dream of any primitive society [but] … The simple philosophy of the Psalm receives qualification even in the Old Testament and certainly in the New Testament" (185).

However, a few scholarly commentators present a literal reading of the fruitful verses as helpful wisdom for contemporary readers, or as God's word for today. When dealing with other issues raised by Old Testament verses (for example, slavery or the status of women), the same scholars might be more cautious, but they seem not to regard natalism as ethically problematic. They sometimes attempt to move directly from Old Testament original meaning to modern application, without interposing the lens of Christian tradition.

Daniel Estes is a Professor of Old Testament at Cedarville University, but also Director of the Center for Biblical Integration, and he teaches courses in Christian Worldview. So he is one of those wanting to bridge the gap between ancient text and modern ethics. Estes focuses on the arrow imagery in Psalm

---

26 For example, in 1560s Geneva efforts by some Calvinists to follow biblical law led to the judicial punishment, including one execution, of children for the offense of insulting their parents (Kingdon 361).

127, which he thinks refers to all kinds of conflict: legal, social, and armed. He notes that others have construed the sons as "defensive protection" but points out that arrows, being missile weapons, are more apt for "offensive action," as in Psalms 11:2 and 64:3 (306-07). Estes also extends the idea of "long-range effect" to the temporal dimension. "As arrows shot from the bow are propelled toward a remote target according to the desire of the archer, so children when properly nurtured extend the effect of their father into human society of the next generation." This is a "future hope" of "social immortality," because these children "can perpetuate his activity as they reflect his values" (310). Estes identifies this as the Psalm's theme.

Near the end of his article, when Estes offers contemporary "application of the psalm," he transforms and reduces its message to this: "the individual can make a positive contribution to society by the careful, godly nurture of children" (311). Estes here elides most of the distinctive features that he identified earlier, for example the emphases on male offspring, on conflict, offensive action, and the importance of quantity of offspring. The reader may be left wondering whether his evaluation that the Psalm offers a "positive message" for today (311) includes those features or only his final summative application. Estes' silence leaves the modern applicability of those features in doubt. They have consequences: if every man needs a son, then over twice as many offspring are needed.[27] Further, having just one son is precarious for the immortal social effect, so any man following the original intent (as presented by Estes) will desire many sons. And his emphasis on gaining influence and immortality through offspring contradicts the message of early Christianity explored in my chapter on Augustine.

David Petersen is Professor of Old Testament at Emory University's Candler School of Theology, and also a church minister. In his Presidential Address to the Society of Biblical Studies he challenges the conservative Americans who suppose that their modern "family values" self-evidently derive from the Bible by looking at the married lives of key biblical characters in Genesis. He encourages his peers to see that "biblical scholars have a role to play in the current debates, since who better than one of us is in a position to talk about family values as they are depicted" in Scripture (5).[28] His goal is to identify

---

27 Because one or more daughters may appear before any son. Demographers identify "son preference" as a major cause of high birth rates, even today: in Pakistan, for example, where men often desire at least two sons (Hussain 384).

28 Petersen's first paragraph observes that some "organizations spend vast sums of money to promulgate their views on issues such as pro-natalism and gay marriage," but he does not revisit the issue of contemporary American pro-natalism.

original meanings, and he finds three "family values" in Genesis. The first is "defining family in expansive terms" (22); the second is "the need for an heir, someone to whom the family's property may be passed" to maintain the "lineage" (17) so that God's promises might not fail; and the third is "conflict resolution without physical violence" (22) through strategies such as "distancing" (Genesis 13:8), a binding agreement to stay apart (Laban and Jacob 31:52), gift-giving, and clever words (Jacob and Esau 33:10).

Petersen claims that "these three values have not been part of the contemporary conversations; and they should be" (22), but some natalists do stress the continuing importance of patriarchal lineage, the second value. Petersen admits the difficulty of applying "Genesis family values" directly, and characterizes them as "a resource for thinking about family values" (15). However, he elsewhere claims that "these values are ... important today" and are "of immediate relevance" (22). Petersen finds the third value most helpful for ethics, and applies it to spousal abuse, urging readers to "deploy this biblical family value" (23). Readers might expect the second value, a need for male heirs, to have some application to marriage, but Petersen is silent. Instead he transforms the first value into a message that humankind is one family, and uses that to briefly present a globalized version of the second value, the virtue of avoiding human extinction by (swiftly returning to his third value) non-violent international relations. These results illustrate the incompleteness of a contemporary ethics derived from the Old Testament (and humane reason) alone, without input from Christian tradition which regards the church as one family and sees the purpose of Abraham's biological lineage fulfilled in Christ's birth.

Just before completing this book, I discovered Jamie Viands' 2014 publication *An Old Testament Theology of the Blessing of Progeny*, though I am unable to do justice to it now. The book is strictly confined to original meaning, but the final page hints at contemporary application. With regard to contraception, he suggests that "Birth control and reproductive and fertility technologies are not treated in the OT since these possibilities have only arisen with modern science[29] ... but a firm conviction that children are blessings will inevitably shape attitudes toward these issues" (288). This seems to assume that Old Testament theology can have direct application to contemporary ethics, though it is unclear how beliefs about blessing would

---

29 The first claim is not completely accurate since birth control, and even technologies (such as herbal pessaries), were known and used in the ancient Near East (Jutte).

shape a couple's decisions about the *number* of offspring they choose to have. Viands also comments on ecological concerns:

> An OT theology of the progeny blessing does not directly address the modern overpopulation debate either. Nevertheless we have seen that the prophets occasionally depict overcrowding in cities (Isa 49:19-21; Zech 2:8[4]; 8:4-5) or territories (Zech 10:8-10), but always portray this as a positive development. Moreover, proliferation and the filling of the land is always a blessing from Yahweh, never a curse, possibly calling into question the very concept of "overpopulation." However since an overflowing population is accompanied by ideal societal conditions in these descriptions, it is unclear how much they have to say to modern societies where proliferation is accompanied by broken and corrupt leadership, poverty, and a scarcity of resources. (Viands 288)

Cautious enough, but I would add a reminder of the great difference between then and now: population numbers in the ancient world were much lower than today and their ecological impact then did not approach anywhere near planetary boundaries (such as the nitrogen cycle, greenhouse gas concentration, and biodiversity loss) which are now transgressed by the total impact of seven billion humans. Perhaps appropriately in a technical work of Old Testament scholarship, Viands' own view is difficult to detect, but his perspective emerges in the final paragraph, which rejoices that "the God of Israel, continues to bless humanity even today ... expanding the human race across the face of the earth" (288). The word "expanding" here must refer to the increase of the world population,[30] suggesting that Viands regards continuing global population growth as beneficial.

In conclusion, the cultural, economic, political, and theological context of the Old Testament fruitful verses limits their plausible appropriation by modern natalism. Pro-fertility ideas in the ancient Near East are unsurprising given the demands of immortality through patriarchal lineage, agricultural subsistence in the Judean highlands, and a small people struggling to retain thier national identity against hostile empires. None of these are relevant motives for modern Christians in the U.S.

Even for Israel in the Old Testament, fecundity was just one aspect of a divine agenda for creating a holy nation in the promised land. It was most important in the earliest stages, before the sons of Israel were numerous enough to become a people, a nation. But once it was substantially fulfilled (in Exodus 1), other dimensions of the agenda (land and holiness) became

---

30 It may also refer to geographical expansion of the land area used by humankind and the corresponding contraction of wild areas.

more important. Though a notion that Israel is exclusively formed by the biological descendants of Jacob persists in some writers, it is often challenged in Old Testament theology by visions of a holy people constituted by covenant and spiritual renewal.

Old Testament specialists who treat the fruitful verses present insights into "what it meant" for the ancient Israelites. Most do not venture to say "what it means" for Christians today. Those who have attempted direct ethical application either discard most of the distinctive features of the fruitful verses, or produce lessons that conflict with traditional Christian interpretation. Their results lend support to my view that the search for original meaning should be only a first step for those wanting to use the Old Testament as a guide to modern life. The next chapter is the second step, looking at a classic Christian reception of the fruitful verses.

5. Augustine on Fruitfulness

In the early centuries of Christianity, the significance of reproduction was intensely debated. The writings of Augustine (354-430) dominated subsequent western Christian reflection on the topic until the 16th century. In part, that simply reflected Augustine's predominance in Christian thought generally,[1] but it was also because later Christian leaders valued his innovative resolution of tensions concerning the origin, past, present, and future of human reproduction.

Today most heirs of Augustinian thought are selective. Catholicism has mostly abandoned his hope that lay Catholic women could aspire to a higher vocation than motherhood. Though it still esteems vowed celibacy above marriage, even that has become weak or muted, especially after the scandals of recent years. Its episcopacy and some laity still hold to Augustine's anti-contraceptive teachings, but have modified them to allow the rhythm method (or rather its scientific variant in Natural Family Planning), which he condemned as a Manichean custom. Protestants mostly reject all this, but in other areas they lean on Augustinian ideas transformed by Luther and Calvin. My *ressourcement* from Augustine in this chapter is a helpful step in evaluation; it does not stand by itself as a viable modern Christian approach to reproductive ethics, but it offers helpful insights toward such a development.

Chronology and writings

Augustine was born in 354 in Numidia (roughly where Algeria is today), a prosperous Roman province near Carthage, the second largest city of the

---

1   For example, the standard medieval Catholic compilation of Bible commentary, the *Glossa ordinaria*, is dominated by quotations from Augustine (AE 383).

http://dx.doi.org/10.11647/OBP.0048.05

western Empire. He worked as a teacher of Rhetoric there and later also in Rome and Milan. He was brought up as a Catholic by his mother Monica, but as a teenager he investigated various philosophies and became a 'hearer' of the Manichean sect for nine years[2] until he moved on to Neoplatonism. While in Milan Augustine heard the preaching of bishop Ambrose which, alongside the inspiring example of Christian monks, led him to return to Catholicism and be baptized in 387. After returning to Numidia, he was ordained a priest in 391 and made an assistant bishop in 395. He soon became the bishop of Hippo Regius, a city on the north coast of Africa, and worked there until his death in 430.

Augustine commented on the Genesis creation narrative in five of his writings: *De Genesi adversus Manichaeos* in 388, *De Genesi ad litteram imperfectus liber* around 393, books 11-13 of *Confessiones* around 400, *De Genesi ad Litteram* between 401 and 415, and parts of *De Civitate Dei* between 413 and 427.[3] However, he also wrote much about reproduction elsewhere, in his other writings against Manicheism,[4] during the controversy about Jovinian and Jerome,[5] and against Pelagianism. Helpful insights also appear in *Sermones*, especially his Christmas sermons reflecting on the Virgin Mary, and in *enarrationes in Psalmos*, especially the sermons on Psalms 127 and 128. The 544 surviving sermons,[6] and the 299 letters in *Epistulae* constitute, by length, almost half (45%) of Augustine's writings, but they have been relatively neglected (Kretzmann and Stump 23, 11). In some areas of thought, Augustine's thinking did change during his Christian career, but the aspects important for my discussion, including his spiritual interpretations of the fruitful verses, remained constant.

The intended audience of his writings was ordained people and elite laity. The sermons, however, were preached in church, mostly at Hippo and sometimes in Carthage. One contextual feature alluded to later is that

---

2   Hearers were second-rate Manicheans who settled for a less than perfect life.
3   The last is the most popular of Augustine's writings today, *The City of God*. For consistency of referencing I use the standard abbreviation of Latin titles.
4   Two books by Augustine contradicting individual Manichean teachers, *Contra Adimantum* and *Contra Secundinum*, were published for the first time in English in 2006 as part of a new multi-volume translation entitled *The Works of Saint Augustine* (WSA I/19:12). My citations from that translation use the standard format WSA series/volume:page.
5   Especially in *De bono conjugalis* which was written in 401.
6   New sermons have been discovered since 1989, and twenty-six of them were translated in WSA III/1:16.

Augustine often signals in sermons that he is turning to address different parts of the congregation. Standing near the front were the virgins, and behind them the consecrated widows, with the married people further back. Also, before and after Easter, he might address the *competentes* (those who had asked for baptism), the *catechumens* (those in preparation for baptism), or the *infantes* (those recently baptized), who were mostly adult converts.

Historical context of Augustine's thought

Philosophical ideas about reproduction

State-sponsored natalism was common in ancient Greek and Roman cities for strategic reasons. Reproduction sufficient to maintain the population was essential, especially as city dwellers often suffered higher mortality from plagues than their rural compatriots. The word for the poor, the *proletarius*, means "one who produces offspring." However the real problem was encouraging the upper class to reproduce itself sufficiently. Stoic philosophers argued that citizens had a duty to produce legitimate offspring. The ideal constitution designed by Cicero banned singleness: *On the Laws* 3.3.7 states that *"caelibes esse prohibunto"* (Daube 27).

The belief that sexual acts should always aim at reproduction (and be contained within marriage) was discussed in chapter 1, which noted its origins in Pythagorean and Stoic eugenic philosophy, its religious transformation in Philo, and its adoption into Christianity by Clement of Alexandria (94, 255). Augustine inherited this "Alexandrian rule" as traditional (Brakke 186), but his version was milder than Clement's. It became the main source of subsequent Catholic teaching. For example, Augustine wrote that "to demand the debt from your marriage partner more than is required for the procreation of children is indeed a sin, though a venial one." He commented on the Old Testament patriarchs: "So chaste were they in their relations with their wives … that they never went in to them for carnal intercourse except for the sake of procreation" (*serm.* 51.22 tr. WSA III/3:34, 33). This is a minor feature in Augustine's thought and though it does shape his ideas about reproduction, his non-natalist attitude is rooted less in his antipathy to sexuality than in deeper themes of salvation history and eschatology, the supreme good, and the consequent relative value of different vocations.

Christian, Encratite, and dualist attitudes to reproduction

Reproduction featured in Augustine's writings because of tensions within the canon of Scripture that generated diversity in Christianity. Under the Old Covenant the patriarchal genetic line and sexual reproduction had been important, but the New Covenant prioritized the church "family," spiritual kinship, and personal resurrection. The contrast was heightened by an early Christian orientation toward a heavenly rather than an earthly vocation. Celibacy and asceticism were part of Christianity from the 1st century, but the form we call monasticism emerged in the 3rd. Augustine's encounter in Rome with a house of monks and the *Life of Antony* played a part in his conversion (*conf.* 8), as did bishop Ambrose, a mediator of the ascetic spirituality of Origen, Athanasius, and the Cappadocian Fathers. Augustine told his congregation in Hippo that before he became a bishop "I … came to this city as a young man … looking for a place to establish a monastery, and live there with my brothers" (*serm.* 355.2 tr. WSA III/10:165). Augustine founded in Hippo a special type of monastery, attached to his main church, for priests as well as lay brothers (H. Chadwick 63). In the West, the only earlier "cathedral" monastery was founded *circa* 363 by the bishop of Vercelli (Harrison 184). Augustine was a pioneer of monasticism in the province of Numidia.

The ancient orthodox (those Christians deemed orthodox by the later Catholic Church) wrote about reproduction mainly when reacting against other groups that identified themselves as Christian while forbidding marriage. The latter can be placed in two categories labelled dualist and encratite. For those in the first category, who included Marcionites and many Gnostics, their denigration of marriage was one aspect of a dualist denigration of the physical world (Cohen 243). Married people could not be baptized in Marcionite churches since only unmarried (or divorced) people were eligible for full membership (Lieu 40). Those in the second category, encratism, worked with common early Christian beliefs about a hierarchy of spirit and flesh, an idea that humankind as originally created was not sexual, and an eschatological reading of Paul's words which led to the idea that marriage was obsolete and celibacy a command. Some churches in Syria where Tatian was a leader, and some in Egypt led by Hieracas, required *catechumens* to vow celibacy (Hunter, *Marriage* 132). Augustine reported that "they are also called Encratites … they do not admit into their number anyone, whether man or woman, who is living a married life" (*haer.* 25 tr.

WSA I/18:38).[7] Irenaeus, Tertullian, Clement of Alexandria, Epiphanius of Salamis, Origen, John Chrysostom, and other orthodox Fathers also wrote against such ideas, laboring to affirm marriage (and marital reproduction) even though almost all of these orthodox writers were themselves celibate.

Historians call others "moderate Encratites" who claimed that the "original things have passed away" (2 Corinthians 5:18), or even that "male and female" are abolished (Galatians 3:28), but did not step over the line into heresy by forbidding marriage (D'Angelo 1). "Encratism predominated for a time in the Churches of eastern Syria and Mesopotamia, without those Churches being considered heretical" (Price 122). Aphrahat, a leading Syriac Christian, regarded celibacy as the only path to holiness (Koltun-Fromm 386). In the West, the anonymous treatise *De castitate* (*circa* 400) argued that the marriage of Adam and Eve (Genesis 2:24) symbolically prefigured the relation of Christ and the church (Ephesians 5:31), and therefore marriage no longer had any function and should be expected to pass away (Clark 358). Even so, these moderate Encratites stayed within the orthodox consensus that celibacy was a voluntary evangelical counsel rather than a command.

The three controversies that were the immediate causes prompting Augustine to develop his theology of reproduction were Manicheism, the controversy over Jovinian and Jerome, and Augustine's long-running debate with Julian of Eclanum. His efforts to shake off his opponents' accusations that he was a secret adherent of Manicheism are a thread running through all three of these controversies.

Manicheism, real and imagined

In the 3rd century AD, in Persian Mesopotamia, a preacher named Mani broke away from a Jewish Christian sect called the Elcasaites who condemned virginity and made marriage compulsory. Mani instead began teaching a dualist cosmogony in which divine light (he revered the sun) was trapped in earthly bodies and sought to escape to the heavenly realm. He called it the "religion of Light," but outsiders named it Manicheism. He deprecated reproduction because conceiving a baby imprisoned a fragment of divinity, a soul, in flesh (AE 239 citing *mor.* 2.18). There were two levels of Manichean: the 'elect' were celibate, while the married 'hearers' were encouraged to

---

7   *Encrateia* is the Greek word for abstinence or continence.

practice contraception.[8] As a young man, while a hearer, Augustine had persuaded many Catholic friends and pupils to join the Manicheans, but now he urgently desired to call them back, and by 411 he had written approximately fifteen anti-Manichean works. These anti-Manichean writings include *Contra Adimantum Manichei disciplum* in 393/4, and *Contra Faustum Manichaeum* in 397/9. David Hunter observes that these polemical writings are more pro-marriage (and, I would add, more pro-reproduction) than his other works written during the same period such as the *Confessiones* ("Introduction" WSA I/9:9-11).

In their apologetics, Manicheans quoted the Scriptures used by Christians.[9] They liked the New Testament, especially Paul's letters, but regarded the Old as carnal. Adda (called Adimantus in the Latin West) claimed that the New Testament and Old Testament were incompatible. While the New looked to eternal rewards, the Old focused on temporal rewards. To show this, he juxtaposed verses from the two that he found contradictory, for example contrasting Deuteronomy 28 and Matthew 16:24. Augustine responded that the older pattern was appropriate to its time. "Carnal and temporal rewards were suitably promised to a people that was still carnal" (*c. Adim.* 18.1 tr. WSA I/19:212). That era lived under different rules and standards, for "when God commands polygamy it is virtue" (*conf.* 3.7.12). Augustine wanted to reject any idea that lust played a part in Old Testament polygamy: the patriarchs "only have wives for the sake of getting children" (*serm.* 51.23 tr. WSA III/3:34). Augustine also challenged the Manichean dichotomy between the Testaments: referring to Isaiah 56:4 he observed that "even in the Old Testament … they have the great promises made to eunuchs, lest the Manicheans think that they were praised by the Lord only in the New Testament" (*c. Adim.* 3, tr. WSA I/19:180).

Faustus the Manichean ridiculed a scripture (Deuteronomy 25:5) that obliged a man to perpetuate the name of his dead childless brother by marrying the brother's widow and begetting a male offspring, a boy regarded as being the dead man's son. In its defence, Augustine deployed allegory: "every preacher of the gospel should so labor in the Church as to raise up seed to his deceased brother, that is, Christ, who died for us, and that this

---

8   WSA I/19:11. In 373, a year after Augustine took a common-law wife (concubine), their son Adeodatus was born. Around that time he joined the Manicheans, and Kim Power speculates that the non-appearance of subsequent children during the 17 years of Augustine's faithful concubinage indicates their use of contraception (AE 222; cf. *b. conjug.* 5).

9   For example, Faustus' *Apologia* includes many references to the Bible, but none to any Manichean scriptures (Lieu 120).

seed should bear His name" (*c. Faust.* 32.10). In other words, converts are named Christ-ian after Christ. The text prefigures the gospel. Thus, in varying ways, Augustine justified the emphasis on marriage and reproduction in the Old Testament.

At the time when Augustine was a bishop, to be accused of Manicheism was dangerous. In the late 3rd century Mani's teachings had spread to the Roman empire, but its foreign origin and "immoral" teachings provoked emperor Diocletian in 302 to order the burning of Manicheans and their scriptures (Lieu 6). That decree had lapsed, but emperor Theodosius in 381 issued a new law tasking "members of the secret service" with prosecuting the Manichean elect (Lieu 111). Priscillian of Avila and two other bishops in Hispania (modern Spain) were accused by their local peers of Manicheism. They travelled to Rome to appeal to the Italian bishops, but the emperor beheaded them in 385 (Hunter, "Resistance" 50). Priscillian was not a Manichean, but he was ascetic and he urged Christians to avoid marriage (Lieu 114). Ambrose of Milan was "plagued" in his later years (he died in 397) by accusations of Manicheism (Clark, "Heresy" 100), and in 412 two ascetic bishops in southern France were forced to retire after similar false accusations.

Augustine was unusually vulnerable because he really had been a Manichean in his younger years. When Augustine first became a priest, Megalius the archbishop of Numidia did not trust him, and his promotion to the junior episcopacy in 395 was enabled by his mentor bishop Valerius of Hippo (M.T. Clark 11). It was common knowledge that Manichean hearers were adept in religious camouflage. Cyril of Jerusalem had warned, in his book about heretics, of the danger of accepting repentant Manicheans into the church too easily. Augustine, in a letter written after he became a bishop, reported to Deuterius that he had exposed and punished Victorinus, a subdeacon, as a secret Manichean:

> After he confessed that he was a hearer in the Manichees, he in fact asked me to bring him back to the path of truth, which is Catholic doctrine. But I admit, I was aghast at his pretense in the guise of a cleric, and I took measures to expel him from the city after chastising him. (*ep.* 236 tr. WSA II/4:135)

It is unsurprising that Augustine "lived his entire Catholic life in dread of being branded a crypto-Manichean" (Coyle 18; also see H. Chadwick 65). His reputation, influence, and legacy were all at stake.[10] In such circumstances it is remarkable that Augustine dared to write anything less than entirely

---

10 *Retractationes* indicates that Augustine was concerned to safeguard his legacy.

positive about marriage and marital reproduction. That he sometimes did compare it unfavorably with celibacy suggests he was confident he could show that his ideas were firmly anchored in the New Testament and mainstream Christian tradition.

The controversy over Jovinian's teachings

The teachings of Jovinian (d. 405) have been reconstructed from Jerome's response to him, and from Ambrose's letter to Siricius. Jovinian argued that virgins and widows would not receive a greater reward in heaven than married people, because "baptism with full faith" confers equal merit on all recipients, and so in heaven all will receive the same reward (Hunter, "Resistance" 45). Jovinian had been provoked by liturgical innovations that elevated celibacy, for example the use of the text "I espoused you to one husband" (2 Corinthians 11:2) in the veiling of women who took vows of Christian celibacy (Hunter, *Marriage* 33). The wider context of the controversy was that Siricius as bishop of Rome (from 384 to 399) was calling for all priests to be celibate: many were but it was not compulsory. Siricius mentioned in a letter that some Italian bishops opposing his proposal to change canon law were using the precedent of married priests in the Old Testament. Jovinian accused Siricius and his ally bishop Ambrose of being Manicheans.[11] Jovinian argued that marriage's goodness was modelled by the patriarchs of Genesis and confirmed by Christ in Matthew 19:5 (Jerome *adv. Jov.* 1.5 tr. NPNF2 6:348). He won supporters in Rome among priests and the senatorial class: some were named by the papal condemnation of Jovinian in 393 (Hunter, "Resistance" 48, citing Siricius *ep.* 2.2.3).

Jerome's intemperate response seemed to vindicate Jovinian's claim that advocacy of celibacy inevitably led to denigration of marriage. Augustine addressed the problem in 404 with two books that should be read together: *De bono conjugali*, "On the Good of Marriage", and *De sancta virginitate*, "On Holy Virginity."[12] The first book identified what he called the "three goods of marriage" which were: *bonum sacramenti* (enduring union as a symbol of Christ and the church), *bonum fidei* (the friendship between husband and

---

11 In the late 380s, in Rome, the Manichees conducted an evangelistic campaign, and their superior asceticism was advertised. Christian ascetics may have been trying to counter the appeal of Manicheism by outdoing them (Hunter, "Resistance" 50, 53).

12 Previously dated to AD 401, Hombert and Hunter now date these two books to 404.

wife), and *bonum prolis* (offspring brought up in the Christian faith). Augustine asserted that marriage is good, and celibacy is better. He advised that one "must not flee from marriage as if it were a pit of sin, but must pass over it as a hill of less grandeur, to settle on the higher mountain of celibacy" (*virg.* 18 tr. WSA I/9:78). He warned virgins that they should not:

> disdain the early fathers and mothers of God's people ... who served the future Christ even by having children ... [as] future events ... were still being prepared and brought to birth, and even their married life had the character of prophecy ... In the present times, however, those to whom it is said, If they are unable to be continent, they should marry ... do not need our encouragement, but our sympathy. (*virg.* 1 tr. WSA I/9:68)

Some of Jovinian's arguments were similar to those that Augustine had used against the Manicheans, but he went further. Jovinian claimed that "Sarah, who was a type of the church ... exchanged the curse of sterility for the blessing of childbirth" (Jerome, *adversus Jovinianum* 1.5, tr. Hunter, *Marriage* 33). Augustine perceived Jovinian's error as being in the opposite direction from the Manichean error (Hunter, "Reclaiming" 325), so he adjusted his earlier arguments defending the Old Testament patriarchs to point out clearly the dispensational differences between old and new covenants, and the dangers of praising external features of the patriarchs' lives as if they were suitable models for Christian readers to imitate.

Augustine affirmed the belief in differences in heavenly reward (homily on John 14 tr. NPNF1 7:324; also see Matthew 16:27; 25:14-30; Romans 2:5-6; and 1 Corinthians 3:11-15). Augustine did query Jerome's reading of the thirty, sixty, and hundred fold yields in the parable of the sower (Mark 4:3-20) as three levels of reward with the greater corresponding to widowhood and celibacy. Elizabeth Clark cites this as evidence of Augustine elevating marriage, but it is only his hesitation about Jerome's reading of one text, "God in his kindness grants many gifts, and some are greater and better than others ... should we conclude that there are too many for them to be divided into three kinds?" Yes, there are more than three gifts: a list can include martyrdom, virginity, widowhood, and non-virginal celibacy (Augustine was in this category), as well as continence within marriage and marital chastity (that is, married people who only engage in sex for reproduction). Married women, even if senior in age and senatorial in class, have a lower place than virgins. These are real differences, but, Augustine urged, they should not provoke pride or jealousy:

See how that Lamb walks on the path of virginity! ... the faithful who are
unable to follow the Lamb this far, will see you ... but they will not be jealous.
They will not be able to sing that new hymn that is exclusively yours, but they
will be able to hear it and to share your enjoyment ... Those who have less
will not be resentful toward you. Where there is no envy, there is harmony
in diversity. (*virg.* 29 tr. WSA I/9:86)

The dispute with Julian of Eclanum

In the twenty years before Augustine's death in 430, most of his polemical
works were aimed at Pelagianism.[13] These included his controversies with
Julian of Eclanum, a bishop who refused to accept the condemnation of
Pelagius in 417 by Zosimus, bishop of Rome. Augustine's first anti-Pelagian
work was *De peccatorum meritis et remissione et de baptismo parvulorum*, "On sin
... and infant baptism," in 411. Others cited here are *De nuptiis et concupiscentia*,
"On marriage and the sinful nature," written between 418 and 420, and *Contra
Julianum*, "Against Julian," in 422.

Julian claimed that everyone is born with the power to choose right or
wrong, with free will, just like Adam before the Fall: a fresh start for every
newborn baby. In his view, human nature was not altered by the Fall, so
phenomena such as the pain of childbirth and man's domination of woman
were original features of creation and not results of the Fall. Julian identified
the root of the sinful character that enslaved each generation as depraved
human culture (rather than nature), which was passed down from parents
to children by example and imitation. In theory, anyone could live a life
without sin if they so chose.

Augustine answered that Adam's nature was corrupted by the Fall, and
all his descendants were born with a fallen nature, lacking the ability to
live a sinless life. The corrupt nature was in the "vitiated seed" and was
unavoidably passed on from parents to children. Augustine complained
that his Pelagian critics

keep shouting in a most hateful manner that we condemn marriage and the
divine work by which God creates human beings from men and women. One
of their reasons is that we say that those who are born from such a union
contract original sin ... we claim that, regardless of the sort of parents from
whom the children are born, they are still under the power of the devil, unless
they are reborn in Christ. (*nupt. et conc.* 1.1 tr. WSA I/24:28)

---

13 Pelagius was a British monk who claimed, among other ideas, that babies are born free
   of sin. Augustine construed the ideas of Pelagius and his followers as Pelagianism.

Julian and others labelled this as Manichean. Augustine observed: "You say I praise the celibacy of the Christian era, not to inspire men to virginity, but to condemn the goodness of marriage" (*c. Jul.* 16(65) tr. FC 303), and he rejected this claim. Julian's focus on Genesis 1:28 (and 2:24) and on reproduction (Clark, "Heresy" 120) ensured that Augustine kept writing on this topic and these verses to the end of his life. He died before finishing his second book against Julian, the *Opus imperfectum*.

Reproduction: past, present, and future

Previous scholarly discussion of Augustine's thought on reproduction has focused on his change of mind about its origin, expressed in his innovative exegesis of Genesis 1:28. Earlier Christian thinking about the origins of reproduction was based on the principle that whereas mortals reproduce a new generation to take their place, immortals do not reproduce, and they believed that the first humans were created immortal. They also believed that the eschatological human condition would restore what had been lost through the Fall.[14] Given that post-resurrection humans will be "like the angels" (Mark 12:25) and not conceiving babies (Luke 20:35), this implied that the first humans were originally like that. Gregory of Nyssa reasoned that "the resurrection promises … the restoration of the fallen to their ancient state … If then the life of those restored is closely related to that of the angels, it is clear that the life before the transgression was a kind of angelic life" (*The Making of Man* 17.2 tr. NPNF2 5:66). In the creation narrative it was not until after the expulsion from the garden that the first instance of sexual reproduction was reported (Genesis 4:1), and so Christian tradition accepted an idea from the Jewish book of *Jubilees* in which the garden of "Eden was like a temple and sex was not possible within its precincts" (G. Anderson 62).[15] As for "be fruitful" (Genesis 1:28), commentators suggested that God had foreseen the Fall and made provision for it in advance, or alternatively they interpreted it spiritually as the fruit of the spirit.

Augustine at first accepted those beliefs, but later decided that reproduction must have been original. That change in his exegesis has been closely tracked

---

14 There was diversity in earlier ideas. Cohen finds three views: 1) sexuality in Eden was allegory, represented by Origen; 2) mortality and sex were a result of the Fall, represented by Gregory of Nyssa; and 3) humans in Eden were not yet immortal and not ready for sexuality, represented by Irenaeus of Lyons and Theodore of Mopsuestia (Cohen 235-42).

15 There are many parallels between Old Testament descriptions of the garden of Eden and the temple sanctuary (Wenham, "Sanctuary"), indicating their similarity.

by historians. His earliest comment on "be fruitful and multiply" was in 388, when he asked: "Should we understand it carnally or spiritually? For we are permitted to understand it spiritually and to believe that it was changed into carnal fecundity after sin." He suggested that "before they sinned" the first humans had been intended to generate "spiritual offspring of intelligible and immortal joys filling the earth" (*Gn. adv. Man.* 1.19(30) tr. FC 84:77-78). A decade later in *Confessiones,* he suggested: "If we consider these words as intended figuratively, which I rather think Scripture intended ... we would understand ... human procreation in terms of matters conceived intellectually, on account of the fecundity of reason" (*conf.* 12.36).

The change began in 401 when Augustine expressed "many different opinions" about the original human condition in Genesis 1:28, including the possibilities that "the first parents both were mortal in their original state" and would have reproduced, and that they could "have children in some other way, without physical union." However, he affirmed the principle that "sexual union is possible only for mortal bodies" (*b. conjug.* 2 tr. WSA I/9:33). Then in *De Genesi ad Litteram,* in 405, he decided that the original plan must have been sexual reproduction by immortals (Harrison 163). Later, looking back in his *Retractationes,* he wrote that "I do not at all agree" (Cohen 243) with his earlier views. According to his new theory, if the Fall had not happened then sexual reproduction would have been rational and limited, until "the determined number would be complete" (*Gn. litt.* 9.3). In this hypothetical scenario:

> children ... would succeed their parents, who themselves would not be destined to die. Thus, finally, the earth would have been filled with immortal men, and when this just and holy society would be thus brought into being, as we believe it will be after the resurrection, there would be an end to the begetting of children. (*Gn. litt.* 1.16 tr. ACW 41:97)

Significance of the changed exegesis

Three questions are considered here. Why did Augustine change his mind about Genesis 1:28? What significance, if any, did his changed ideas about origins have for his attitude to contemporary reproduction? Did it imply a rejection of his spiritual exegeses of this and other Old Testament fruitful verses? Patristic scholars disagree about his motive and the implications. Peter Brown sees it as part of a turning away from the Platonic hierarchy of spirit and flesh, but Margaret Miles responds with examples of a soul/body hierarchy from later writings by Augustine (Brown and Donovan 5-9, 19). Susan Schreiner considers that by setting Paradise in the continuum of real history, he "attacks Neo-Platonic devaluation of history" in order to defend the transcendence of God ("Eve" 158). David Hunter claims that the change was provoked by Julian, but Elizabeth Clark argues it was a response to Jovinian ("Heresy" 108), which is more plausible given the timing of the change in 405. In any case it is unlikely that Augustine's motive was pro-reproductive.

Augustine's changed view about the historical origins of reproduction never detracts from his belief that it has no future, and that this points to a proleptic celibate ideal for the present. Virginity is "a foretaste of eternal incorruptibility" (*virg.* 13 tr. WSA I/9:74). Augustine affirms in the 420s that "in the resurrection there will be no generation" (*civ. Dei* 15.17 tr. Bettenson 627): reproduction will cease in the future. Augustine preached at Lent *circa* 420:

> As for those of you who have taken vows ... you are leading the life of angels on earth. Angels, you see, don't get married ... That's what we shall all be like, when we have risen from the dead. How much better you people are, then, who already begin to be before death what everyone will be after the resurrection! ... God is keeping for you your respective honors. The resurrection of the dead has been compared to the stars ... (1 Cor.15:41-42). There will be one splendor there for virginity, another for married chastity, another for holy widowhood. (*serm.* 132.3 tr. WSA III/4:327)

Augustine's shift in exegesis of Genesis 1:28 was a move from one scheme of primordial history to another. It did not, *contra* Jeremy Cohen, supersede figurative and spiritual exegeses of Genesis 1:28. Cohen claimed that medieval exegetes such as Aquinas and the *Glossa Ordinaria* compilers were contradicting Augustine when they rehearsed both his literal and spiritual readings. In this argument, Cohen wrongly assumed that a text could have only one meaning, but Augustine explained why they are compatible: in *de Genesi ad litteram*, he noted

> three generally held opinions about this topic; one held by those who think Paradise should only be understood in the literal material sense, another by those for whom only the spiritual sense is true, the third by those who take Paradise in each way[16] [i.e. in both ways] ... it is the third opinion which I favor. (*Gn. litt.* 8.1-2 tr. WSA I/13:346)

---

16 Here, "in each way" means in both ways, allowing multiple meanings.

The historical literal meaning is the first elementary and preliminary step. In itself it may not be edifying, but a wealth of figurative, typological, and other spiritual interpretations await beyond it. Augustine wrote in the same commentary that

> In the case of a narrative of events, the question arises as to whether everything must be taken according to the figurative sense only, or whether it must be expounded and defended also as a faithful record of what happened. No Christian will dare say that the narrative must not be taken in a figurative sense. (*Gn. litt.* 1.17 tr. ACW 1:39)

He continues: "in this book I wanted to see what I could accomplish in the laborious and difficult task of literal interpretation." Accordingly, at a later point, he arrests himself from straying into figurative exegesis: "But this is to give an interpretation, a thing which I did not set out to do in this treatise, I have started here to discuss Sacred Scripture according to the plain meaning of the historical facts, not according to future events which they foreshadow" (*Gn. litt.* 1.17.34 tr. ACW 1:41).

He had written in his first Genesis commentary that "this whole discourse must first be discussed according to history, then according to prophecy" (*Gn. adv. Man.* 2.3 tr. ACW 1:95). His attempt at the historical approach in *Genesi ad litteram imperfectus liber* (394) had halted at Genesis 1:26; subsequently, he worked on prophetic exegesis in *Confessiones* chapters 12-13; and now, in *Genesi ad litteram*, he fills in the missing history. The spiritual exegesis that he made (and will continue to make) is not superseded. Except for the specific point about when reproduction began, *De Genesi ad litteram* supplements his earlier (and later) spiritual interpretation. He commented late in life (*circa* 421) on Genesis 1:28 that "all of these things can appropriately be given a spiritual meaning" on top of the historical meaning (*civ. Dei* 14.22). Spiritual exegeses of the fruitful verses continued in his later writings, and some will be mentioned in the remainder of this chapter.

Progress from old ways to new life

Augustine used two complementary models, both drawn from earlier writers, to explain why the meaning of the imperative "be fruitful" is historically contingent. The first is a binary model: the Old Testament commanded marriage, but the New Testament does not. This is evident from Jesus' example and in Paul commending singleness: the challenge is to explain the difference without disparaging the Old Testament. Augustine preached in

409 about other differences between the two covenants, using a metaphor of the Word as doctor. "The doctor visits the patient, and says, 'Take this one in the morning, and that one in the afternoon.' ... So in the same sort of way, then, some things were good for the benefit of the human race in earlier times, other things are good in later times." Augustine imagines an objection to this argument: "the patient comes back to the doctor with, 'Why not the same one in the afternoon as in the morning?' ... my dear sick man, don't start giving the doctor advice!" (*serm.* 374.16 tr. WSA III/11:402). Ultimately only God knows why He divided history into a time before and after Christ's birth, and why many of the rules given in the Old Testament have been abolished.

Augustine nevertheless attempted an explanation of the old compulsion. The most important purpose of reproduction in God's plan was Christ's birth. The messianic lineage that would ultimately lead to the singularity of Advent depended on the mothers of Genesis: "since it was necessary that Christ come in the flesh, both the marriage of Sarah and the virginity of Mary served to propagate that flesh" (*contra Secundinum* 22; Hunter 323). Augustine, also concerned to defend as much as possible the morals and motives of Old Testament patriarchs and matriarchs, suggested that they were aware of this divine purpose. He wrote in 418 that "Abraham was fully imbued with faith in the incarnation" (*gr. et pecc. or.* 2.27; Hunter 333). A secondary purpose was symbolic: the biblical accounts of patriarchs' marriages existed to serve figuratively as prophecies of the marriage of Christ and the church, and the promises and narratives of their childbearing and genealogies served as prophecies of the gospel's spread. "Not only the words of these holy men ... but also their lives, their wives, their children, and acts ... signified spiritual mysteries closely associated with Christ and the Church of which those saints were members" (*cat. rud.* 19.33). Now that the reality foretold by those symbols has come, the canon is closed and the old symbols are past.

In the progressive model, the urgency of reproduction had already gradually been diminishing during the Old Testament period. In the earliest period after Adam and again after Noah, the number of humankind was tiny and tasked with spreading a human presence to unpopulated lands. Also, the chosen people descending from Abraham were at first very few in number and survived precariously. Therefore early practices such as marriage to close relatives and polygamy were virtuous at first but later prohibited even before Christ. Genesis indicated that "men took their sisters as wives ... a decent procedure under the pressure of necessity; but it became reprehensible in later times" (*civ. Dei* 15.16 tr. Bettenson 623). Childbearing was necessary to create Israel and produce the prophets who brought revelation. "Sarah too should be seen as acting from the pious motive of wanting the Israelite race to be increased" (*c. Faust.* 22.30-31, 47 tr. WSA I/19). That became less important after the nation was established, and after the prophets had written. And now the people of God is not limited to the Israelite race. Augustine wrote in 421 that:

> This propagation of children which among the ancient saints was a duty for begetting a people for God, amongst whom the prophecy of Christ's coming had precedence over everything, now has no longer the same necessity. For from among all nations the way is open for an abundant offspring to receive spiritual regeneration, from whatever quarter they derive their natural birth. (*nupt. et conc.* 1.13)

Augustine also suggests that the progressively diminishing importance of human fertility continues during the Christian era as the gospel spreads, beginning with Jesus, then Paul, and now with the growing evangelistic celibate movement of his own time: "For who does not know that the multitude of Christian men of perfect continence is daily spreading farther and farther, throughout the entire world, and especially in the East and in Egypt" (*mor.* 1.65). Elizabeth Clark observes that from Augustine's perspective the greatest outpouring of the Spirit so far was in the 4th century (147). The rules, methods, and permissions appropriate for the dawn of human history were no longer necessary.

Advancing from reproduction to continence

This progress could be mirrored in individual life histories. Within the span of their marriage, a couple might begin with reproduction but a few years later, while still biologically fertile, become continent (that is, abstain from conjugal sexual relations). In the 4th century Western church, married men ordained in middle age often became continent. Bishop Ambrose expected that although these men "have had sons," they should "not continue to make sons" (Harrison 188). Augustine *circa* 420 recommended this custom as an option for non-ordained people.

He also praised married couples in which husband and wife "observe a perpetual abstinence" (*nupt. et conc.* 12 tr. NPNF1 5). At least since Irenaeus, some leaders had affirmed the perpetual virginity of Mary,[17] and Augustine emphasized that Joseph and Mary had a true marriage even if they were celibate. A similar pattern was found in the story of Moses and Zipporah. He wrote in 418 that "we know many brothers and sisters bearing much fruit in grace, who by mutual consent withhold from each other in the name of Christ the desire of the flesh, but do not withhold from each other their mutual married love. The more the former is held in check, the stronger grows the latter" (*serm.* 51.21 tr. WSA I/24:33). Examples known to him included Therasia and Paulinus, and also Melania the Younger, who wished her marriage to be continent from the beginning but agreed to her husband Pinianus' wish to produce one male heir for his family's sake. After one daughter and a dead infant son, they became celibate marriage partners (Brown 409).

Roman society, mainly to maintain property inheritance, disapproved of this behavior and sometimes intervened legally to dissolve such marriages. Augustine defended them and wrote: "Heaven forbid that in the case of those who have decided by mutual consent permanently to abstain from the use of carnal concupiscence the marital bond between them is broken. In fact, it will be stronger to the extent that they have entered more deeply into those agreements with each other" (*nupt. et conc.* 1.11 tr. WSA I/24:35). However, he emphasized the need for mutual agreement and by letter he reprimanded Ecdicia, who dragooned her husband into continence, which he at first accepted, but then when she started giving away their money he turned to adultery. Augustine reminded Ecdicia of Paul's teaching on the "marital debt" owed between husband and wife (*ep.* 262 tr. WSA II/4).

Augustine also advised that after the death of a spouse, it is good for the surviving partner to remain single. This was a counsel and not a command. He criticized Tertullian for making it a rule and condemned the "Catharii or Novatians ... [who] do not allow second marriages" (*haer.* 38 tr. WSA I/18:111). Augustine commended a widow who was "at an age when she could still marry and have children if she wanted to, and she then embraced chastity as a widow" (*b. vid.* 14 tr. WSA II/4:124). When Augustine's own sister became a widow she joined a celibate community of women in Hippo Regius and became their abbess (AE 354 citing *ep.* 211.4; and Possidius, *vita Augustini* 26).

---

17 Jesus' siblings were presumed to be from Joseph's previous marriage.

Spiritual exegesis and celibate fertility

Throughout his career, Augustine used figurative, allegorical, and other kinds of spiritual exegesis to find deeper meaning in Scriptures that, on the surface, concerned biological fertility. In the 420s, reading the promise to Abraham that "I will make your offspring as the dust of the earth" (Genesis 13:16), Augustine first noted that it was "hyperbole ... [for] how incomparably greater is the number of the sands than the number of all human beings can possibly be, from Adam himself to the end of the world." The text has a double meaning, with the initial reference to offspring having a deeper reference to spiritual descendants, the church, "the whole seed of Abraham" (*civ. Dei* XVI.21 tr. Bettenson 679). Looking at another promise, "count the stars ... so shall your offspring be" (Genesis 15:15), Augustine emphasized the spiritual meaning: "God's promise refers to a spiritual posterity in heavenly beatitude" (*civ. Dei* XVI.23 tr. Bettenson 681).

Augustine also used allegory. Preaching on Psalm 127:3-5, he presented the man with a quiver full of sons as Christ, the sons as the twelve disciples, and the arrows sent far by the Lord's bow as the apostles (*en. Ps.* 126.10 tr. WSA III/20:93).[18] Another text he considered best interpreted spiritually was Psalm 128:3: "Your wife will be like a fruitful vine within your house; your children will be like olive shoots around your table." The wife is the church, and the children are the peacemakers (through an intertextual reading with Matthew 5:9), for it is they who shall be called the children of God (*en. Ps.* 127[8].13 tr. WSA III/20:111). Augustine also offers an alternative interpretation of the children and grandchildren in verse 6 of the same Psalm, the blessing "May you live to see your children's children":

> What do your children represent? The works you perform here. Who then are your children's children? The fruits of those works. If you give alms they are your children; but because you gave alms you receive eternal life, and that is what your children's children stand for. (*en. Ps.* 127[8].16 tr. WSA III/20:115)

Words such as "children" and "son" when used in Scripture do not always refer to biological offspring. Augustine wrote in 428: "The name of sons is interpreted in three ways in the Scriptures." Apart from the obvious way "according to nature," a person can have sons "according to teaching, as the

---

18   The difference in Psalm numbering (126 for 127, and 127 for 128) is due to the old Latin numbering which Augustine used. There is one fewer between Psalms 10 and 148 than in Hebrew and in modern English Bibles (Green, Preface xxiv).

Apostle calls his own sons those to whom he has taught the Gospel." The third way is "according to imitation," when someone hears about or sees a saint's faith and life and follows their example (*retr.* tr. FC 60:94). Augustine earlier had explained that "virginity is no obstacle to fertility" because "No one gives birth to consecrated virgins except a consecrated virgin" (*virg.* 2, 12 tr. WSA I/9:69, 74). Spiritual fecundity refers not only to the number of other people led to Christ, but also to personal fruits of the spirit:

> Nor should you count yourselves barren because you remain virgins; since this very integrity of the flesh, chosen for love, contributes to the fruitfulness of the mind. Do what the apostle says: since you are not thinking of the affairs of the world, how to please husbands, think of the affairs of God, how to please him in all things, so that instead of wombs fruitful with offspring, you may have minds fruitful with all the virtues. (*serm.* 191.4 tr. WSA III/6:44)

Ressourcement contrasted with natalism

What is the highest good that a person and a society ought to seek? Augustine's answer is that "eternal life is the Supreme Good, and eternal death is the Supreme Evil" (*civ. Dei* 19.4). Temporal, this-worldly blessings are good, but not if they distract from pursuit of the supreme good. On reproduction, Augustine reflects upon material interpretations of the "fruitful wife" and the "children like young sprouting olives" in Psalm 128 and warns: "do not lose heavenly happiness by pursuing temporal, earthly well-being" (*en. Ps.* 127[8].2 tr. WSA III/20.99).

Augustine would also not accept the idea that more of a temporal good is necessarily better. For all things there are appropriate limits "by measure, number, and weight," and Augustine liked the maxim, "nothing in excess" (AE 204). He advised that the "indulgence of the bodily appetites is intended to secure the continued existence and the invigoration of the individual or of the species. If the appetites go beyond … the limits of temperance, they become unlawful" (*c. Faust.* 22.29 tr. NPNF1 4). There he is writing about food, but the idea could well be applied to reproduction. The broader concept of *incontinentia* covers any inordinate love and accumulation of God's good gifts and has been related to greedy consumption and ecological sustainability by Gerald Schlabach. Those who become addicted to the experience of raising infants and want to spend their adult life repeating that good moment are incontinent.

Perpetuating family, nation, and species

Reproduction enables the continuity of clan lineages and nations. At the small scale of a family line, to seek perpetuity was a common goal among ancient Romans. The consul Cassius Dio rejoiced *circa* 225, "Is it not blessed, on departing from life, to leave behind as heir to your line and fortune one that is your own, produced by you, and to have only the mortal part of you waste away while you live on in the child?" (Rawson 100). Augustine commented on the text "see your children's children" in Psalm 128:5 (whose figurative exegesis was treated above):

> And consider this: Have your children been born to you in order to live with you on earth? Or to supplant you and oust you? Can you rejoice over the birth of those who are born only to push you aside? All new-born children tacitly say to their parents, "Get out of the way, it's our show now." (*en. Ps.* 127[8] tr. WSA III/20:112)

This was no path to immortality but a delusion. All that survives is the family name and a similarity of appearance, and the dead individual does not live beyond death that way: the only path to immortality is resurrection.

The wish to perpetuate a human society (whether it be a nation, city-state, or clan) is at minimum the hope that some will reproduce so that society continues. This hope does not seek exponential or absolute increase in population and does not impose an obligation on particular individuals. Augustine in 388 deployed against Manichean denigration of reproduction an argument that the continuity of species is a benefit of reproduction, for all species "by that blessing preserve their kind by giving birth" (*Gn. adv. Man.* 15.50 tr. FC 84:180). Responding to the controversy over Jovinian in 401, he similarly accepted that reproduction does "contribute to the continuation of the human race" (*b. conjug.* 9 tr. WSA I/9:40). However, he added:

> It is good to bear children and be the mother of a family; but not marrying is better because to have no need of this task is even better for human society ... There is no shortage of offspring ... so holy friendships may be fostered. What this means is that in the earliest ages of the human race, especially because of the need to propagate the people of God, through whom the Prince and Savior of all peoples would be proclaimed and be born, holy persons had a duty to make use of that benefit of marriage ... Now, however, since among all peoples everywhere there is an abundant provision of the spiritual kinship required for creating a true and holy society, even those who desire to marry solely for the sake of having children should be advised to avail themselves rather of the greater benefit of abstinence. (*b. conjug.* 9 tr. WSA I/9:41)

Augustine does not make clear whether the "holy society" envisaged is the whole communion of saints across all ages, or only those walking the earth at a particular moment. Are there already enough regenerated people for the holy society, or must production be maintained in each future generation? If the latter, then an implication would be that if at a future time there were very few new offspring being born, one would either have to rescind commendation of singleness or discard this particular argument. Augustine did not consider this implication, but in the 13th century, Latin scholastic writers did entertain such questions (Biller 120).

The perpetuation of the whole species was a philosophical concern, but at the smaller scale of a nation or city it was a common worry of ancient politicians, as noted earlier. Aware of the accusation that Christianity had weakened the empire, Augustine in general emphasized patriotic duty (AE 197 citing *ep.* 91.1), but this did not extend to reproduction. He wrote that "if it is part of a wise man's duty (and this is something which I have not yet discovered for certain) to devote himself to children, the man who takes a wife for this sole reason can seem to me worthy of admiration, but not of imitation" (WSA I/9:10). In any case, in later years Augustine gave less weight to patriotism.

Cornucopians claim that a rising population stimulates economic growth. The vision of continuous increase is uniquely modern, but a *ressourcement* against this secular eschatology can be made by comparing it to the Roman imperial ambition with which Augustine engaged in his analysis of Roman history. The driving force of the "City of Man" is *libido dominandi* (the will to power), which is not a virtue. The sinful and delusional nature of this imperial *libido* was a key concept in Augustine's writings (Markus, *Saeculum* xvi; Kretzmann and Stump 23).

Strengthening the visible church

Some natalists advocate Christian fecundity as a long-term project to grow numerically and politically relative to other religions. Augustine makes a comparison between his "two cities" motif and the Old Testament genealogies of Seth and Cain which seem at first sight amenable to the natalist vision. He outlines his book *The City of God* as "a summary of the origins of both these cities" that would go on to "describe their development from the time when that first pair begin to produce offspring up to the time when mankind will cease to reproduce itself" (*civ. Dei* 15.1 tr. Bettenson 595). Later in the book, he refers to the "two lines of descent of the human race" and observes that "the genealogies of the two societies are recorded separately, one deriving from Cain the fratricide, the other from the brother called Seth" (*civ. Dei* 15.8 tr. Bettenson 608). This does sound like a tribal vision because none of the godly species are descended from Cain.

However, only some of Seth's descendants were godly. Augustine suggests that the names listed (Enos, Cainan, Mahalaleel, Jared, Enoch, Methuselah, Lamech, Noah) are the lone men from each Sethite generation who turned to godliness. Given the advanced age of the fathers recorded at the time of the births of each of these men, Augustine concludes that there were large numbers of Sethite offspring (*civ. Dei* 15.20 tr. Bettenson 631), but only a few good ones. Further, they "all became bad enough to be wiped out by the Flood, except for one righteous man" (*civ. Dei* 15.8 tr. Bettenson 608). Of the period before Abraham, he asked "whether the progress of the Holy City can be traced in a continuous line after the Flood" and noted that "the record is silent about any righteous men ... [for] more than a thousand years" (*civ. Dei* 16.1 tr. Bettenson 649). So there is no genetically inherited righteousness here. Augustine later clarified that his contrast between the descendants of Cain and Seth merely "gave an appropriate picture of the two cities" (*civ. Dei* 15.21 tr. Bettenson 635 Cf. Genesis 4:26.), and that it was a rhetorical device in Genesis. When Augustine writes that "the City of God has even in this world many thousands of citizens who abstain from the act of procreation" (*civ. Dei* 15.20 tr. Bettenson 625), this is not a lament for competitive disadvantage but a sign of hope.

Some modern natalists argue that biological reproduction is the most effective way of adding members to the church. But *circa* 420, Augustine wrote: "No longer is God's people to be propagated by carnal generation; but, henceforth, it is to be gathered out by spiritual regeneration" (*nupt. et conc.* 15 tr. NPNF1 5:270). He discerned that the time for reproducing had been superseded by a time for gathering those people already sown. One of the arguments Jovinian used in support of his claim that marriage has as much merit as celibacy was that it produces Christians.[19] Augustine countered with this *reductio ad absurdum*:

> What then if some rich woman spends a great deal of money on the good work of buying slaves of various nations in order to make them Christian? Will she not procure the birth of members for Christ more abundantly and

---

19 Jovinian alone used this to argue that marriage has as much merit as celibacy.

fruitfully than would be possible from her womb, however fertile? She still will not dare to compare her money to the gift of holy virginity. Yet if physical motherhood truly makes up for lost virginity, because the children born become Christians, there will be even more to be gained from this enterprise if the loss of virginity is in return for payment of a large sum of money. With that money a much greater number of children can be purchased, to become Christians, than could be born from one woman's womb, however prolific. (*virg.* 9 tr. WSA I/9:72)

Though slave-buying or motherhood could add people to the church, the better way was preaching and holy life. Augustine wrote of the apostles "begetting children through the preaching of the gospel" (*en. Ps.* 44.23 tr. WSA III/16:301). Commenting on Psalm 40:6, "I proclaimed and I spoke; they were multiplied beyond counting," he claimed that "it's happening now; the gospel is being proclaimed, Christians are multiplying beyond counting" (*serm.* 229m.1, Friday before Easter 412, tr. WSA III/6:316).

Augustine observed that in his time "the human race is converging on the name of the crucified and streaming together ... It's high time for all and sundry to be inside. Now just a few have remained outside" (*serm.* 354a.25 tr. WSA III/11:382). His motive for bringing everyone inside was that *extra ecclesiam nulla salus – none can be saved outside the church.* He did not think all those inside would be saved. Membership was necessary but not sufficient for salvation. The two cities are both inside the church for "many reprobate are mingled in the Church with the good. Both are collected in the net of the Gospel ... [and] both swim ... in the net until brought ashore" on Judgement Day (*civ. Dei* 18.49). Markus notes Augustine's "protest against the readiness to see within any society the ultimate eschatological conflict prematurely revealed" (*Saeculum* 101). Since one cannot even identify or count the true members of the City of God mingled inside the visible church, a sectarian project to outnumber outsiders is not viable or meaningful.

Some natalists argue that increasing the number of people is intrinsically good, regardless of how many are redeemed, because everyone is made in the image and likeness of God. However, following a major strand of Christian tradition, Augustine argued that the original "likeness" to God was lost in the Fall (AE 441 citing *retr.* 2.24) and though a "spark" of reason shows that the *imago Dei* "has not been utterly quenched," it is broken (*civ. Dei* 22.24). The likeness can be restored only by Christ, and therefore increasing the quantity of births does not in itself increase the quantity of the divine image unless those born are subsequently regenerated.

Eternal destination of Christians' offspring

A few natalists argue that increasing Heaven's population is a benefit from fecundity. My counter-argument inspired by Augustine's writings considers the consequent parallel increase in Hell's population. The question is whether a rise in biological reproduction adds more to endless torment than to eternal bliss? Will most (or at least half) of church members' offspring ultimately be added to Heaven's population? There are various ways to make that scenario imaginable, but Augustine suggests problems in each line of reasoning.

If all the offspring of Christian parents were automatically born Christian, as Julian of Eclanum argued, that would be a good start toward a Heavenly majority. Augustine, however, responds that "our offspring are born as children of the present world" (*nupt. et conc.* 1.18; *c. Jul.* 6.13.40). Biological reproduction cannot transmit regeneration. Due to Adam's sin, "the whole of mankind is a *massa damnata*; for he who committed the first sin was punished, and along with him all the stock which had its roots in him" (*civ. Dei* 21.12 tr. Bettenson, 989; *c. Jul.* 16.4 tr. FC 35:111). Augustine offers an illustration from horticulture: seedlings from cultivated grafted olive trees always revert to the wild form, which is comparatively fruitless (*nupt. et conc.* 2.58). Our "parents, in giving us birth, bear us to eternal death, because of the ancient fault" (*serm.* 216). Christian parents are not privileged, because "what is born of the flesh is flesh … if they do not receive that rebirth [baptism], righteous parents will do them no good" (*pecc. mer.* 2.9 tr. NPNF1 5:88).

Baptism removes the guilt and penalty of original sin (*retr.* 199), but even if all parents had their infants baptized, only a minority would ultimately be saved. First, Augustine was aware that many die before baptism, either in the womb or in the days after birth. He observed in 411 that "mothers come running to church when their babies are ill" (*en. Ps.* 51 tr. WSA III/17:418). He discerned that "God does not wish to admit to His kingdom that immense number of infants who die without baptism" (*c. Jul.* 6.43 tr. FC 35.206). Julian responded that if it were so, it would be better if they had never been conceived. Augustine refused to concede this: "I do not say that children who die without the baptism of Christ will undergo such grievous punishment that it were better for them never to have been born … who can doubt that non baptized infants, having only original sin and no burden of personal sins, will suffer the lightest condemnation of all?" (*c. Jul.* 5.11.44, tr. FC 35:285). Nevertheless, the punishment would be endless in duration, and Augustine in a letter to Jerome in 415 expressed his distress regarding "the condemnation of so many thousands of souls, which in the deaths of infant children leave this world without the benefit of the Christian sacrament" (*ep.*166 tr. NPNF1 1:525).

Even if those dying before baptism are set aside as a special case,[20] infant baptism does not solve the problem of the hell/heaven balance because it does not guarantee salvation. In early 5th century Roman Christianity there may have been a popular idea that people were "incorporated" into the church "by birth and (infant) baptism, not by an act of conscious and deliberate decision ... no longer made but born" (Markus, *Christianity* 26). Augustine, however, rejected the idea that baptism automatically saves recipients (*civ. Dei* 21.19; 21.25; Daley 223). He regarded the visible church as a *corpus permixtum* (mixed body) composed of both wheat and tares (Harrison 220 citing *en. Ps.* 61.6), for "the identity of the predestined elect of the city of God is unknown in this life ... [and] they share ... in some cases, the same family" (*civ. Dei* 19.17; also see 21.23; 22.24). Preaching at the Easter vigil after 412, Augustine advised:

> Don't be surprised, either, at how many bad Christians there are, who fill the church, who communicate at the altar ... The Church of this time, you see, is compared to a threshing-floor, having on it grain mixed with chaff, having bad members mixed with good ... Every day people who seemed to be good fall away and perish; and again, ones who seemed to be bad are converted and live. (*serm.* 233.2 tr. WSA III/7:210)

So the destiny even of baptized children is unknown. Augustine, responding to Julian, referred to "the pious parents you so eloquently urge to procreate" and noted wryly that "we must attribute to parents their wish to have children, although they know nothing of their future" (*c. Jul.* 5.11.44 tr. FC 35:285-6). That uncertainty might give parents reason to hesitate before conceiving.

Natalists might press on with confidence that at least more will be saved than lost, but Augustine suggests a chilling thought: perhaps even among the baptized less than half will be saved. By the 410s most people within the Roman empire were members of the church, and from 416 imperial law required the baptism of infants. Yet still in the mid-420s, Augustine considered that the godly were "a mere few, in comparison with the multitude of the ungodly" (*civ. Dei* 16.21 tr. Bettenson 679), and he discerned that "there are many more condemned by vengeance than are released by mercy" (*civ. Dei* 21.12 tr. Bettenson 989). "There are a few among Christians who live good lives ... This threshing floor is going to be winnowed, there will be a huge

---

20 Which modern Catholic and Lutheran theology does.

pile of chaff, but there will also appear a shining mass of saints" (*serm.* 299a.9 tr. WSA III/11:271). The idea that even among church members the saved are few compared to the chaff is an additional argument against the idea that high birth rates serve the ultimate good by adding to the sum of eternal joy.

Augustine, following earlier Christian writers, believed that God had planned before the foundation of the world a fixed number of the redeemed to fill heaven. If Adam had not fallen, "there would have come into being a number of saints sufficient to complete the muster of that Blessed City" (*civ. Dei* 14.23 tr. Bettenson 585). After that, God "did not fail to have a plan whereby he might complete the fixed number of citizens predestined in his wisdom even out of the condemned human race" (*civ. Dei* 14.26 tr. Bettenson 591). This predetermined number is the cumulative total across all generations. Augustine was not eschatologically anxious about how many of the redeemed might be born in his lifetime, as he contemplated the possibility of the secular order continuing for 6,000 years or even "600,000 years, if the mortal state of humanity, with its succession of birth and death, should last so long, and our frailty, with all its ignorance, should endure" (*civ. Dei* 12.13 tr. Bettenson 487). The birth rate would make no difference to the number of the elect.

Choosing the greater blessings

Natalists argue that children are a blessing, "the more the better" (Provan 28). Augustine identified differing kinds of blessings, spiritual and temporal, greater and lesser. In many cases one has to choose between blessings. In a sermon to celibates at Christmas, *circa* 412, he pointed to the example of the Virgin Mary: "Setting at nought earthly marriages, you have chosen to be virgins … Imitate her as far as you can; not in her fruitfulness, because you cannot do this and preserve your virginity. She alone was able to have both the gifts, of which you have chosen to have one" (*serm.* 191.2 tr. WSA III/6:43).

The blessing in Psalm 128 superficially refers to biological offspring, but Augustine shows that logically it must refer primarily to spiritual blessings:

> How will this God-fearer be blessed? By seeing his wife like a fruitful vine against the sides of his house, and his children like young sprouting olives around his table. Does this mean that people who for God's sake have renounced marriage have missed their reward? Perhaps a celibate will say, "God blesses me in other ways." But that will not do: either he blesses you like this or he

does not bless you at all, for the psalm plainly says, Lo, this is how anyone who fears the Lord will be blessed." What does it mean then, brothers and sisters? (*en. Ps.* 127[8].1 tr. WSA III/20:98)

Augustine warned that "carnally-minded persons … may be tripped up rather than built up by this psalm" if they fail to unpack the "wrapped-up parcel" of its figurative meaning (*en. Ps.* 127[8].1,2), since:

It would be disgraceful … to refer the promises in our psalm to this-worldly happiness. That would be to say of any faithful follower of God … who, though married, does not happen to have any children, "That man clearly does not fear the Lord." … If we talk like that, we show ourselves to be carnally-minded … trapped in the love of earthly things.

Augustine then imagined a debate with someone who points to the case of a godless man who acquires many grandchildren as a contradiction of the Psalm:

If you look for those good things with earthly eyes, you will be expecting hordes of children and grandchildren, and a wife who is fertile and frequently pregnant. But these are not the good things of the eternal Jerusalem; they are the good things that belong to the land of the dying … Beware of running after blessings that are not from Zion … Yes, these temporal things truly are blessings from the Lord … but do you not see that he has given them to animals as well? That blessing cannot originate *from Zion* … Remember how even the birds were bidden, Increase and multiply. Can you rate so highly a gift conferred equally on birds? If you are given these temporal blessings, make good use of them; but give more thought to how you are going to bring up the children already born than to having even more. Happiness lies not in merely having children but in having good ones. If they are already born to you, work hard on their upbringing; if they are not born, give thanks to God, because you will perhaps have fewer worries. (*en. Ps.* 127[8].15 tr. WSA III/20:101)

Of the three goods of marriage, the good of offspring is the least and is not essential. Marriages that are infertile or perpetually continent completely lack the *bonum prolis*, and yet Augustine considered them to be true marriages nonetheless. The *bonum sacramenti*, symbolizing Christ and his bride, shines from every married couple. The *bonum fidei* can be achieved by every couple "helped by the grace of God." But if a couple's offspring are not saved (which is manifest if the children leave the church, and uncertain even if the children stay within the visible church), then for those parents there would ultimately be no *bonum prolis*, but only (I coin the term) a *malum prolis*.

Ordinance of God and nature

Some natalists invoke "be fruitful" as a command for people today. Augustine, as discussed earlier, limited the command to the Old Covenant. Instead he poses a choice: "the married, the widowed, the virginal ... Let each of you choose from these three kinds of life whichever you wish" (*serm*. 61.2 tr. WSA III/3:196). This had to be a choice because individuals had different levels of ability and faith in this area. Augustine's advice closely followed Paul's in 1 Corinthians 7. He advised that "the only ones who should marry are those who are unable to be continent, in accordance with that advice of the same apostle" (*b. conjug*. 42). Similarly, *circa* 426, he referred to "those men to whom the apostle permitted as a matter of indulgence to have one wife because of their incontinence" (*doc. Chr*. 18/26). For those who are capable, singleness is the better option.

The idea that humankind was originally designed for reproduction does not in Augustine's thought lead to a "law of nature" requiring obedience to natural urges. In the 420s Augustine wrote that although "man .. is brought [down] to the level of the beasts, and he breeds like the beasts," the created natural order now conveys only "the possibility, not the necessity, of propagation" (*civ. Dei* 22.24 tr. Bettenson 1071). Biology does not dictate behavior when the Holy Spirit rules. For natalists, the default life-path is marital fecundity, but Augustine reverses this: singleness is the default way of life, the norm. He wrote: "Do not look for a wife, is a statement of advice, not a commandment; hence to marry is not something wrong to do, but it is better not to do it" (*virg*. 15).

Modern natalists (like Luther in the 1520s) marginalize celibacy as a rare exceptional gift rather than a life-choice. Augustine admitted that "unless God grants it, no one is able to be continent" (*cont*. 192). However, this is equally true for married faithfulness: it also is only possible by grace, so rarity is not a valid argument against volunteering for either state. Augustine often refers to celibacy as something one may choose. For example, in sermons at Christmas he addressed the celibate members of his church, remarking in 411 that "you have chosen to be virgins" (*serm*. 191.2 tr. WSA III/6:43), and in 412 that "for Christ's sake you have declined to give birth" (*serm*. 192.2 tr. WSA III/6:47), and in the 410s that "virgins decide against being mothers" (*serm*. 188.3 tr. WSA III/6:33).

Julian of Eclanum used this acknowledged freedom as an argument for the power of the will to Christian perfection, but Augustine answered, you say as though to test me: "If you are really inviting men to strive for continence, you will admit that the virtue of chastity can be possessed by those who wish, in such a way that whoever wishes may be holy in body and soul." I answer that I admit it, but not in your sense. You attribute this to the powers of the soul itself; I attribute it to the will helped by the grace of God. *(c. Jul.* 16 tr. FC 35:303)

Celibate singleness is an "evangelical counsel" that any Christian may choose to accept. Elaine Pagels found that a "theme of human freedom ... dominates patristic exegesis of Genesis 1-3," and although she argued that in some ways freedom was "buried" by Augustine because of his teaching on the fallen state as "not able not to sin" ("Politics" 68), elsewhere she admits that "freedom from cosmic necessity ... expresses itself most powerfully ... in ... choosing celibacy" ("Freedom" 93). In this respect, compared to the ideas Luther presented in the 1520s, Augustine is an apostle of freedom from necessity. Mary Clark argued that for Augustine, "free choice itself was not lost ... human will is never held 'in bondage'... and he did not use the expression 'natural law'" (52, 55).

God's means of forming disciples

Many natalists regard parenthood as a necessary discipline for adults and the intentionally childless as selfish. Augustine agrees that all must be consecrated to service but adds that this can be oriented toward the neighbor as understood in a broad sense. In comparison with Christian love that extends even to enemies, Augustine regarded parental love of offspring as merely natural and instinctive. He preached in 397 on the distinctive quality of the true Christian love of neighbor as compared to the pagan love of blood relatives, offspring, and family:

> Can't you see how mutual love holds sway among irrational animals ... So what's so great about what you're doing, if as a human being you want to be with another human being? It's still no different from the animals in your stable. I don't know whether that's the sort of love that God requires of us. Perhaps you'll say, "I do love my neighbor; after all. I love my son, and as myself." That's easy enough too. Tigers love their cubs. After all, none of these animals would reproduce, unless one were loved by another. Go beyond [animal behaviour]. *(serm.* 90a.6 tr. WSA III/11:79)

Seven years later in 404, he preached: "Nor are human beings to be praised for a quality that is to be found in dumb animals ... what is so wonderful about a man loving his son?" (*serm.* 159b.4 tr. WSA III/11:149). Such love was unimpressive as a witness, as an example of distinctively Christian love.

Some natalists regard childrearing as a formative discipline that is good for the soul. Augustine has no such idea, but he agrees that childrearing is onerous. Enquiring into the "supreme good" in *City of God*, he observed "the number and the gravity of the ills which abound in society and the distresses of our mortal condition? Our philosophers should listen to a character in one of their own comedies ... I married a wife; and misery I found! Children were born; and they increased my cares" (*civ. Dei* 19.5 tr. Bettenson 858). Parenthood is just one of the sources of distress in this world, and these troubles do not function as a purifying penance but only as a distracting worry. He wrote in 404 that marriage should be regarded as

> [not] something bad and forbidden, but as something burdensome and worrying... In the present age, however, when bearing children physically does not contribute toward the future physical birth of Christ, to undertake for the sake of having a marriage the burden of those afflictions of the flesh that the apostle pronounces to be the lot of those who marry would be utter foolishness. The only exception is for those who lack self-control, if there is danger they will ... fall into mortal sin ... Is there anyone, among those who have tied themselves with the bonds of marriage, who is not tossed and torn by those cares? (*virg.* 16 tr. WSA I/9:76)

Elizabeth Clark finds in Augustine a "proreproductive and anticontraceptive marital ethic" ("Vitiated" 396). That represents two separate claims because, as I showed earlier, there is no logical connection. The second claim is obviously true: Augustine is anti-contraceptive. As to the first claim, by comparison with the Marcionites, Manicheans, Encratites, and many of the Fathers preceding him, Augustine is less antipathetic to sexual reproduction. But when compared with modern natalists, he is anti-reproductive. Strands in early modern and especially 19th-century Catholicism, influenced by nationalism, developed a two-tier model of vocation with a small celibate elite and a lay married majority encouraged to have big families. That model would be alien to Augustine, and to most medieval Christians. Augustine wanted all to aspire to as high a spirituality as possible, to continence within marriage if not to celibacy.

Augustine's ideas about reproduction developed in the context of various controversies. Against the Manicheans he justified the reproductive obsessions of the patriarchs of Genesis by finding their purpose in salvation history. To oppose Jovinian, he clarified the dispensational distinction between the Old

Testament and Christianity. Augustine argued that marriage is good, and celibacy is better. Against the Pelagians he claimed that Christians are not able to give birth to Christians and that baptism does not guarantee salvation.

Ressourcement from Augustine offers much help in critiquing natalism. A secular pragmatism about reproduction is found in Augustine's writings, but it is minimal and trumped by his focus on eternity. Christians have no obligation to perpetuate the City of Man. The church's future is assured not by biological but by spiritual reproduction. The human future is assured not by sexual reproduction but by the general resurrection of the dead. Motherhood is a blessing but non-reproductive lives are more blessed. Nature does not dictate motherhood (or fatherhood), and grace enables anyone to follow the apostolic counsel of singleness. Earlier rationales for Christian celibacy had been vulnerable to criticisms like those made by Jovinian, but Augustine stabilized the tradition and forestalled any emergence of aggrandizing natalism within Christianity, at least until Luther's demolition work in the 1520s.

So there is much to use against natalism in Augustine's thought as it stands, but without the anti-contraceptive ideas he inherited from Alexandria there would be even more. If one imagines Augustine's thought without that, his high esteem of celibacy would remain, and some of the benefits he perceived in continent marriage could then be ascribed to contraceptive marriage, if it was devoted to rational and spiritual fruitfulness. Augustine's non-natalist view is not rooted in his antipathy to sexuality but in his sense of vocation, in God's purposes in history and eschatology, and his relative valuation of different blessings.

6. An Ecological Critique of Natalism

I will here complete my evaluation of natalist interpretations of the fruitful verses, which I previously weighed against their original Near Eastern context and then compared with Augustine's thinking about human fruitfulness. Now a constructive ecological response to natalism will be offered, bringing together Scripture, Christian tradition, and the 21st-century context of North American and global population growth and ecological footprints to produce an alternative interpretation of the fruitful verses, one shaped by concern for biodiversity and ecological sustainability. This chapter considers the purpose and context of human fecundity, as well as the concepts of abundance, limits to growth, and what it means to "fill" the earth. As in the previous two chapters, there follows a section which evaluates the major natalist arguments, supported by further *ressourcement* from patristic and classic Christian thought.

Ecological crisis and the role of population

Population size is a multiplier of ecological impact. One way to quantify that impact is the 'ecological footprint' (EF), developed by the Global Footprint Network since the 1990s. It sums up how consumption of all types (e.g. food, construction, travel, and manufactured goods) uses renewable resources such as fresh water, trees, and crops. The sum of consumption is the ecological footprint. The annual production of each resource is also calculated and is called biocapacity. For example, wood from trees grows each year, so it is a renewable resource. If trees are felled faster than they grow, that part of the footprint exceeds its biocapacity and means that the stock of trees shrinks that year. All kinds of resources are converted into standard units called

http://dx.doi.org/10.11647/OBP.0048.06

global hectares (gha), and the planet has around 12 billion gha available each year to be shared among the human population. Calculations in 2010 suggested that humankind was using about 18 billion gha. Not living within our means, we incur detriment each year, for example by lowering aquifer water tables and reducing soil depth.

Ecological hermeneutics

Consciously ecological approaches to biblical interpretation, hereafter referred to as eco-biblical,[1] are a recent innovation. Brief comments on local environmental problems and animal welfare appear in exegetes of the 19th century and earlier, but the first instance I have found addressing broader environmental problems features in a 1957 commentary on Genesis by David Stalker of Edinburgh University. He sees soil erosion and the depletion of whales as symptoms of human "exploitation" of nature and suggests that "a profitable discussion could be held about the guidance which Genesis has to offer on this problem" (28). Joseph Sittler after 1955 pioneered an ecotheology that included exegetical remarks on New Testament letters, and later on Psalm 104 (Bouma-Prediger and Bakken 20, 32, 38, 51). The trickle of eco-biblical work increased after the 1967 article by Lynn White which blamed western Christian reception of Genesis for the ecological crisis (1205) and provoked substantial responses by Old Testament scholars, including James Barr in 1973 and Bernhard Anderson in 1983. The volume of eco-biblical research has continued to grow: it was surveyed by Gene McAfee and Gene Tucker in the 1990s, and by Ernst Conradie in 2006. Diverse approaches to eco-biblical interpretation have developed. I will describe these under three headings and identify which one offers the most appropriate methodological resources for the particular requirements of this project.

One type of eco-biblical work can be characterized as recovery or "apologetics" (Horrell, *Bible* 11), aiming to show that Scripture is full of ecological wisdom or at least that it does not promote an exploitative attitude. A radical objection to this approach is that it is anachronistic to expect ecological awareness among the ancient biblical writers. For example, James Nash claims the Bible is "ecologically unconscious," especially with regard to biodiversity (214). Eco-biblical apologetics is also criticized for unacknowledged selectivity from the canon, ignoring the diversity of biblical

---

1   The term eco-Bible appeared in 1993 in the title of an article by Walter Wink (465).

voices (Conradie 296). Celia Deane-Drummond agrees that these criticisms are deserved responses to unsophisticated portrayals of ecological concern as the original meaning of a wide range of biblical texts,[2] but considers that most work by Old Testament scholars has avoided these defects (272). The recovery approach is often helpful: for example, the message of caring for the land is clearly rooted in the Old Testament context of good husbandry of poor and easily ruined land (Wright; Habel, *Land*; Davis, "Learning"; Marlow). However, with regard to the issue of high fecundity, I demonstrated in chapter 4 that the Israelite writers had little experience of overpopulation and normally desired fecundity, so the recovery approach is not likely to be sufficient for my purposes.

A second approach, influenced by the hermeneutic of suspicion and ecofeminist ideological criticism, emerged in the late 1990s. It is best represented by the *Earth Bible* project, which is based on six "ecojustice principles" that are summarized by Norman Habel as the intrinsic worth of all creatures, purpose, interconnectedness, mutual custodianship, earth's voice, and resistance to injustice ("Challenge" 125). This approach has many virtues: it helpfully engages with science and politics, and is designed to facilitate dialogue with people of any faith or none. However, for my project, where the aim is evaluation of Christian reception, it is less suitable. The ecojustice approach rejects dominion, hierarchy, and dualism (Habel, "Challenge" 128), whereas a nuanced affirmation of those concepts is necessary here; otherwise, a basis for calling humankind to responsible behavior would be lacking. According to some biologists, humankind, like any other species, should reproduce as much as it can, regardless of limits to growth and without concern for impact on other species, sacrificing individual welfare for aggregate prosperity (Sideris 56). Justifying an intelligent limitation of human fecundity for the sake of biodiversity depends on perceiving a special human status and responsibility for other living creatures, which David Clough calls "instrumental anthropocentrism" (Horrell, *Bible* 131). Even dualism must be redeemed, as transcendence of instinct is required. So the ecojustice approach is not sufficient as a methodology here.

---

2   In defence of practitioners of unsophisticated eco-Bible, one should note that, first, their approach is similar to much other devotional use of the Bible, and that, second, popular literature disseminating such interpretations not only encouraged some who were already convinced environmentalists, but also persuaded some conservative Christians to engage with ecological issues and change their lives (Maier; and my experiences working for Evangelical environmental groups).

A third way, which I do adopt in this chapter, was developed by Ernst Conradie and the Exeter University project on "Uses of the Bible in Environmental Ethics." David Horrell argues that even the most ecofriendly verses are "ambivalent and ambiguous," and he points to contrary interpretations by Beisner and other foes of environmentalism (*Bible* 117, 14). He is also concerned that much work of the *Earth Bible* type is not persuasive to conservative Christians. His response begins by noting that interpretation normally uses doctrinal lenses, for example Augustine's rule that all exegesis should foster love of God and neighbor, and Luther's key principle of justification by faith (*Bible* 123). Horrell suggests a method for constructing a new lens by "consciously bringing certain texts and themes into central focus, [and] marginalizing or resisting others" (*Bible* 128). Drawing on numerous Old and New Testament verses, he proposes several interpretive principles: the goodness of creation, its interconnectedness (the inclusion of all creatures in covenant, praise, and reconciliation), and a unique human role (*Bible* 129-36). Horrell acknowledges a need for awareness that this selection of principles is prompted by contemporary environmental issues, and we should not "pretend that the doctrinal lenses emerge solely from the texts, nor even the tradition, alone" (Horrell, Hunt, and Southgate 236). This "acknowledged circularity" is unavoidable.

My use of Christian tradition needs clarification. There is no consensus in the tradition about reproduction or the fruitful verses, as my chapter on Luther illustrated. I have prioritized the early Church Fathers because of their importance in the tradition and their proximity to the formation of creeds and canon. Whereas chapter 5 looked in depth at one Church Father's thought in historical context, this chapter draws on a wide range of patristic writings without revisiting their context. However, none of the ideas presented here are peculiar to one Church Father, and most of them represent a majority patristic view. This *ressourcement* applies these ideas beyond their original context, but that is a characteristic of any effort to "rediscover and renew the Christian tradition" (Conradie 295), and the tradition develops in every age precisely by its encounter with whatever issues are then contemporary.

The role of contemporary context also needs clarification. Eco-Bible is informed by ecological science (especially its contribution to calculating the limits of earth systems and the vulnerability of particular species to extinction), but the commitment to an ethic of biodiversity derived from Genesis 1 here takes precedence. The ecologists consulted by the *Earth Bible* team considered the ecojustice principles appropriate (Habel, "Challenge"

126), but other observers of nature might find different principles there, such as ruthless competition or purposeless futility (Sideris 2). With regard to fecundity, there is no ecological reason to prefer a regime of low fertility and low mortality to one in which both rates are high. Rather, since evolution requires variation and selection fuelled by the early deaths of infants and pre-reproductive individuals, a regime of high fertility and high mortality could be deemed a good ecological pattern for society. Further, many ecologists judge the success of an individual life by its genetic contribution to the next generation, the number of biological descendants, according to which criterion Genghis Khan (a polygamist with many descendants) is held up as a paragon of human behavior (Zerjal 720) and Jesus of Nazareth is regarded as an abject failure. Karl Barth (ix) and the Church Fathers warn us that Christian ethics should not be based upon examining nature.[3]

A danger in eco-Bible, as in environmentalism, is neglect of connected interests such as those of women and the poor. The camps of political exegetes rebuke each other for neglect of other dimensions of liberation: one example is Womanist (black) criticism of early feminism for ignoring racial oppression. Such conflict causes fragmentation but also mutual awareness, and hopefully it leads to efforts at convergence so that one liberative reading does not act unwittingly against another. Therefore a critique of natalism should avoid, for example, a denigration of early Judaism which plays into the hands of anti-Judaists. Another caution for practitioners of eco-Bible in general comes from those ecofeminists who identify a series of connected dualisms such as man/woman, human/animal, spirit/body, Heaven/Earth. They claim that eco-Bible only functions properly under the umbrella of ecofeminism. I take this as a warning that an eco-biblical treatment of the fruitful verses should not denigrate motherhood or blame women for high fecundity.

Population and environmental impact

Eco-biblical writings are often prefaced by a survey of ecological crises, and here they sometimes do mention population. For example, one of the five causes of the ecological crisis identified by Martin-Schramm and Stiver is "too many people" (Horrell 5). However, after such introductions eco-biblical writings rarely engage with the population issue or the fruitful verses. For example, of the imperatives in Genesis 1:28 there is far more eco-biblical

---

3   Barth adds that only the incarnation reveals nature's meaning.

writing about "subdue [the earth]" and "have dominion" than about "be fruitful and multiply, fill the earth." This is sometimes due to a downplaying of the significance of population, but even those acknowledging its impact rarely apply ecological hermeneutics to the fruitful verses.

Catherine Keller observed that "among Northern ecumenical Protestant Christians – ethicists, feminists, eco-spiritualists, liberation theologians, and justice activists – there seems to reign an unstated assumption that population is never worth highlighting" (110). Since the 1970s, wider academia has normally been reluctant to highlight population as ecologically problematic, and eco-Bible followed that fashion with good reason. Since the 1950s, many who emphasize overpopulation as the cause of environmental crises have been motivated by anxiety about rich nations' power and national security. The affluent North was responsible for most ecological impact, but many of the voices against overpopulation focused on high birth rates in the global South, and Andy Smith discerns in this a prejudice against colored women (75). Evangelicals and Catholics are also wary because of institutional links between family planning and abortion. So it is unsurprising that eco-biblical readings have rarely focused on any of the fruitful verses.

A dualism contrasting the ecological impacts of consumption and population associates the poor with the issue of population (Hynes 43). Population is regarded (wrongly) as only an issue for poor nations, so those who (rightly) regard affluent people as the main cause of ecological impact consider it inappropriate to focus on population as a problem (Smith 77). Ernst Conradie, a South African theologian, regards contemporary debates about relative impacts of population and consumption as reflecting "tensions between North and South," and so to highlight population is to side with injustice, because that choice "implies that the impoverished countries ... carry a special responsibility" for the crisis (*Christianity* 21). However this dualism is defective. First, it fails to notice exceptions, notably the U.S., where numbers of births each year substantially exceed deaths. Due to higher per-person greenhouse gas emissions, the natural increase of the U.S. population each year generates more additional emissions than the (much larger) combined natural increase of all Africa. At a smaller scale, in the UK births also exceed deaths. For example in 2012 there were approximately 813,000 births compared to 569,000 deaths (ONS).

Second, and more widely applicable for most developed countries, the dualism is based upon a focus on present rates of population growth rather than historical population increases. For example, the U.S. population in

1800 was 5.3 million; by 1900, it was 76 million; today it is over 300 million. Many observers assume that U.S. population growth was mostly due to immigration, but most additions to its population have been births in the U.S. Using annual data that begins in 1909, one can calculate the number of U.S. births from 1909 to 2012 to be 359.5 million.[4] Across the same period, the number of legal immigrants was only 52.4 million,[5] so the number of U.S. births was nearly seven times greater. By analogy with climate justice models of "contraction and convergence," which take historical emissions into account, rich nations have a large total impact on the environment due to past population growth. A responsibility to "contract" the U.S. national ecological impact could be met through a lower birth rate. So highlighting population size as an ecological problem is not intrinsically biased against poor countries.

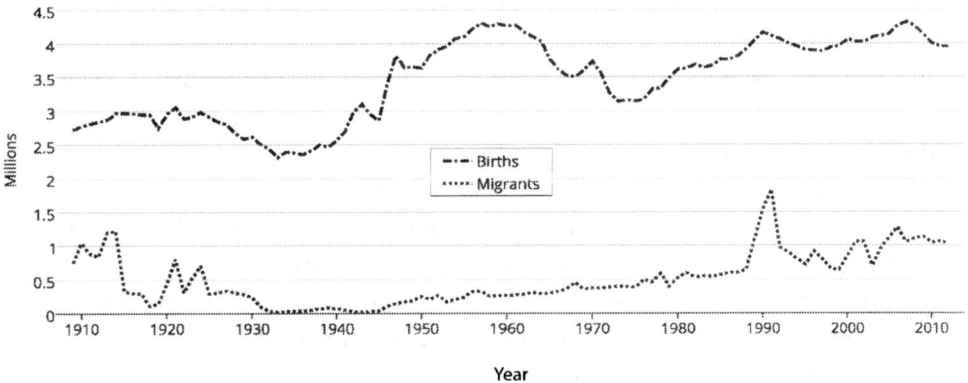

Figure 6. Addition to U.S population: births in the U.S. compared to immigration, 1909-2012.

Ecofeminists are divided on the question of the significance of population size. Some would rather ignore it. For example, Patricia Hynes claims that the equation for ecological impact, I=PAT, gives a false impression that poor people are equally responsible by including population.[6] Her suggestion to delete P (population) from the equation (40) is, however, a rhetorical step too far. Population is a multiplier of impact. For greenhouse gas emissions, there

---

4   http://www.cdc.gov/nchs/data/statab/natfinal2003.annvol1_01.pdf
5   http://www.dhs.gov/immigration-statistics
6   I=PAT stands for Impact = Population x Affluence x Technological efficiency.

has been research on population's effect. One study by Dietz and Rosa finds a 1.15 global ratio of change (elasticity). This means that if there were a 10% rise in population it would cause 11.5% more emissions. Anqing Shi finds a global average elasticity of 1.42, but with regional variation (35, 39). For the U.S., Michael Dalton finds that the "effect of smaller population size on emissions is somewhat more than proportional" (90).[7] Those figures are just for emissions: the elasticity for ecological footprints is less well established, but it is safe to say that impact is roughly proportional to population. In future, to achieve higher affluence[8] for the poor, the future reduction of the total ecological footprint requires some mix of new technology, lower consumption in rich nations, and population shrinkage everywhere.

Another reason for the lack of eco-biblical treatment of the fertility theme is a belief that biblical reception does not affect birth rates. Eco-Bible began from a conviction that exegesis can affect attitudes toward the environment and that ecofriendly interpretation can therefore make a difference (Horrell 6-7). By contrast, many assume that birth rates are governed by economics (the common belief is that poor people will have high fecundity until they become richer), and that religion makes no difference. However, the demographer Massimo Livi Bacci finds that "cultural factors ... seem to be more significant to fertility decline than economic factors" in developed countries (116). Eric Kaufmann and other social scientists have found that in developed countries religiosity is more important than education as a predictor of the number of children born to a woman. As noted in chapter 1, the birth rate among fundamentalists is higher than among moderate U.S. Protestants, and that difference is partly caused by religious differences.

Ecological perspectives on fertility

The design of life on earth seems harsh to individual creatures, but supportive of biodiversity. Globally there are around 1.75 million named species, and over the last 200 million years the number of diverse species has been slowly increasing (Eldredge 12). The common pattern of life on earth is profligate reproduction and equally high mortality, especially among the young. The

---

7   John Harte argues that elasticity may worsen as population rises due to a host of nonlinear thresholds; for example, given a ceiling on annual production of natural gas, extra demand by a rising population may result in greater use of coal (234).

8   Or at least, following the UN Millennium Development Goals, to raise everyone's HDI (human development index). Reducing inequality within a nation provides more HDI per unit of affluence.

selective cycle repeats in each generation, and there is competition between species.[9] One might expect frequent loss of species, but the normal rate of extinction is low: the lifespan of a species is typically 1 to 10 million years (Baillie, Hilton-Taylor, and Stuart 41). Five brief episodes of mass extinction (the most recent happening 65 million years ago) each wiped out more than half of all the species of those moments, but all these episodes had external physical causes[10] and none of them was caused by one or a few species multiplying so much as to crowd out many others. In the most recent few thousand years, often called the Anthropocene (human era), a sixth episode of mass extinction has begun, caused by human impact.

The flourishing of a species or a local subpopulation is measured ecologically by quantity, health, and genetic diversity. Geographical range is also important, but a species limited to one region (endemic), or even to a single island, can still flourish in that place, though it is more vulnerable than a widely distributed species. Number is important because too small a population is endangered, at risk of local extinction (Ranta, Kaitala and Lundberg 214). However, as numbers rise above that minimum the additional gain to a species' chance of survival diminishes. At high levels, number conflicts with health; for example, with a local absence of predators, reindeer numbers and density will increase to the point where individuals' health deteriorates. By contrast, wolves are slow to reproduce, and even when food is abundant they tend to maintain steady numbers and good health (Rockwood 150). Robert Attenborough notes that "natural historians have long been impressed by the persistence and relative numerical constancy of many natural populations" (190).

The population of each species is regulated by external influences in a diverse ecosystem. Some species rapidly increase in numbers to the limit of local resources and then fall precipitously; for example, cinnabar moths often strip their food plant (ragwort) and then crash with most larvae dying (Moss, Watson, and Ollason 35-37). That, however, is not the norm. Even at the end of summer, tree foliage is rarely all eaten because leaf-eaters do not increase to anywhere near the limit of their food, mostly because of mortality from predation and disease. Populations are regulated by mortality but also by fertility.[11] Reproduction is controlled by variables such as mating,

---

9 Alongside examples of mutualism or symbiosis (Vandermeer and Goldberg 221).

10 Likely causes of the mass extinction episodes include meteor impact, volcanic eruptions, and solar disruptions, mostly affecting life through climate changes.

11 Obviously, fertility regulation is harder to observe and measure than mortality, but even so it has been detected in many species.

conception, and brood size. For example, territorial behavior means that only those individuals who secure a territory mate in that season. Honeybee queens adjust their egg-laying rate to match food supply, reducing it when flowers are poor. In nature, local population growth often follows a logistic curve: the rate of growth slows as population density approaches a certain level, and the population size then flattens out or peaks.

In nature, density-dependent effects on mortality and fertility usually prevent overcrowding, but in laboratories many experiments have put a population of a species (for example fruit flies, mice, or rats) in a confined space while supplying unlimited food. In all species tested, beyond some high population density, the birth rate (and/or infant survival) began declining to a low level. Various mechanisms were observed: fruit flies laid fewer eggs and mice neglected their young, leading to infant mortality rates above 90%. Some rats engaged in non-reproductive sex, while others became homosexual or asexual (Rockwood 66).

The stability and longevity of a species is dependent on the biodiversity of the surrounding ecosystem. The flourishing of life as a whole is defined by number of species, number of individuals (and their mass), overall geographical spread, health of ecosystem services, and diversity. The persistence of biodiversity is mysterious but at least partly explained by species being limited to ecological niches and constrained by particular local food supplies rather than total global resources.

Homo sapiens has exceptional ability to adapt and occupy additional niches, and to modify environments to be like familiar habitats. Local studies find that rising human population density only slightly reduces biodiversity up to a certain level, but beyond that, threshold biodiversity falls rapidly and the numerical size of nonhuman populations also declines (Cincotta 69). A sixth episode of mass extinction began (gradually) at least ten thousand years ago, largely due to human population growth (McKee 61), but 20th-century growth in consumption *per capita* hugely multiplied the effect, so the extinction episode has become increasingly acute (Eldredge x). One measure of biodiversity based on vertebrates, the Living Planet Index, fell by 30% between 1970 and 2003. Data for earlier decades is patchy but suggests "large losses" in the mid-20th century (Loh et al. 20). The human ecological footprint (including large U.S. and European components) crowds out many nonhuman species.

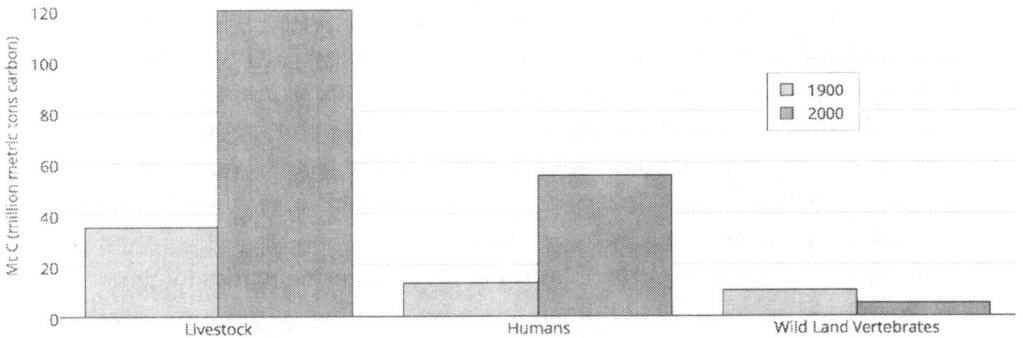

Figure 7. Fall in combined mass of wild land vertebrate species from 1900 to 2000. Data source: Vaclav Smil, "Harvesting the Biosphere: The Human Impact." *Population and Development Review* 37.4 (2011): 613-36.

Fertility in eco-biblical perspective

The hermeneutic lens used here is drawn from selected Scriptures, with a special focus on Genesis 1. One reason for giving that chapter priority is its canonical position at the beginning of the Bible, making it familiar to contemporary readers. Another is that Christian tradition regards the first two chapters of Genesis as depicting how life on Earth was originally intended to be prior to the sin of humankind. It portrays an ideal world, but it is also more realistic than many other creation stories insofar as it constitutes wisdom literature based on the ancient writers' awareness of the created world. Some features of the story are recognisable to a modern scientific worldview. However, it differs in being a vision of an ideal world that is more ordered and peaceful than the writers' known world (Bauckham, *Ecology* 25). Genesis 1-11 is also an aetiology, showing how the original creation became the world known by its early readers. The ostensible scope is the whole of creation and humankind in general, not only Israel.

Principles relevant to the question of fecundity's relation to sustainability can be derived from the text. Genesis 1 provides a pattern for reproduction. Its purpose is the perpetuation of each species, and it is designed to work in parallel with a great variety of different species reproducing at the same time within the same world. That provides a context for human fecundity as one species within that created plan, but there is also a unique human role and vocation to uphold this purpose of the creator. As implications of those principles, the following additional concepts are explored: the limits to growth, the idea that abundance is only one aspect of flourishing, and the metaphor of "filling" a land. These will be illustrated from Genesis chapters 3-11 and other biblical texts that portray the world after sin, in which relations are broken and fertility has become ambivalent.

David Horrell's seven principles for ecological hermeneutics in general can be related specifically to human fecundity. Biodiversity is intrinsically valuable to God (Bauckham, *Ecology* 78) because of the goodness of all creation and the nonhuman calling to praise God (principles 1 and 5). The importance of perpetuating every kind of creature is explicit in God's covenant with all creatures (principle 4). Limits to growth are implicit in the connectedness of life in failure and flourishing, and in humankind's membership of the Earth community (principles 3 and 2). A human vocation to facilitate the diversity of species and their flourishing is one aspect of eschatological reconciliation (principle 7).

Perpetuating diverse species

Genesis shows a great variety of species being created and sustained. The major categories mentioned are grass, herbs, trees, life that swarms in the waters, flying winged creatures,[12] livestock, creeping things, and wild beasts. Applied to each of these categories is the phrase "according to their kinds" (1:11, 12, 24, 25), implying many different forms within each. Elsewhere in the Old Testament over 120 kinds of animal are named, and the writers probably knew of many others that did not happen to feature in Scripture.[13] They were perhaps aware of stories of yet more varieties unseen, especially

---

12 Most water-dwelling animals are not "fish" and not all flying species are "birds." Most commentators use those terms, but the Hebrew is more generic, referring to "every living creature that moves" in the waters and "every winged flying creature" (1:21). Finding short English terms for the categories of Genesis 1 is difficult. The attributes of moving and flying feature in the text, so we might use the words swimmer and flyer. However, no distinctive locomotion spans all of the 6th day's species. Some translations (following the KJV) have "creeping" things, but the word *ramas* just means "moving." A designation based on the spatial zones of sea, sky, and land works for sea-creatures and land-animals, but sky-animals is inadequate because these are also linked to the land (1:22).

13 A possible upper limit is the 500 described by Aristotle, the father of zoology.

hidden in the seas. A divine intention for this variety to persist is implicit in the assessments that "it was good" (1:12, 21, 25), and is explicit in the Flood story where God commands that from "every kind" of living creature a breeding population must be saved "to keep them alive" (6:19-20, ESV).[14]

The purpose of fruitfulness is the perpetuation of distinct species. That is the meaning of the phrase "bearing fruit ... each according to its kind" (1:11, ESV).[15] The idea is not explicitly repeated until Genesis 5:1 when "Adam ... fathered a son in his own likeness, after his image," but it can be assumed that each kind in chapter 1 is fruitful in its own likeness, perpetuating that species. This suggests that the original creatures brought forth at God's command by the waters and the ground (1:20, 24), the first generation, were not immortal and their continuity depended on the reproductive capability incorporated in each species.

Abundance or quantity of creatures is one aspect of God's design, as indicated by the words *shrtz*, "swarm" or "teem" (1:20, 21), and *rbh*, "increase" (1:22, 28), used in the imperatives that God speaks to nonhuman species. Geographical extension is another aspect, as indicated by the distribution "on the face of the whole earth" (1:29, NIV) of the vegetation which is designed to be food for all the animals (1:20), and by the word "fill" spoken to nonhuman species (1:22). The species are intended to spread across the sea and the land. These words are spoken to all kinds of creature so the abundance and spatial extension of "living creatures" must work in tandem with maintaining diversity. Algae alone carpeting a sea, or bindweed covering a continent, would satisfy both the numerical and spatial criteria, but would not comply with God's intention for biodiversity, and so would not be good.

All species are intended to multiply and fill simultaneously. I initially consider only aquatic species as the formula differs for others. On the fifth day, "God blessed them, saying, Be fruitful and multiply and fill the waters of the seas" (1:22, ESV). The framing as a blessing and the context of chapter 1, especially regarding its orderliness, suggests that the simultaneous multiplication of all these species is not designed to cause rapid extinctions. When one species multiplies and fills the seas it does not prevent other species from doing the same. Flying creatures are similarly addressed. God creates

---

14 A wide diversity of species is essential for ecosystem functions, but even if a form of human existence accompanied only by a small subset of the currently living species of fish, birds, reptiles, and mammals were possible, while it might be designated "sustainable," it would contradict this creative word.

15 The NLT paraphrase, "the seeds will then produce the kinds of plants and trees from which they came" (1:11), expresses the meaning clearly.

"every winged bird according to its kind … God blessed them, saying … let birds multiply on the earth" (1:21-22, ESV). Again, many different species of bird increase in parallel. It is reasonable to suppose that a similar design applies to the nonhuman animal species created on the sixth day.

Beisner makes a counter-argument that the Earth is divided into three domains: sky, sea, land; and the land is reserved for humankind. Beisner finds a "difference between what God told Adam and what He told the fish and birds: He told Adam to be fruitful, multiply, and fill up the earth, i.e. the land or ground, not the sea or the sky" ("Imago" 191).[16] His idea interprets the biblical phrase "birds of the air" but fails to account for the blessing, "let flying creatures multiply in the land" (1:22), which uses the same word, *'rtz* (land), as the blessing of the sixth day (1:28). The author of Genesis is well aware that birds do not live off thin air but feed and nest on the land. God intends them to multiply in the same zone as humankind.

Beisner's attempt to remove flyers from the land fails exegetically and has few supporters, but a similar idea that excludes land animals from living space is given credence by some biblical scholars. They interpret the omission of a separate blessing for land animals (the nonhuman creatures of the sixth day) as indicating that the parallel flourishing of many species, while appropriate in the sea and air, is not appropriate on land. Nahum Sarna comments on the "absence" of blessing that "whereas the natural habitat of fish and fowl allow for their proliferation without encroaching adversely on man's environment," on land the wild animals are "a menace" (11). This might seem plausible since there was conflict between large carnivores and livestock keepers in the Old Testament world (Ezekiel 34:8) as there is today. However, it does not fit the setting of Genesis 1 where all kinds of animals eat plants (1:30). Also, the livestock-hunting large carnivores are only a small subset of all the nonhuman creatures living on the land.

Even if a conflicted context were imagined, the interpretation fails because the categories supposed by those exegetes to be unblessed in 1:24 include the "cattle" which Israelites and Old Testament writers would want to be blessed with prolific reproduction. Gordon Wenham finds the unblessing idea unconvincing and considers it more likely that "the blessing on man (v.28) covered all the works of the 6th day, including the land animals" (*Genesis* 26). John Calvin also comments on the lack of a second blessing on the sixth day: "Why does God here not also add his benediction? I answer:

---

16 Even if Beisner's argument were accurate, overfishing that damages species' health in the domain of the sea would still contradict Genesis 1:22 as he construes it.

What Moses previously expressed on a similar occasion is here also to be understood, although he does not repeat it word for word" (24). The omission of a repetition is comparable with other variations in chapter 1, which is not exhaustively repetitive. Seven elements of a daily formula appear on the first day, and subsequent deviations from strict repetition, including the omission of "it was good" on the second day, and "it was so" on the fourth, may be regarded as "elegant stylistic variation" (Wenham, *Genesis* 17, 19, 23).[17]

In any case, God later explicitly calls upon every kind of creature disembarking from the Ark to "be fruitful and multiply on the earth" (Genesis 8:17). This includes wild creatures. There is a small number of kinds of domesticated animals, but most of the kinds told to "multiply on the earth" are wild, the beasts, reptiles, and insects for which humans had no practical use. And the space in which God instructs these kinds to multiply is explicitly "the earth." Richard Bauckham points to God's allocation of food to all species (Genesis 1:30) and deduces that it is not the Creator's intention for humankind to excessively multiply or fill "to an extent that competes with the livelihood of other living creatures" (*Ecology* 17).

Limits to growth

Reproduction has two modes: the expanding mode is appropriate where there are empty spaces, while the replenishing mode is for spaces that are already filled. In the world of the biblical narrative, there are two moments when the expanding mode is active globally for all species. The first moment is the time after God created the world. In the beginning in the Priestly text the earth is "void" (1:2), and in the Yahwist's story it is a time before rain, when "no bush of the field was yet in the land" and "no man" (2:5, ESV).[18] The initial spatial distribution of the first "living creatures" and their number are not specified in chapter 1. In chapter 2, the first human is located in one place, and the male-female pair from each kind of animal may similarly be the first ur-animals.[19] So in both creation stories there is a progression from an originally empty earth to its occupation.

The second moment of universally expansive reproduction is the time after the dry land re-emerges around Noah's ark. Since in the narrative all

---

17 The Septuagint translators inserted the latter, "missing" clause.

18 The narratives of chapter 1 and chapters 2-3 are different in style, and biblical scholars usually call them the Priestly and Yahwistic creation stories.

19 Christian tradition assumes a pair of each kind in Genesis 2.

living creatures have been wiped out (except in the sea), the earth is empty and must be repopulated by the male-female pairs[20] after they disembark from the ark. From a single point location (8:4), the multiplying animals will slowly spread out across the whole earth (7:9; 8:19). In this moment of re-colonization each kind of animal and bird will increase in total number as well as spatial extent until the earth is filled. The ancient Israelites assumed that the process had been completed before their time, for the psalmist observes that "the earth is full of your creatures" (Psalms 104:24, NIV). The writer of Genesis perceived that animals had completed filling the earth many years before his time, and chapter 1 looks back to the beginning before that happened.

The replenishing mode is the continuing fertility that maintains diverse species on a filled earth. Ancient people were aware that while the number of birds would fluctuate from one year to the next, they did not keep growing in number generation after generation. The blessing "be fruitful and multiply" (1:22) is active in the present as well as the past. In the present, the word "multiply" or "increase" refers to that replenishing reproduction by animals and birds that maintains each kind.

That is the picture for the world as a whole, for nonhuman kinds and perhaps also for humankind, though they had been slower to fill the world. Ancient Israelites imagined that humans had settled in most of the inhabitable regions of the known world. At spatial scales smaller than the whole earth, a land or a place could still be empty. A land that had in the past been filled by people might become uninhabited as had happened on the plain of Jordan (Deuteronomy 29:23; Genesis 13:10). The most important local exception to a full earth was Canaan, which had become notionally empty because the Canaanites had forfeited their right to live there. Colonization by the sons of Jacob, and the gradual birth of the Israelite nation depicted in the Old Testament, warranted a rhetorical return to the expansive population growth associated with moments of origins.

Land allocation and boundaries

The principle that more people need more land is implicit in Old Testament texts: God tells Moses to "distribute the land by lot according to your clans" (Numbers 33:54a, NIV). "To a large tribe you shall give a large inheritance,

---

20 Seven pairs for "clean" kinds of animal and one pair from each of every other kind of animal (Genesis 7:2).

and to a small tribe you shall give a small inheritance" (Numbers 33:54b, ESV). The same idea underpins the complaint by Ephraim and Manasseh that the amount of land allocated to them is unfair compared with the land allocated to smaller tribes (Joshua 17:14).[21] Since more people need more land, boundaries are proxies for ultimate limits on population size. The geographical boundaries between Israelite tribes are detailed in Joshua 12:6 to 22:9, and their purpose is to prevent disputes. The areas are large and mostly unconquered, so the boundaries are at first experienced as targets, not as limits. Near the end of Joshua's life God says that "there are still very large areas of land to be taken over" (Joshua 13:1, NIV). However, for intra-Israelite relations there were limits: if one tribe reproduced faster than another Israelite tribe, then the boundaries would become constraints.

Boundaries also existed that subdivided the land for each clan and family. At these smaller scales, the limit can be more acute because it is far more likely that one family would grow more than another, than that a whole tribe would grow faster than another tribe (due to statistical averaging with larger totals). The land allocation text for each tribe repeats the phrases "clan by clan" (Joshua 13:15; 13:24; 13:29; 16:5; 15:20) and "by their families" (17:2). Scripture does not systematically describe the subdivisions of land, but a few are mentioned incidentally, for example Timnath for Joshua (24:30) and Gibeah for Phinehas (24:33). These boundaries were tangible in topographic features and marker stones, and were not changeable. "Do not move your neighbour's boundary stone set up by your predecessors" (Deuteronomy 19:14, NIV). Alteration by a growing clan that wanted more land is forbidden. The allocation was fixed, in the ideal picture presented in Scripture at least, so a clan that became more fecund after the allocation could not be awarded additional land.

Looking beyond inter-clan relations, the principle of limits on encroachment is sometimes applied to inter-national boundaries. God specified to Moses the borders for the ancient Israelite nation: "This will be your land with its boundaries on every side" (Numbers 34:12).[22] The ancient Israelite kingdoms never occupied all the land: Sidon, though allocated to the tribe of Asher, was not captured, and even Solomon did not capture Gaza. Actual borders did not reach the prescribed borders and this mismatch explains some

---

21 The historical reality of the land allotment is disputed, but in any case the ideal suggests awareness of the issues discussed.

22 Alternative verbal maps of the ideal boundaries of the Israelite nation appear elsewhere in the Old Testament, including in Joshua.

instances of expansive language. Later after the Assyrian invasions which destroy the northern Israelite kingdom, Isaiah rejoices at the success of the southern kingdom of Judah: "You have gained glory for yourself; you have extended all the borders of the land" (Isaiah 26:15, NIV).

A clear idealized vision of stable inter-national borders can be construed from the Table of Nations (Genesis 10) in which nations descended from seventy named grandsons of Noah are allotted specified places in the geography of the known world. A later remembrance confirms that stability of spatial allocation was intended. "When the Most High gave to the nations their inheritance, when he divided mankind, he fixed the borders of the peoples according to the number of the sons of God" (Deuteronomy 32:8, ESV). In early Jewish tradition the number of nations remained at seventy, a number symbolizing plenitude. Arguably, it is a divine arrangement that should not be transgressed. How then may Israel be created as a new nation when the earth is already full of nations? How can space be made? One answer from the Old Testament is that the extreme wickedness of the Canaanites (Deuteronomy 9:5) justified their dispossession, so Israel inherits the land which had been allotted to them. It is a special case, and it is a replacement not an expansion. These texts speak against the expansionist ideology of empire.

Quantity is not an absolute good

Reproductive abundance is normally regarded as good in the Old Testament, but it is occasionally portrayed negatively. There are concepts of excess, and a contrast between orderly and disorderly reproduction. The Old Testament writers noticed that some species misbehave more than others. Moses prophesied that "the river will teem (*shrtz*) with frogs" (Exodus 8:3). Back in the creation story, the same verb *shrtz* featured positively: "let the water teem with living creatures" (Genesis 1:20, NIV), but when the frogs *shrtz*, it has a negative connotation and is identified as a "plague" (Exodus 1:19). One difference between the two texts is that whereas in Genesis all kinds of water creatures teem together (which is good), in Exodus one species teems disproportionately in the waters.[23] So the frogs burst out from their normal habitat and invade the houses of the Egyptians. When locusts multiply, that also is a plague. "They covered all the ground until it was black ... They devoured ... everything growing in the fields and the fruit

---

23 Commentators looking for realistic explanations of the plagues have speculated that the frogs temporarily exceed predator control.

on the trees" (Exodus 10:15, NIV). Many texts lament the damage caused by swarms of locusts (Joel 1:4; Amos 7:1; Deuteronomy 28:38, 42; 2 Chronicles 7:13; Psalms 105:35). The ultimate result is mass death of the species with disorderly reproduction. The locusts are blown into the sea (Exodus 10:19). The frogs die in heaps and the land reeks of their death (8:13).

People are often pictured in the Bible using metaphors from nonhuman creatures, including locusts. This can refer to behavior: "your plunder, O nations, is harvested as by young locusts; like a swarm of locusts people pounce on it" (Isaiah 33:4). It can also refer to human numbers: "the children of the east lay along in the valley like grasshoppers for multitude" (Judges 7:12, KJV). A longer comparison of humans with locusts features in a prophetic oracle against the Ninevites. Nahum taunts the men of Nineveh:

> Look at your troops, they are all weaklings ... Draw water for the siege, strengthen your defenses! ... There the fire will consume you; the sword will cut you down – they will devour you like a swarm of locusts. Multiply like grasshoppers, multiply like locusts! You have increased the number of your merchants till they are more numerous than the stars in the sky, but like locusts they strip the land and then fly away. Your guards are like locusts, your officials like swarms of locusts ... (Nahum 3:13-17, NIV)

Nahum prophesies that Nineveh will be besieged. His taunt is that even if the number of Ninevite soldiers multiply, it will not help them but only magnify the number slain by God's wrath as embodied in the attacking army: "the fire will devour you ... and like grasshoppers consume you," so go ahead and "multiply like locusts" (3:15, ESV), it will not help. The locust-like swarming of Ninevites also features in another way, as a magnifier of their rapacious greed and the damage they have caused. "You have increased the number of your merchants till they are more than the stars of the sky, but like locusts they strip the land and then fly away" (Nahum 3:16, NIV). The allusion is to one of the fruitful verses, in which offspring number like the stars (e.g. Genesis 26:4), but here it has a negative connotation of excess. The problem of greed is compounded by the number of greedy people.

In an early narrative, the problem perceived by the Israelites was large numbers of other peoples intruding and consuming the produce of the land. "Whenever the Israelites planted their crops, the Midianites, Amalekites and other eastern peoples invaded the country. They camped on the land and ruined the crops all the way to Gaza and did not spare a living thing for Israel ... They came up with their livestock and their tents like swarms of locusts. It was impossible to count them" (Judges 6:3-5, NIV). The sheer number of people and their livestock generated a detrimental consumption so that "Israel was greatly impoverished because of the Midianites" (6:6, KJV). In the next chapter an allusion to a fruitful verse is added to the account of this intrusion: "the other eastern peoples had settled in the valley, thick as locusts. Their camels could no more be counted than the sand on the seashore" (Judges 7:12, NIV). This last metaphor is the same as in the promise to Abraham of "descendants as numerous ... as the sand on the seashore" (Genesis 22:17, NIV), but here multitude has a negative connotation. The people settle in the valley "thick as locusts": the density of population causes detriment.

Myths of abundance and scarcity

Some theologians claim that a worldview imagining unlimited abundance is more helpful than worrying about not having enough for everyone. Regina Schwartz in *The Curse of Cain* sees in the Old Testament and its modern reception[24] a "tragic principle of scarcity," because in the text most people do "not receive divine blessings ... as though there were a cosmic shortage of prosperity" (xi). Her focus is national identity, expressed in the biblical text through sibling rivalry for divine favor, but in her chapter on "land" she also suggests that our perception of material scarcity or limits is an illusion. One reviewer, Catherine Madsen, agrees that "nature, in good health, is lavish and wasteful," but she rejects Schwartz's idea that scarcity is an illusion, because people do "need to live on and use land" (147).[25]

Walter Brueggemann in a review of *The Curse of Cain* confessed that "no other book in my field has instructed me as much" (535). Schwartz found a "myth of scarcity" dominating the Old Testament, and only briefly observed "glimpses" of "plenitude" there (Schwartz xi). In his 1998 review, Brueggemann agreed with that assessment, but one year later he reversed his view and chose to present a "liturgy of abundance" as the biblical norm ("Liturgy" 342). In later work he extends his claim: "the root of reality is a limitless generosity that intends an extravagant abundance. This claim is exposited in Israel's creation texts, sapiential traditions, and ... flies in the face of the theory of scarcity" (*Unsettling* 171). These two different perceptions suggest that abundance and scarcity both exist as motifs in the Old Testament. To evade the inconvenient truth of this reality is misguided.

Brueggemannn, unlike Schwartz, focuses on applying the abundance paradigm to material resources. He speculates that if today we "trust

---

24 Schwartz finds a principle of scarcity in biblical scholarship, which was formatively influenced, in her view, by 19th-century German nationalism (11).

25 Schwartz and Madsen both mention Israel/Palestine, and that conflict seems to be an important context for their discussions of scarcity and land.

abundance" then this "causes the earth to produce more," and though he admits this sounds "absurd," he suggests that our reactions may "signify nothing more than the totalising power of the ideology of scarcity" (*Unsettling* 171). Brueggemann claims that Genesis 1 "denies scarcity" and that the idea first appears only when "Pharaoh dreams that there will be a famine in the land. Pharaoh introduces the principle of scarcity" ("Liturgy" 342). But in the biblical narrative Pharaoh's dream is presented as a true message from God, and the predicted famine really happens, though its effect is mitigated by wise precautions after Joseph interprets the dream.

Brueggemann also extends the paradigm to fecundity, writing that Genesis begins "with a liturgy of abundance ... In an orgy of fruitfulness, everything in its kind is to multiply" (342). He also perceives "the contest between the liturgy of abundance and the myth of scarcity" recurring four hundred years after Joseph, when the Israelites multiply and a different "Pharaoh decides that they have become so numerous that he doesn't want any more Hebrew babies" (343). However, the narrator tell us what Pharaoh's motive is: "let us deal shrewdly with them, lest they multiply and if war breaks out they join our enemies and fight against us and escape from the land" (Exodus 1:10, ESV). The issue was not scarcity but the political fear that a large Israelite population might turn against Pharaoh. He is not worrying about them overpopulating Egypt: rather, he fears that these useful laborers may become strong enough to escape and leave Egypt.

Brueggemann's declared aim was to rebuke consumerism, to persuade his readers that the U.S. need not compete with rival nations for resources, and to encourage international justice. Those motives are good but his denial of limits is unhelpful, and results in language that is almost cornucopian. Brueggemann's dichotomy of "abundance and scarcity" could be reformulated as "generosity and greed," and that would serve his purpose better. It is precisely because material limits do exist that neighborliness is needed, and one aspect of this virtue is self-restraint of fecundity by individuals and nation-states.

Vocation informs reproduction

Though all species are blessed with fertility, for humankind the words of that blessing are given in the context of a unique vocation for the government of other species and the land: the same verse says "be fruitful" and also "have dominion" (Genesis 1:28). Jeremy Cohen advises that the syntax of this verse warns against any "neat division" between procreation and dominion (13), therefore the exercise of human fecundity should be guided by this vocation.

Even if human dominion over nonhuman creatures were intended to be tyrannical, a king must have subjects to be a king, so a fecundity that leads to the extinction of the subjects cannot be intended. Further, the scope of biblical dominion is "every living thing" (1:28), so a fullness of dominion requires that no kind of creature should be exterminated.

Many biblical scholars contend that *rdh* (rule) here is not meant to be tyranny. Elsewhere *rdh* is used only of relationships between humans, but in Genesis 1:28 it is applied to relations between humans and animals. Leviticus 25:43 uses *rdh prk* to express "rule harshly," but *rdh* alone simply means "rule" with the context indicating its character. Most instances of *rdh* refer to rulers' actions, such as extracting forced labor (1 Kings 5:16), but the word can also be used neutrally (Psalm 68:27). The context of Genesis 1:28 indicates the character of human rule. First, since God says the creatures are good, dominion is unlikely to be a licence to destroy. Second, they are given this responsibility because they are made in the image of God to reflect His character. To many modern readers kingship has negative connotations, but theologically the concept needs to be put into the context of the rule of God. God's rule is sustaining and nurturing (Psalm 104:10-26; Psalm 145:9, 16), therefore to rule in his image is to do likewise (Bauckham 31). The ideal king is a shepherd (Ezekiel 34:2-5; Lohfink 12) and a servant (1 Kings 12:7). The word *rdh* appears in messianic texts (Psalm 72:8), and Jesus the anointed one (i.e. king) is central to a Christian understanding of *rdh*, connecting the "suffering servant" with kingship.

Reinforcing the universal human vocation, a special responsibility carried by the chosen people can be derived from the call of Abraham. God foretells that "in you all the *clans* of the earth shall be blessed" (Genesis 12:3).[26] Clearly the primary reference is to other peoples, but the word clan gives room for a wider ecological interpretation. This word *mishpachah* is not the usual term for family households and is often translated as "clan," as for example in "clans of Levi" (Numbers 26:58) where it denotes all the branches descending from the named progenitor. Therefore "clans of earth" can be read as all creatures that God created from the earth. The idea of

---

26 The translation is notoriously difficult and controversial. Westermann sees here a promise that Abraham's descendants will be famously blessed, admired so others will wish "that I might be blessed like them." Or, in other words, "The nations will not be blessed by Abraham (and his family) – the patriarchs will not function as the agents of blessing – but the nations will bless themselves in him (them) – the patriarchs will serve as examples of blessing" (Biddle 603). However, tradition (based on Acts 3:25) insists that Abraham's (spiritual) progeny, Christ and the church, will bless others.

earth as progenitor comes from the text, "these are the generations of the heavens and the earth" (Genesis 2:4). This is the first of a series of verses using the word *toledot* (descendants), which derives from a verb meaning "to give birth," and that function as headings to structure Genesis (Hamilton 5). There are ten *toledot* verses: the second is "these are the generations of Adam" (5:1), and the third is "these are the generations of Noah" (6:9). Since the first *toledot* (2:4) introduces the "generations" from the earth[27] as all kinds of living creatures which God commanded the land and sea to bring forth (Genesis 1:20, 24), the "clans of the earth" to be blessed can be understood to encompass every species. This is an adventurous ecological reading reinforced by the usage of *mishpachah* (clan) at Genesis 8:19 with a generic sense that refers to nonhuman creatures.

Responding to natalist arguments

Perpetuating humankind

Most patristic writers consider the preservation of the species the only valid justification for procreation. For example, John of Damascus in the 8th century discerns that "to prevent the wearing out and destruction of the race by death, marriage was devised that the race of men may be preserved through procreation of children" (*Exposition of Orthodox Faith* 4.24, tr. NPNF2 9:97). Patristic writers suggested that reproduction had over time become a less pressing necessity. Cyprian contrasts earlier times with his own time (the 4th century AD): "While yet the world was uncultivated and empty ... we increased for the extension of the human race ... Now when the earth is filled and the world is peopled, they who can, receive continence" (ANF 5.436). This could imply that if the number of humans dwindled toward extinction then reproduction would become more necessary. Thomas Aquinas is unusual in making this idea explicit, and concedes a collective duty to perpetuate the human species, though not any individual obligation, for "the precept given concerning procreation pertains to the entire collective of human beings ... It therefore suffices ... if only certain people meet the needs of bodily reproduction while others abstain" (Cohen 291).

---

27 The phrase "the heavens and the earth" (Genesis 2:4) is a merism that encompasses the sky, land, and sea: the whole world, the biosphere.

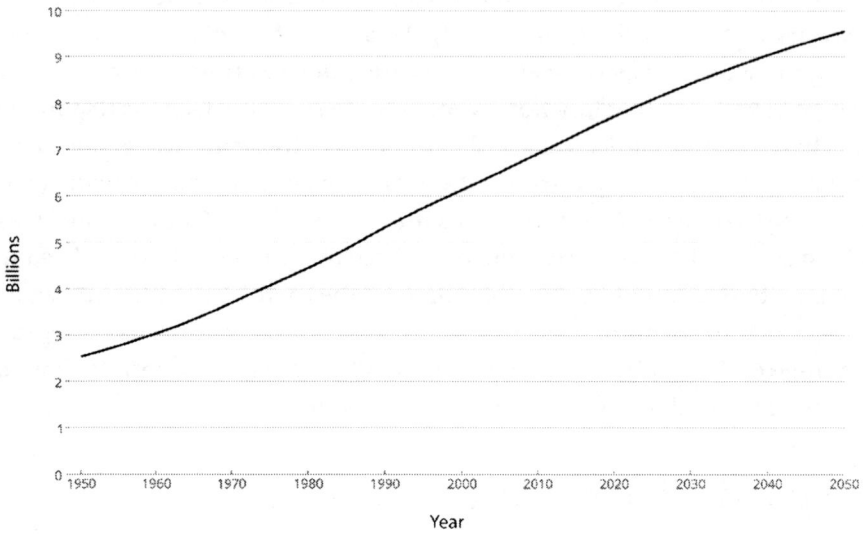

Figure 8. World population from 1950-2010 and UN medium projection to 2050. Data source: *World Population Prospects: The 2012 Revision* (New York: United Nations, 2013).

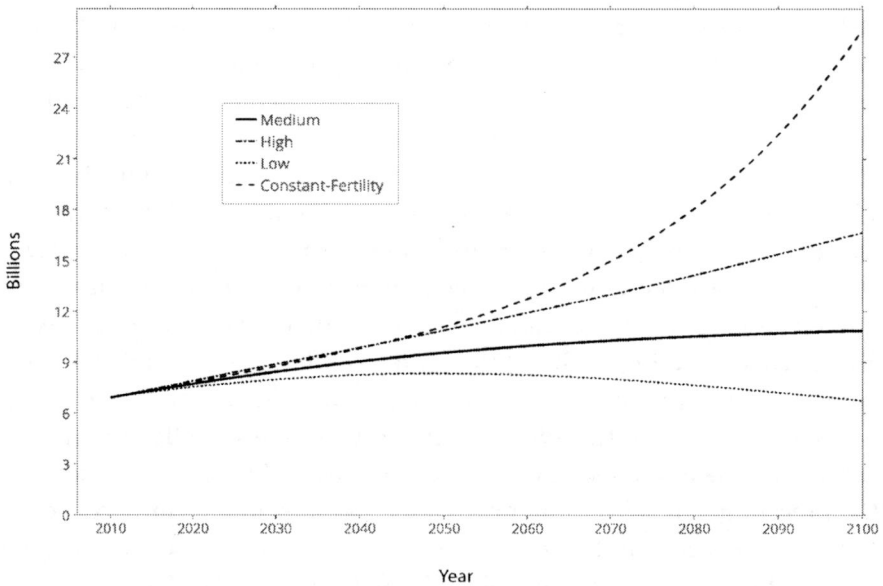

Figure 9. The four UN projections of future population size, 2010 to 2100. Data source: *World Population Prospects: The 2012 Revision* (New York: United Nations, 2013).

There is in reality no prospect that, due to insufficient reproduction, *Homo sapiens* will decline to anything like the number (less than 1 million) that would make our species vulnerable to extinction. The human population in Cyprian's time was under 200 million. Today it is over 7 billion and still growing. The UN produces forecasts (projections) of population with different scenarios based on what might happen to birth rates. The medium scenario (the unbroken line on the graph above) is what the UN considers most likely and is based on fertility (TFR) in the "Less Developed Regions" diminishing from 2.63 (the 2010 average) to 2.25 by 2050. Even with that decline in birth rate, the global population grows to more than 9.5 billion.The high and low variant forecasts are based on TFRs being slightly higher or lower than the medium variant. Furthermore, if birth rates stay the same as they are now in each nation, this will lead to the "Constant Fertility" scenario and a population of 28 billion by 2100. Thankfully it is unlikely, but it serves to illustrate that all other U.N. scenarios already have anticipated falls in birth rates built-in. Only in other, fantastically long-range projections can serious global shrinkage of population be seen. One study extrapolated to 2300 simulating with different rates of global fertility and different levels of maximum life expectancy (Basten, Lutz, and Scherbov). They found that a global average TFR of 2.0 leads to a 10.17 billion population in 2300. If instead TFR slowly converges to 1.5 everywhere, then nearly 300 years from now the global population will be 870 million. Even if that far-fetched scenario occurred, the population in 2300 would still be four times greater than it was when Cyprian was bishop of Carthage.

Since the human footprint exceeds global biocapacity, population shrinkage is desirable; but if the rate of change were too rapid it could arguably be detrimental to human welfare. An earlier long-range projection (UN, 2003) gives predicted rates of population change up to 2300. In this, the fastest rate of annual decrease is 0.15%, and it happens between 2100 and 2125. The UN long-range forecast includes a low fertility variant which has a 0.46% rate of shrinkage in the quarter century to 2075 and then 0.75% until 2125. For comparison, Russia has experienced 0.5% annual decrease since 1991. Whether such rates are too fast is hard to assess as they are a new phenomenon. Lower population density would raise average welfare through reducing land prices (Turner, "Population" 3016).[28]

One effect of shrinkage would be to increase the structural ageing already caused by lengthening life expectancy, which for men in the UK has risen 8 years in the last 25 years (ONS). Adair Turner, the former Chair of the UK Pensions Commission, explains how this could be ameliorated by changes in tax and

---

28 Low fertility and population shrinkage also increase the average inheritance of capital, which raises average welfare.

pension rules, and by raising the retirement age so some of the added years of lifespan are shifted into working years. It is viable because "health at any given age is increasing rapidly"; for example, in the 1990s an average French woman of 75 was as fit as a woman aged 62 was in 1900 (Turner, "Population" 3011). Much can be done to ameliorate the effects of structural ageing through reducing avoidable causes of infirmity, so rapid population shrinkage need not be so detrimental to welfare.

There is a chronological mismatch in the argument that a hypothetical future decrease of population warrants high birth rates now. Today, population is not only too high but still rising. Even in the low variant scenario, rapid decrease (greater than 0.5% annually) would not happen until after 2075. Birth rates can change rapidly, for example in the UK child tax credits stimulated a 15% rise in fertility among recipient couples within one year of their introduction (Brewer, Ratcliffe, and Smith). In the U.S., fertility rose from 2.1 to 3.7 between 1937 and 1957. So there is no need to promote natalism a half-century or more in advance of a situation that might perhaps justify it. The only remaining argument is that nations whose TFR is below 1.5 are stuck in a "low fertility trap" that causes fertility to keep falling due to momentum and cultural transmission of a low ideal family size (Lutz and Skirbekk, 701). The trap theory was challenged after 2000 by rising fertility in such nations (Goldstein, Sabotka, and Jasilioniene 644). In any case, this argument was never relevant to the U.S. or UK. The time to debate whether local social natalism might be helpful would be much nearer to 2075, and even then only if the UN low variant scenario seemed to be happening. So far, the gap between numbers of births and deaths which generates population growth has (as shown by the figure below) not diminished much. There are still more than twice as many births as deaths each year globally. We are a long way away from needing to worry about too few births.

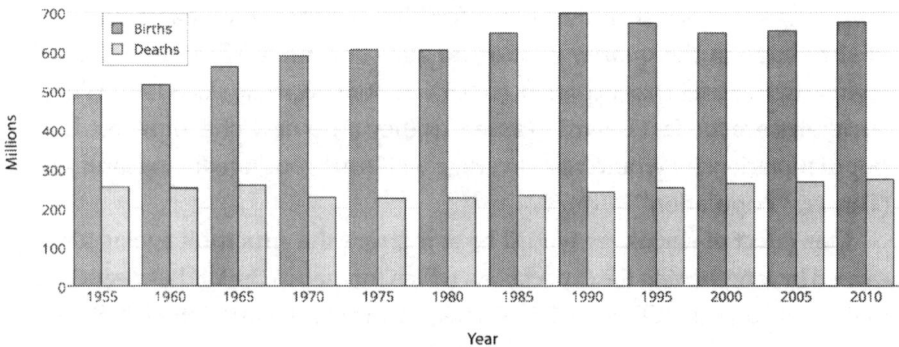

Figure 10. Births and deaths in all nations, five-year total from 1950-2010. Data source: *World Population Prospects: The 2012 Revision* (New York: United Nations, 2013).

National welfare

The question of whether local circumstances can justify encouragement of higher local fertility cannot be ignored. Karl Barth suggests "there may even be times and situations in which it will be the duty of the Christian community to awaken either a people or section of a people ... that to avoid arbitrary decay they should make use of this merciful divine permission and seriously try to maintain the race. But a general necessity ... cannot be maintained on a Christian basis" (268).[29] This is not for the sake of nationhood *per se*, but for human welfare. Some natalists claim this circumstance applies today, so high fertility is now a patriotic duty as a means of avoiding national suicide. Allan Carlson claims: "Europe is dying ... America is not far behind" (65). However the median projection (including net migration) is that the U.S. population will grow to 439 million by 2050 (Census Bureau).

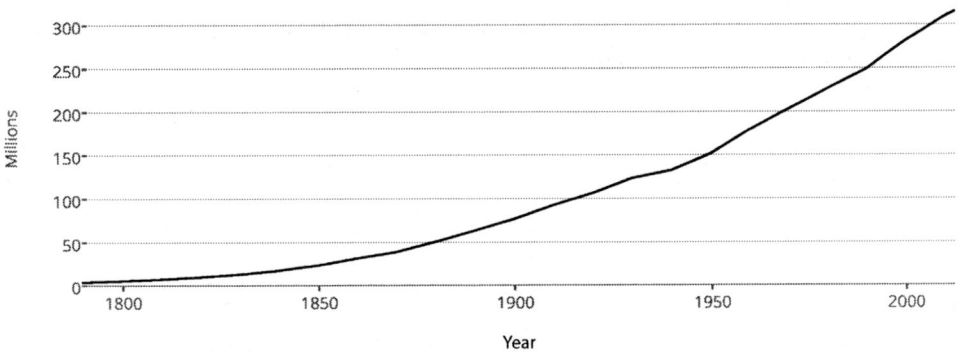

Figure 11. Census of U.S. Population, 1790-2010. Data source: http://www.census.gov/population/censusdata/table-16.pdf (Census Bureau).

The case of Europe must be considered, not least because natalist outreach is often targeted at European Christians. The population of the EU is rising slowly and is projected to peak in 2035 (EuroStat). But though it seems that remedial local natalism cannot be justified at present, one can imagine some counter-arguments.

Nativists may complain that the population projections cited above include immigration continuing at present levels. Nativism is a fantasy: in European states, and even more so in the U.S., a large part of the so-called

---

29 This is a proviso within a long section in which Barth demolishes the notion that there is any Christian obligation to reproduce.

old-stock people descend from immigrants if their families are traced back a few centuries.[30] However, even if, for the sake of argument, one allows nativists to focus on "natural increase" without including migration data, the U.S. has more births than deaths: for example 4.25 million births and 2.47 million deaths in 2008 (Census Bureau).

Al Mohler laments a "disastrous fall in European birthrates" ("Birthrates"), but in fact Europe currently has slightly more births than deaths. That is especially so in the UK which in 2009 had 790,000 births and 491,000 deaths (ONS).[31] Granted, some nations, notably Russia, Italy, and Germany, do have fewer births than deaths, but natalists exaggerate their shrinkage. Carlson and Mero claim that by 2050, Italy's population (currently 59 million) will fall to 41 million (65), but Italy's statistics agency predicts it will rise to 61.7 million by that date (ISTAT). Even if migration were excluded, the natural decrease would only reduce Italy's "native" population to 53.5 million by 2050. That was the total in 1968 and it was not regarded as being too low then. Further, since Italy's total footprint is now 290 gha, whereas its national biocapacity is only 60 gha (GFN), some decrease in Italy's population would be a step toward sustainability.

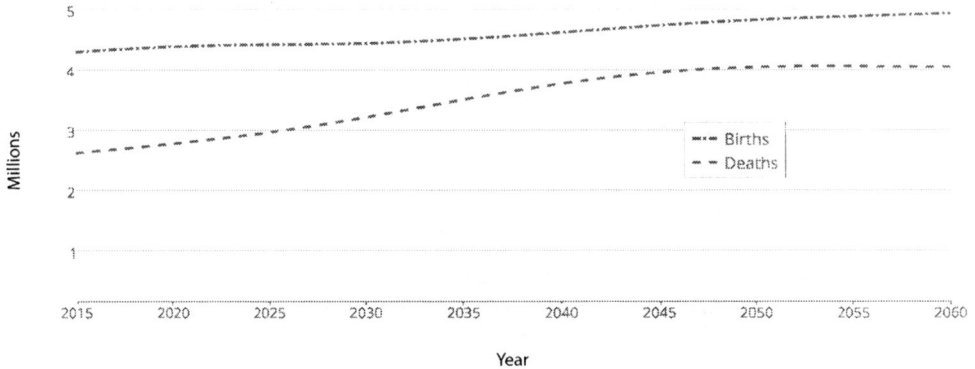

Figure 12. Forecast of U.S. births and deaths from 2015 to 2060. Data source: http://www.census.gov/population/projections/data/national/2012.html (Census Bureau).

Some point to the more distant future. It is projected that by 2070 Europe will return to the population total it had in 2010. Since the ecological footprint of Europe is already running at over 200% of its biocapacity, that scenario

---

30 U.S. natalist writers with recent European ancestors should be aware of this.
31 UK population growth was and is more a result of natural increase (births) than of net migration, except in the years between 2000 and 2007 (ONS).

would be beneficial for sustainability. Nations do fear a diminution relative to other global regions; for example, the European Parliament in 1984 expressed concern about "the declining share of Europe's population in the world total, and ensuing effects on Europe's standing and influence in the world," and so it resolved to promote fertility (Demeny 169). Such motives are unworthy for Christians.

Building the church

Continuous numerical growth on a finite planet is not sustainable. Many religions and denominations have become accustomed to numerical growth in their membership that is partly just a product of background population growth. But when global population peaks, as it will sooner or later, those who want to see numerical growth will have to focus on conversions. Church increase by conversion has no impact on total population size, whereas endogenous growth by sexual reproduction is ecologically unsustainable. One natalist writer argues that better-reared Christian children who are less addicted to consumerism are also better for the environment (Pride, 62-63). That may be true, but any benefit would be outweighed by the rise in total numbers inherent in the endogenous approach. For example, given a national population (of any size) which is 10% Christian, and assuming no natural increase among the non-Christians, to make the nation 20% Christian by using the endogenous method would increase the overall national population by 11.25%. To make the nation 50% Christian would require an 80% increase in the total national population.[32] If the ecological footprint of our hypothetical nation has already overshot its biocapacity, as most countries have, endogenous church growth would be harmful to human welfare. For those wanting a numerically larger church, growth by conversion is the better way.[33]

Relying on endogenous growth predictably changes the character of a religion or denomination. There are many cases in religious history of groups that began as open movements attracting outsiders but which turned inward decades or centuries later and started relying on their children to

---

32 Also, the nation would never become fully Christian if only the endogenous mode applied, for there would also be some descendants of the non-Christian people.

33 Denominations and missions should report the numerical progress of Christianity in percentage terms rather than by counting heads. In contexts of population growth the latter may look good, but if population shrinks (as it will, preferably sooner, but otherwise later) the reporting of progress as percentage share of the nation will be more encouraging.

perpetuate the institution.[34] For example, few outsiders join the Amish or Hutterites today. It is a recurring temptation for churches to transform themselves into ethnic groups. This is not really easier – in fact it is hard labor (pun intended) – but the new natalists appear to regard it as a dependable human strategy. They thus seem to "put confidence in the flesh" (Philippians 3:4-5), but they should instead consider that the Holy Spirit reaches out to whomever He will, regardless of ancestry and parentage, and that high birth rates are incompatible with increasing longevity and maintaining quality of life within ecological limits.

Populating heaven

Natalists look at temporal fluctuations of membership numbers, but tradition points to a cumulative number that includes not just those currently walking the earth, but all Christians who ever lived and share in resurrection: the "communion of saints." The stars in heaven are a metaphor for saints and suggest characteristics for their reproduction. Genesis 1 depicts spaces created on days 1-3 and then filled with creatures on days 4-6. Stars are created on day 4 and this is the only case where God creates each one directly and individually, rather than creating pairs to reproduce. "He determines the number of the stars, and calls them each by name" (Psalm 147:4, NIV). Ancient observers regarded the stars as numbering about three thousand, not increasing but immortal.[35] Patristic writers favored stars as a more suitable metaphor for Christians than dust, sand, or grass, the other Old Testament metaphors of fecundity and far more numerous than stars. Dust and grass have connotations of mortality, but stars are fixed in number like the elect. Christians are compared to stars: "become blameless and pure, children of God without fault in a warped and crooked generation. Then you will shine among them like stars in the sky" (Philippians 2:15, NIV). And even

---

34 Or alternatively disappearing. Shakers are often cited (by evolutionary biologists) as an example of what happens to religious groups that do not reproduce biologically. But that misrepresents history: the early Shakers were open and evangelistic and despite being celibate from the 1750s, they continued growing in number for almost a hundred years by attracting adults from outside. Only after turning inward and recruiting fewer converts did they begin to decline. Those who apply evolutionary theory to religion need to be aware that many religious groups began as voluntary affiliations, even though some might look like ethnic groups today.

35 Modern astronomy identifies about 3,000 stars visible from any one location on the spherical earth under perfect viewing conditions.

today, from a scientific viewpoint, stars are very long-lived, and new stars are born from the debris of past dead stars, which is like reproduction. So stars can still be a good metaphor for a stable population with a very low rate of mortality and a very low rate of fertility.

Created order

The pattern of early marriage and frequent reproduction favored by natalists is commended as natural, and some look to lessons from nature. Watters (35) advises readers to "Ask the animals and they will teach you" (Job 12:7). The normative order of creation is depicted as all individuals forming couple bonds that produce many offspring, but some features of the prescribed pattern are not universal. Examples supporting the pattern natalists advocate can be found, but nature encompasses a variety of reproductive strategies, and contrary examples also exist. In some species few adult males ever reproduce; for example, only 1% of male elephant seals gain a harem and become fathers. This is presumably not a model for human emulation. The created order is more diverse than natalists imagine.

Natalists regard any downward change in birth rates as unnatural, but such changes can be found in nature in those species which have a density-dependent fertility that declines when population density approaches a certain level (Rockwood 42). High fertility with low mortality causes a population to grow rapidly. The norm in human history until recently was both high fertility and high mortality. Natalists praising the former as "natural" should realize it is inseparable from the latter. In a limited biosphere, higher fertility will eventually produce higher mortality (which means a lower life expectancy).

Science has a valuable ancillary function. Knowledge about earth systems, biodiversity, and ecological sustainability provides feedback on global and local scales which informs us about the consequences of different levels of human population size, and whether they are beneficial (that is, a blessing) or not. Science does not, however, provide moral values. For example, where population density is reducing average individual human welfare but increasing the total number of human beings, we may ask if that is good or bad. An eco-biblical hermeneutic suggests an answer. If the size of a nation's ecological footprint exceeds a fair share of global biocapacity and so exacerbates global ecological overshoot, then it is too high because it is causing extinctions among other species and detrimentally affecting welfare in other nations.

7. Conclusion

This book has explored the role of biblical interpretation in exhortations to higher fecundity by U.S. Protestants. Earlier critics of natalist exegetes have regarded contraception as the central issue of interest, and emphasized the difference between rejection of family planning (portrayed as problematic legalism) and planning a large family (portrayed as one reasonable application of a Christian model of parenthood). They have rarely critiqued natalism *per se*. From my perspective, the anti-contraceptive ideology is separate in theory and peripheral in practice since large families can be planned. All natalists use similar arguments for high fecundity, based on the same Bible verses, regardless of whether they allow contraception or not.

Luther's ideas about marriage and family have been much studied, but little attention has been given to his thoughts on human fertility and the Old Testament fruitful verses except by Yegerlehner, and by the natalist writers Provan and Carlson. This is the first study to test natalist appropriation of Luther's words against their immediate literary context, his pastoral and theological concerns, and 16th-century demography. Natalists claim that Luther taught a reproductive law of nature, but I have shown this to be rhetorical hyperbole responding to crises of the 1520s, including Luther's battle with vowed celibacy; a different idea can be found elsewhere in his writings. Furthermore, his short temporal horizon was incompatible with natalist demographic ambitions. On the other hand, Luther's presentation of parenthood as a penitential discipline offers support to the natalist idea that the trials of child-rearing form parents in Christian character, although this has not been noted by natalists.

Biblical scholars comment on all the fruitful verses, and historians of ancient Israel discuss fertility and population in that culture. By undertaking a systematic evaluation of each natalist argument using recent Old Testament scholarship, this book has challenged some attempts by Old Testament scholars to apply the fruitful verses to contemporary Christians. I have

http://dx.doi.org/10.11647/OBP.0048.07

demonstrated that while ideas about fecundity as a material blessing to parents and the nation echo ancient Near Eastern culture and are plausible as original meanings of the fruitful verses, the Old Testament writers regarded offspring as a reward, and so the verses should be read as promises, not exhortations. Further, an Old Testament theology drawing on the wider canon relativizes fecundity by identifying it as only one aspect of a broader divine plan, and subordinated to holiness.

Augustine's thoughts on human reproduction have been intensively researched with reference to theological topics such as original sin, and to various modern issues including gender and sexuality. However, researchers interested in fertility or population have, because of the widespread conflation of anti-contraception and natalism, often regarded his legacy as part of the problem. In order to refute natalist arguments, I undertook the first *ressourcement* from Augustine's writings directed against natalism. This approach challenged recent scholarly efforts to portray Augustine as pro-reproductive by highlighting his insistence that the church is built by the Word and regenerated by the Spirit, not by reproduction. Moreover, Augustine reminds us that although secular social preservation is a good, the ultimate future of humankind is assured by the general resurrection of the dead. My study of Augustine's writings also underlined his belief that spiritual blessings are more important than parenthood, and his concern that pursuit of what is good should not lead to loss of what is better.

Ecological hermeneutics have been applied to many parts of the Bible, but only briefly to the fruitful verses, for example by Lohfink, DeWitt, and Bratton. Taking U.S. demographic exceptionalism as the primary context for my analysis, this book has offered an innovative development of previous work, countering specific natalist interpretations with an eco-biblical hermeneutic. This ecological approach suggests that natalism would only be appropriate in special circumstances: if a too rapid shrinkage of the population became detrimental to welfare, or if it were necessary to avoid the extinction of the human species. At present there is no prospect of either circumstance arising on a global level, or nationally in the U.S. or UK.

Possible directions for further research

Social-scientific research on U.S. natalism is needed to provide data on the number of people affected, the degree of influence, and their geographical distribution.[1] Some questions posed by Goodson in her 1996 survey of Protestant seminaries (including her three alternative interpretations of "be fruitful and multiply") could be repeated to allow comparison. The commonly used measure of belief in inerrancy is rather indirect, so a better and more specific measure of how strongly behavior is shaped by the Bible is needed. To link this with natalism, further questions would be needed to uncover views about ideal family size and how far they is governed by biblical norms and prescriptions, or only by personal preference. A similar survey in the UK would also be helpful.

Case studies of natalism within a congregation would be helpful in clarifying the relative importance of internal and external influence, from peers and teaching, from sermons, books, and other media. This could be done in one of the groups with a significant natalist presence: the Presbyterian Church of America (PCA, a 1970s conservative splinter from mainline Presbyterians), the Lutheran Church Missouri Synod (LCMS, a Southern branch of Lutheranism), or the SBC.[2] Anthropological research could investigate questions beyond those used in national surveys, such as whether leaders and laity differ. Whereas natalist Old Testament reception is minimal in published Catholic sources, there is evidence of Catholic natalism, and further investigation would be desirable.

The association of natalism with ideas about gender could be investigated. A minority among natalists affirm views which Kathryn Joyce labels patriarchal, for example emphasizing the wife's submission to her husband. Other natalists, while distancing themselves from patriarchy, are not egalitarian with regard to gender roles. A review of Joyce's book by Nathan Finn criticizes her for using the word "complementarian" to describe the Quiverfull movement.[3] Finn emphasizes the difference between "oppressive patriarchy," which is "an extreme fringe" linked with "far-right aberrations," and a biblical complementarian viewpoint which he affirms (48). Finn himself seems not to be natalist, but his review suggests another fracture in natalism: between complementarians and patriarchs.

With regard to further historical *ressourcement*, the writings of John Calvin should be prioritized. Though he is far less significant in the reception history

---

1 Most of my sources are from the southern U.S., but this may reflect a preponderance of conservative Evangelicals in the Bible Belt.

2 Many leaders of the SBC became alarmed after 2003 that SBC church membership had stopped growing. It would be interesting to see if birth rates have changed among Southern Baptist congregations.

3 Nathan Finn is Assistant Professor of Church History at Southeastern Baptist Theological Seminary, North Carolina. His review does not suggest he is natalist.

of the fruitful verses than Martin Luther, many natalists (of both limited and unlimited types) express an affinity with historic Puritans and can be regarded as part of the New Calvinist movement which esteems his writings. Kathryn Blanchard has explored Calvin's ideas about contraception, but research is needed on his exegesis of the fruitful verses and on what views, if any, he expressed about human fecundity. Another avenue of research from historical sources would be a comprehensive study of Christian reception of the metaphors (grass, dust, stars) that were used in the Old Testament to signify numerous offspring.

The paradox of those natalists who are also ecologically concerned deserves further attention. While some natalists are cornucopian, others are not. For example, Mary Pride blames consumerism for ecological damage. A striking example is John Jefferson Davis, who teaches natalism and environmental ethics in different parts of the same book (*Ethics* 63-67, 263-73). Also, in an article surveying recent works of systematic theology, he critiques "ecological blind spots" where they fail to consider God's care for the earth (Davis, "Ecological"). This reflects a wider phenomenon discussed in chapter 6: the refusal to treat population size as a factor in ecological sustainability. A closer look at other writings by natalists to identify ecofriendly interpretations of other Scriptures, and statements about environmental issues, would be helpful. The surveys suggested above could include questions on environmental attitudes for this comparative purpose.

Prospects, and value of the research

The scenarios predicted by Eric Kaufmann and others suggest that religious groups practising an "endogenous growth model" will change the U.S. population's character. If trends persist, by the end of this century the nation be dominated by those Christians, Mormons, and others who have a large-but-limited approach to family size. After another century, however, they in turn would be dwarfed by Quiverfull adherents and others practising unlimited fecundity. More importantly from an ecological perspective, the total U.S. population would rise above one billion.[4] The consequent decline

---

4   UN projections use national average fertility for consistency with nations where the only reliable data are aggregate national statistics. However, the fertility differentials of small fecund subpopulations will, if persistent, yield compositional effects eventually making U.S. rates and totals higher than national average data predicts.

in average individual economic welfare would eventually cause reduced fecundity, except among the most "ascetic" natalists, but is there hope for a change in trajectory before that happens? Sectarian techniques such as religious schools and home education do enable retention of most offspring in membership (Kaufmann 27), and "most" is enough for demographic effects. It is not even necessary that children be retained by the particular sect of their birth, only that natalist ideology is transmitted and acted on.

Is there any hope that these scenarios for U.S. population growth will not occur? Extrapolation from the current high fertility of some fundamentalist groups many decades into the future is not a reliable predictor. Many U.S. adults are moving away from Protestant fundamentalism. A transition matrix using GSS data to explore how U.S. citizens changed their religious affiliation after age 16 found that "Protestant Fundamentalists" (a category that includes Missouri Synod Lutherans, "Conservative" Evangelicals, and many types of Pentecostal, according to GSS Methodological Report 43) have a negative -3.3 net flow: fewer convert than leave (Skirbekk, Kaufmann, and Goujon 300). By contrast, the "Protestant Moderates" (which include "Open" Evangelicals) have a positive +10.3 net flow. The fundamentalist churches are unattractive to adults, but their birth rate is higher: though they "lose" more children, they have more to spare and so they can keep increasing despite their losses. However, the endogenous strategy is not reliable in a U.S. context: 44% of Americans "do not currently belong to their childhood faith" (Pew 1). The extrapolators need to remember that religion is more like a voluntary affiliation than a genetic ethnicity.

The widespread cultural and legal assumption that babies by default belong to the parents' (or in some cultures specifically the father's) religion is a mainstay of endogenous growth strategies. Social scientists collude in this when they use the term "apostate" to describe anyone who chooses a different religion from the religion of his or her father. The trend of fundamentalist population growth might be slowed by a legal extension of children's rights to end that presumption. It could entail the regulation of religious curricula in private schools and among homeschoolers. However, such a change is not politically feasible. Other kinds of intervention are unlikely to be effective. If the financial incentives to additional reproduction were reduced (for example, through cutting tax credits after the second child, while mitigating socially regressive side-effects by redirecting the funds to state schools) that might lower birth rates among some types of recipient (Brewer, Ratcliffe, and Smith 245). However, since religious natalists are self-sacrificing in pursuing their perceived duty, they would be less influenced than others. Even if a reduction in state subsidies lowered birth rates overall, it would probably widen the gap between fundamentalists' and others' fertility.

A change in hearts and minds is the best way forward. The journey of individual members, and perhaps of whole congregations, away from fundamentalism and toward mainline historic Christianity is desirable. However, there will be large numbers of fundamentalists in the U.S. for the forseeable future, so a way to help them feel comfortable about choosing smaller family sizes has to be found. If some fundamentalists chose to redirect their energy away from biological fecundity and toward other pursuits such as evangelism and mission (including social concern and creation-care), that would be good for ecological sustainability. One contribution to this would be non-natalist interpretation of the Old Testament fruitful verses that is nevertheless compatible with fundamentalist approaches to the Bible. This book is one more step in that direction, but although more research should be done, a far more important task is popular outreach by non-natalists within each denomination to fellow members of their churches, especially to young people.

There is much potential for immediate and enduring reductions in our ecological impact through lower fertility, given the high U.S. per capita ecological footprint of 7.0 gha (GFN) and the long-term consequences of additional births (Murtagh and Schlax 18). Ecological impact is a product of impact per person multiplied by population size (which is driven by birth rates). And yet while many researchers and activists labor toward reducing the impact per person (which is good and essential because even if the population stabilized, lower-impact living would be needed), often through small efficiency gains, few consider the large and rapid savings achievable through lower fertility. Looking beyond the U.S., there are many types of natalism, including state, religious, and cultural natalisms. If young people were liberated from all natalist pressures and allowed to follow their own inclinations, there would be lower birth rates and less ecological impact. And it is not all-or-nothing: if just one couple influenced by natalism is released from that ideology and has a smaller family, they will personally avoid "many troubles" (1 Corinthians 7:28, NIV) and also help mend the world.

Appendix

The database catalogues biblical references in sources by ten natalist writers: Pride, Provan, Heine, Owen, Campbell, Houghton, Mohler, Akin, Carlson, and Watters. This is a representative selection, with five of the large-but-limited type and five of the unlimited type (those who combine natalism with anti-contraceptive ideology). Each use (by reference or quotation) of a biblical text is a separate entry in the database. The main table had the following fields:

    source_id
    source_page
    usage
    argument
    book_of_bible
    chapter
    verse_range
    standardized_verse

The field "usage" records whether a scripture is quoted in full, in part, paraphrased, only cited, or just appears in a list of scripture references. The field "argument" indicates which type of argument the author supports with the scripture. The fifty codes here map to the smaller set of natalist arguments described in chapter 2. Many biblical references could not be tied to a particular argument and were left unassigned. Citations of non-contiguous verses such as "11, 14" were treated as a single reference. After compiling the database, I noticed counts of popularity were confused by overlapping verse ranges, for example 3-4 and 3-5 (for Psalm 127). I created the field "standardized_verse" to enable production of the verse popularity table below. The few cases where no verse but only the chapter was referenced were also assigned to a standardized verse-range.

Many projects in popular reception of the Bible record allusions, as they lack citations. In this project there was rarely a need to resort to recording allusions as natalists refer to Bible texts explicitly and profusely, except for Mohler who is often allusive. There was originally a field called "weight" in which I tried to quantify how much was done with a Bible citation by a natalist writer, ranging from a one sentence comment up to several pages. I found it often difficult to identify where discussion of one scripture ended and another began, so I abandoned this. If the data could reflect this weighting, my impression is that the preponderance of the two key texts (Genesis 1:28 and Psalm 127) would be stronger than it already is.

The tables below show how many references were made to each Old Testament book, and how many times each verse-range was cited, across the natalist sources that were catalogued. The counts were generated from the database.

Frequency of citation in natalist sources

Count	Book
84	Genesis
12	Exodus
7	Leviticus
1	Numbers
35	Deuteronomy
1	Joshua
1	Judges
2	Ruth
3	1 Samuel
1	2 Samuel
1	1 Kings
1	2 Kings
6	1 Chronicles
1	2 Chronicles
2	Ezra

1	Nehemiah
5	Job
48	Psalms
11	Proverbs
2	Ecclesiastes
17	Isaiah
12	Jeremiah
1	Lamentations
3	Ezekiel
4	Hosea
2	Joel
4	Malachi

Count of Old Testament standardized verse-ranges cited

Count	Book	Ch.	Verse
1	Genesis	1	27
23	Genesis	1	28
1	Genesis	2	18
1	Genesis	2	23
1	Genesis	3	20
10	Genesis	9	1,7
1	Genesis	9	19
2	Genesis	13	16
2	Genesis	15	5
2	Genesis	16	10
1	Genesis	16	2
3	Genesis	17	1-6
1	Genesis	17	15-16
1	Genesis	17	20

1	Genesis	20	18
1	Genesis	22	16-17
1	Genesis	23	3,14
3	Genesis	24	60
1	Genesis	25	21,24
1	Genesis	26	24
2	Genesis	26	3-4
2	Genesis	28	13-14
2	Genesis	28	3
1	Genesis	29	31-34
2	Genesis	30	1-2
1	Genesis	30	22
1	Genesis	30	3
1	Genesis	30	43
2	Genesis	32	12
6	Genesis	35	11-12
2	Genesis	38	9-10
1	Genesis	47	27
1	Genesis	48	4
2	Genesis	49	22,25
1	Exodus	1	12
1	Exodus	1	20
2	Exodus	1	7
1	Exodus	1	9
1	Exodus	12	37
1	Exodus	20	12
3	Exodus	23	26
1	Exodus	23	30
1	Exodus	32	13

1	Leviticus	15	19,28
1	Leviticus	20	13
1	Leviticus	21	17-20
1	Leviticus	22	24
1	Leviticus	26	22
2	Leviticus	26	3,9
1	Numbers	23	10
1	Deuteronomy	1	10-11
1	Deuteronomy	4	27
1	Deuteronomy	4	9-10
1	Deuteronomy	5	16
2	Deuteronomy	6	3
4	Deuteronomy	7	13-14
1	Deuteronomy	7	3-4
1	Deuteronomy	8	1
1	Deuteronomy	10	22
1	Deuteronomy	13	17
1	Deuteronomy	23	1
1	Deuteronomy	25	11-12
2	Deuteronomy	25	6
1	Deuteronomy	26	5
1	Deuteronomy	28	1
2	Deuteronomy	28	18
1	Deuteronomy	28	3
7	Deuteronomy	28	4,11
2	Deuteronomy	28	62
1	Deuteronomy	30	16
1	Deuteronomy	30	19-20
1	Deuteronomy	30	9

1	Deuteronomy	33	6
1	Joshua	7	9
1	Judges	11	37
2	Ruth	4	11
1	1 Samuel	1	10,20
1	1 Samuel	1	8
1	1 Samuel	2	21
1	2 Samuel	12	23
1	1 Kings	4	25-26
1	2 Kings	19	29-31
1	1 Chronicles	4	38
2	1 Chronicles	25	5
2	1 Chronicles	26	4-5
1	1 Chronicles	27	23
1	2 Chronicles	1	9
1	Ezra	9	2
1	Ezra	10	3
1	Nehemiah	9	23
2	Job	5	25
1	Job	10	11
1	Job	12	7-8
1	Job	42	13
1	Psalms	1	3
1	Psalms	33	11
1	Psalms	37	25
1	Psalms	37	26
1	Psalms	37	28
1	Psalms	37	38
1	Psalms	48	13
1	Psalms	68	6

1	Psalms	78	6
1	Psalms	80	11
2	Psalms	92	12-14
1	Psalms	105	24
2	Psalms	107	38,41
1	Psalms	109	10-13
4	Psalms	112	2
1	Psalms	113	9
1	Psalms	115	14
18	Psalms	127	3-5
9	Psalms	128	1-6
1	Psalms	144	12
1	Proverbs	2	17
1	Proverbs	5	18
3	Proverbs	14	28
2	Proverbs	17	6
1	Proverbs	20	7
2	Proverbs	22	6
1	Proverbs	30	16
1	Ecclesiastes	3	1-2
1	Ecclesiastes	12	1
1	Isaiah	8	18
2	Isaiah	9	7
1	Isaiah	11	1
1	Isaiah	26	15
2	Isaiah	27	6
1	Isaiah	29	23
1	Isaiah	38	19
1	Isaiah	48	18-19
1	Isaiah	49	2

3	Isaiah	54	1-6
1	Isaiah	59	21
2	Isaiah	66	22
1	Jeremiah	1	5
1	Jeremiah	10	20
1	Jeremiah	17	7-8
1	Jeremiah	23	3
4	Jeremiah	29	4-6
2	Jeremiah	30	19
1	Jeremiah	32	39
1	Jeremiah	33	22
1	Lamentations	4	3
1	Ezekiel	36	10-11
1	Ezekiel	36	11
1	Ezekiel	47	12
1	Hosea	1	10
1	Hosea	4	10
2	Hosea	9	11-14,16
1	Joel	1	3
1	Joel	1	8
4	Malachi	2	15

Abbreviations

adv. Jov.	*adversus Jovinianum*, by Jerome
AE	*Augustine Through the Ages: An Encyclopedia.* ed. Allan Fitzgerald, Grand Rapids, MI: Eerdmans, 1999.
ANET	*Ancient Near Eastern Texts Relating to the Old Testament.* ed. James B. Pritchard. 3rd edn. Princeton: Princeton University Press, 1969.
ANF	*Ante-Nicene Fathers.* 10 vols. ed. Alexander Roberts and James Donaldson. Edinburgh: T&T Clark, 1867-73.
COS	*Context of Scripture.* ed. William W. Hallo. Leiden: Brill, 2003.
Dem. Evang.	*Demonstratio Evangelica*, by Eusebius of Caesarea
ESV	*English Standard Version*
GFN	Global Footprint Network
GSS	General Social Survey (U.S.)
hab. virg.	*De habitu virginum*, by Cyprian of Carthage
KJV	*King James Version*
JSOT	*Journal for the Study of the Old Testament*
LCMS	Lutheran Church Missouri Synod
LS	*Luther on Women: A Sourcebook.* eds. Susan C. Karant-Nunn and Merry E. Wiesner. Cambridge: Cambridge University Press, 2003.
LW	*Luther's Works.* 55 vols. ed. Jaroslav Pelikan. St. Louis: Concordia, 1955. Logos edition 2007.

NIV	*New International Version*
NLT	*New Living Translation*
NPNF	*Nicene and Post-Nicene Fathers*. 28 vols. eds. Philip Schaff and Henry Wace. New York: Scribner,1886-1900.
New Testament	New Testament
Old Testament	Old Testament
ONS	Office for National Statistics
PCA	Presbyterian Church of America
RTSF	Religious and Theological Students' Fellowship
SBC	Southern Baptist Convention
SBL	Society of Biblical Literature
SPCK	Society for Promoting Christian Knowledge
TFR	Total Fertility Rate
WSA	*The Works of Saint Augustine: A Translation for the 21st Century*. 46 vols. ed. John Rotelle. Hyde Park NY: New City Press, 1990-.

Abbreviations for works by Augustine

c. Adim.	*Contra Adimantum Manichae disciplum*
b. conjug.	*De bono conjugali*
b. vid.	*De bono viduitatis*
cat. rud.	*De catechizandis rudibus*
civ. Dei	*De Civitate Dei*
conf.	*Confessiones*
cont.	*De continentia*
div. qu.	*De diversis quaestionibus octoginta tribus*
doc. Chr.	*doctrina Christiana*
ep.	*Epistulae*
en. Ps.	*enarrationes in Psalmos*
c. Faust.	*Contra Faustum Manichaeum*

Gn. litt.	De Genesi ad litteram
Gn. adv. Man.	De Genesi adversus Manichaeos
Gn. litt. imp.	De Genesi ad litteram imperfectus liber
gr. et pecc. or.	De gratia Christi et de peccato originali
haer.	De haeresibus
c. Jul.	Contra Julianum
mor.	De moribus ecclesiae catholicae et de moribus Manichaeorum
nupt. et conc.	De nuptiis et concupiscentia
pecc. mer.	De peccatorum meritis et remissione et de baptismo parvulorum
retr.	Retractiones (Reconsiderations)
c. Sec.	Contra Secundinum Manichaeum
serm.	Sermones
virg.	De sancta virginitate

These are the standard abbreviations given in AE, except for *sermones* where AE uses the single letter *s.* but I have used *serm.*, following the SBL style.

Works Cited

Adams, Jason. *Called to Give Life: A Sourcebook on the Blessings of Children and the Harm of Contraception*. Dayton, OH: One More Soul, 2003.

Akin, Daniel. "Axioms for a Great Commission Resurgence." April 2009. http://www.danielakin.com

Alexander, T. Desmond. *From Paradise to the Promised Land: An Introduction to the Main Themes of the Pentateuch*. 2nd edn., London: Paternoster Press, 2002.

Allen, Leslie C. *Psalms*. Waco, TX: Word, 1987.

Allison, Dale C. "What I Have Learned from the History of Interpretation." *Perspectives in Religious Studies* 35.3 (Fall 2008): 237-50.

Anderson, Bernhard W. "Creation and Ecology." *American Journal of Theology and Philosophy* 4.1 (1983): 14-30.

Anderson, Gary. "Celibacy or Consummation in the Garden: Reflections on Early Jewish and Christian Interpretations of the Garden of Eden." *Harvard Theological Review* 82.2 (1989): 121-48. http://dx.doi.org/10.1017/s0017816000016084

Andrews, Robert. *The Family: God's Weapon for Victory*. Mukilteo, WA: Winepress, 1996.

Anonymous. *Love Your Unborn Neighbour*. London: Society for the Protection of Unborn Children, 1994.

Assis, Elie. "Psalm 127 and the Polemic of the Rebuilding of the Temple in the Post-Exilic Period." *Zeitschrift für die alttestamentliche Wissenschaft* 121.2 (June 2009): 256-72. http://dx.doi.org/10.1515/zaw.2009.017

Attenborough, Robert. "Ecology, Homeostasis and Survival in Human Population Dynamics." *Human Population Dynamics: Cross Disciplinary Perspectives*. ed. Helen Macbeth and Paul Collinson. Cambridge: Cambridge University Press, 2002: 186-208. http://dx.doi.org/10.1017/cbo9780511542480.012

Livi Bacci, Massimo. *A Concise History of World Population*. 4th edn., Oxford: Blackwell, 2007. http://dx.doi.org/10.2307/2137643

Baillie, Jonathan, Craig Hilton-Taylor, and Simon N. Stuart. *2004 IUCN Red List of Threatened Species: A Global Species Assessment*. Gland, Switzerland: International Union for Conservation of Nature, 2004. http://dx.doi.org/10.1017/s0030605305260489

Bainton, Roland H. *Here I Stand: A Life of Martin Luther*. London: Penguin, 1950.

Baird, David. "Fertility and Ageing." *Human Reproduction Update* 11.3 (2005): 261-76.

Barnes, Robin Bruce. *Prophecy and Gnosis: Apocalypticism in the Wake of the Lutheran Reformation.* Stanford, CA: Stanford University Press, 1988. http://dx.doi.org/10.2307/204093

Barr, James. "Man and Nature: The Ecological Controversy and the Old Testament." *Bulletin of the John Rylands Library* 55 (1973): 9-32.

Barrett, David B., Todd M. Johnson, Christopher R. Guidry, and Peter F. Crossing. *World Christian Trends, AD 30 - AD 2200: Interpreting the Annual Christian Megacensus.* Pasadena, CA: William Carey Library, 2001.

Barrett, David B., George T. Kurian, and Todd M. Johnson. *World Christian Encyclopedia: A Comparative Survey of Churches and Religions in the Modern World.* 2nd edn., Oxford: Oxford University Press, 2001.

Barth, Karl. *Church Dogmatics Vol. 3 The Doctrine of Creation.* trans. G.T. Thomson, ed. Geoffrey W. Bromiley. Edinburgh: T&T Clark, 1999. http://dx.doi.org/10.1177/004057366101800213

Barton, John. *The Nature of Biblical Criticism.* Louisville, KY: Westminster John Knox Press, 2007. http://dx.doi.org/10.1086/590014

Basten, Stuart, Wolfgang Lutz, and Sergei Scherbov. "Very Long Range Global Population Scenarios to 2300 and the Implications of Sustained Low Fertility." *Demographic Research* 28 (2013): 1145-66. http://dx.doi.org/10.4054/demres.2013.28.39

Barusse, Virginie de Luca. "Pro-Natalism and Hygienism in France, 1900-1940." *Population* 64.3 (2009): 477-506. http://dx.doi.org/10.3917/pope.903.0477

Bauckham, Richard. *The Bible in Politics.* London: SPCK, 1989. http://dx.doi.org/10.15695/hmltc.v37i2.3732

— *The Bible and Ecology: Rediscovering the Community of Creation.* Waco, TX: Baylor University Press, 2010.

Baue, Frederic. "Luther on Preaching as Explanation and Exclamation." *Lutheran Quarterly* 9.4 (Winter 1995): 405-18.

Bayly, Tim. "The Place of Childbirth in Christian Marriage: Raising up a Godly Seed." *Journal of Biblical Manhood and Womanhood* 3.4 (Winter 1998): 14-15.

Beal, Timothy K. and David M. Gunn, eds. *Reading Bibles, Writing Bodies: Identity and the Book.* London: Routledge, 1997. http://dx.doi.org/10.4324/9780203433362

Beisner, E. Calvin. *Where Garden Meets Wilderness: Evangelical Entry into the Environmental Debate.* Grand Rapids, MI: Eerdmans, 1997. http://dx.doi.org/10.1525/nr.2001.4.2.362

— "*Imago Dei* in the Population Debate." *Trinity Journal* 18.2 (Fall 1997): 173-97.

Bettenson, Henry. *Concerning the City of God against the Pagans.* trans. Henry Bettenson, Harmondsworth: Penguin, 1972.

Biddle, Mark E. "The 'Endangered Ancestress' and Blessing for the Nations." *Journal of Biblical Literature* 109.4 (Winter 1990): 599-611. http://dx.doi.org/10.2307/3267365

Biller, Peter. *The Measure of Multitude: Population in Medieval Thought.* Oxford: Oxford University Press, 2003. http://dx.doi.org/10.1162/00221950360536657

Blake, Judith. *Family Size and Achievement.* Berkeley, CA: University of California Press, 1989. http://dx.doi.org/10.2307/2579638

Blanchard, Kathryn D. "The Gift of Contraception: Calvin, Barth, and a Lost Protestant Conversation." *Journal of the Society of Christian Ethics* 27.1 (2007): 225-49.

Blenkinsopp, Joseph. "The Family in First Temple Israel." *Families in Ancient Israel*. ed. Leo Perdue, Joseph Blenkinsopp, John J. Collins and Carol Meyers. Louisville: Westminster John Knox, 1997): 8-103.

Blowers, Paul M., Angela R. Christman, David G. Hunter, and Robin D. Young, eds. *In Dominico Eloquio – In Lordly Eloquence: Essays on Patristic Exegesis in Honour of Robert Louis Wilken*. Grand Rapids, MI: Eerdmans, 2002. http://dx.doi.org/10.1353/earl.2003.0052

Bongaarts, John and Griffith Feeney. "On the Quantum and Tempo of Fertility." *Population and Development Review* 24.2 (June 1998): 271-91. http://dx.doi.org/10.2307/2807974

Bongaarts, John and Robert G. Potter. *Fertility, Biology, and Behavior: An Analysis of the Proximate Determinants*. New York: Academic Press, 1983. http://dx.doi.org/10.2307/1973328

Boone, Kathleen C. *The Bible Tells Them So: The Discourse of Protestant Fundamentalism*. London: SCM Press, 1990. http://dx.doi.org/10.1086/488431

Borowski, Oded. *Daily Life in Biblical Times*. Atlanta, GA: Society of Biblical Literature, 2003. http://dx.doi.org/10.1177/001452460411501013

Bouma-Prediger, Steven, and Peter Bakken, eds. *Evocations of Grace: The Writings of Joseph Sittler on Ecology, Theology, and Ethics*. Grand Rapids, MI: Eerdmans, 2000.

Brakke, David. *Athanasius and Asceticism*. Baltimore, MD: John Hopkins University Press, 1998. http://dx.doi.org/10.1177/0040571x9710000225

Bratton, Susan Power. *Six Billion and More: Human Population Regulation and Christian Ethics*. Louisville, KY: Westminster John Knox Press, 1992.

Brecht, Martin. *Martin Luther*. trans. James L. Schaaf. Minneapolis, MN: Fortress Press, 1985.

Brewer, Mike, Anita Ratcliffe, and Sarah Smith. "Does Welfare Reform Affect Fertility? Evidence from the UK."

Brichto, Herbert Chanan. "Kin, Cult, Land and Afterlife: A Biblical Complex." *Hebrew Union College Annual* 44 (1973): 1-54.

Brooks, David. "The New Red-Diaper Babies." *New York Times*, 7 December 2004. http://www.nytimes.com/2004/12/07/opinion/07brooks.html

Brown, Peter R. L. *The Body and Society: Men, Women, and Sexual Renunciation in Early Christianity*. London: Faber and Faber, 1989.

Brown, Peter R. L. and Mary Ann Donovan. *Augustine and Sexuality: Protocol of the Forty Sixth Colloquy*. Berkeley, CA: Center for Hermeneutical Studies in Hellenistic and Modern Culture, 1983.

Brueggemann, Walter. "The Liturgy of Abundance, the Myth of Scarcity." *Christian Century* 116.10 (1999): 342-47.

— Review of "The Curse of Cain." Theology Today 54.4 (January 1998): 534-37. http://dx.doi.org/10.1177/004057369805400417

— *An Unsettling God: The Heart of the Hebrew Bible*. Minneapolis, MN: Fortress Press, 2009.

Bultmann, Christoph. "Luther on Gender Relations: Just One Reading of Genesis?" *Currents in Theology and Mission* 29.6 (2002): 424-28.

Buss, Doris, and Didi Herman. *Globalizing Family Values: The Christian Right in International Politics*. Minneapolis, MN: University of Minnesota Press, 2003. http://dx.doi.org/10.1086/424639

Byrne, Ryan. "Lie Back and Think of Judah: The Reproductive Politics of Pillar Figurines." *Near Eastern Archaeology* 67.3 (Summer 2004): 137-51. http://dx.doi.org/10.2307/4132376

Calvin, John. *Genesis*. 1554. Ed. James I. Packer. Wheaton, IL: Crossway, 2001.

Camiscioli, Elisa. "Producing Citizens, Reproducing the 'French Race': Immigration, Demography, and Pronatalism in Early Twentieth-Century France." *Gender and History* 13.3 (November 2001): 593-621. http://dx.doi.org/10.1111/1468-0424.00245

Campbell, Nancy. *Be Fruitful and Multiply*. San Antonio, TX: Vision Forum, 2005.

Carlson, Allan. *Conjugal America: On the Public Purposes of Marriage*. New Brunswick, NJ: Transaction, 2007.

— "Be Fruitful and Multiply: Religious Pronatalism in a Depopulating America." *This World* 21 (Spring 1988): 18-30.

— "Freedom, Authority, and Family." *Dialog* 20.3 (Summer 1981): 195-99.

— "Children of the Reformation." *Touchstone: A Journal of Mere Christianity* 20.4 (May 2007): 20-25.

— *Godly Seed: American Evangelicals Confront Birth Control, 1873 - 1973*. New Brunswick, NJ: Transaction, 2012.

Carlson, Allan and Paul Mero. *The Natural Family: Bulwark of Liberty*. New Brunswick, NJ: Transaction, 2009.

Census Bureau (U.S.). "Census 2010." http://www.census.gov/2010census/

Chadwick, Henry. *Augustine*. Oxford: Oxford University Press, 1986. http://dx.doi.org/10.1093/actrade/9780192854520.001.0001

Chadwick, Owen. *The Early Reformation on the Continent*. Oxford: Oxford University Press, 2001. http://dx.doi.org/10.1093/0198269021.001.0001

Cincotta, Richard P. "The Biological Diversity That is Humanly Possible: Three Models Relevant to Human Population's Relationship With Native Species." *Human Population: Its Influences on Biological Diversity*. ed Richard P. Cincotta and Larry J. Gorenflo. Berlin: Springer, 2011: 61-73. http://dx.doi.org/10.1007/978-3-642-16707-2_5

Cincotta, Richard P. and Larry J. Gorenflo, eds. *Human Population: Its Influences on Biological Diversity*. New York: Springer, 2011. http://dx.doi.org/10.1007/978-3-642-16707-2

Clark, Elizabeth A. "Heresy, Asceticism, Adam, and Eve: Interpretations of Genesis 1-3 in the Later Latin Fathers." *Genesis 1-3 in the History of Exegesis: Intrigue in the Garden*. ed. Gregory A. Robbins. Lewiston, NY: Edwin Mellen Press, 1988: 363-73. ://dx.doi.org/10.1163/157006797x00152

— "Contesting Abraham: The Ascetic Reader and the Politics of Intertextuality." *The Social World of the First Christians: Essays in Honor of Wayne A. Meeks*. ed. L.

Michael White and O. Larry Yarbrough. Minneapolis: Augsburg/Fortress, 1995: 353-65.

— *Reading Renunciation: Asceticism and Scripture in Early Christianity.* Princeton, NJ: Princeton University Press, 1999.

Clark, Mary T. *Augustine.* London: Continuum, 2000.

Clifford, Richard J. *Psalms 73-150.* Nashville, TN: Abingdon Press, 2003.

Clines, David J.A. *What Does Eve Do to Help? And Other Readerly Questions to the Old Testament.* Sheffield: JSOT Press, 1990.

— *The Theme of the Pentateuch.* 2nd edn., Sheffield: JSOT Press, 1997.

Cohen, Jeremy. *'Be Fertile and Increase, Fill the Earth and Master It': The Ancient and Medieval Career of a Biblical Text.* Ithaca, NY: Cornell University Press, 1989.

Coleman, Simon. *The Globalisation of Charismatic Christianity: Spreading the Gospel of Prosperity.* Cambridge: Cambridge University Press, 2000.

Concordia Press. "Luther's Works American Edition, New Additions to Series." 2009. http://www.cph.org/t-topic-luthersworks.aspx

Conradie, Ernst. "Towards an Ecological Biblical Hermeneutics: A Review Essay on the Earth Bible Project." *Scriptura* 85 (2004): 123-35.

— *Christianity and Ecological Theology: Resources for Further Research.* Stellenbosch: Sun Press, 2006. http://dx.doi.org/10.1163/156853507x230636

— "What on Earth is an Ecological Hermeneutics? Some Broad Parameters." *Ecological Hermeneutics: Biblical, Historical and Theological Perspectives.* London: T&T Clark, 2010. 295-314.

Cotterell, Peter. *Prosperity Theology.* Leicester: RTSF, 1993.

Coward, Harold G., ed. *Population, Consumption, and the Environment: Religious and Secular Responses.* Albany, NY: State University of New York Press, 1995. http://dx.doi.org/10.2307/2137444

Coyle, Kevin. "Saint Augustine's Manichean Legacy." *Augustinian Studies* 34.1 (2003): 1-22. http://dx.doi.org/10.1163/ej.9789004175747.i-348.93

Cunningham, Andrew and Ole Peter Grell. *The Four Horsemen of the Apocalypse: Religion, War, Famine and Death in Reformation Europe.* Cambridge: Cambridge University Press, 2000.

Dahood, Mitchell J. *Psalms III: 101-150.* Garden City, NY: Doubleday, 1970. http://dx.doi.org/10.2307/3263101

D'Angelo, Mary Rose. "The Garden, Once and Not Again: Traditional Interpretations of Genesis 1:26-27 in 1 Corinthians 11:7-12." *Genesis 1-3 in the History of Exegesis: Intrigue in the Garden.* ed. Gregory Allen Robbins. Lewiston, NY and Queenston, ON: Edwin Mellen Press, 1988: 1-41.

Daley, Brian. *The Hope of the Early Church: A Handbook of Patristic Eschatology.* Peabody, MA: Hendrickson, 2003.

Dalton, Michael et al. "Population Aging and Future Carbon Emissions in the United States." *Energy Economics* 30 (2008): 642-75.

Daube, David. *The Duty of Procreation.* Edinburgh: Edinburgh University Press, 1977.

Davidson, Randall T. *The Five Lambeth Conferences.* London: SPCK, 1920.

Davidson, Robert. *The Vitality of Worship: A Commentary on the Book of Psalms.* Edinburgh: Handsel Press, 1998.

Davies, Philip. "The Ancient World." Sawyer, *Culture* 11-27. http://dx.doi.org/10.1002/9780470997000.ch2

Davis, Ellen F. "Learning Our Place: The Agrarian Perspective of the Bible." *Word and World* 29.2 (Spring 2009): 109-20.

Davis, John Jefferson. *Evangelical Ethics: Issues Facing the Church Today.* 3rd edn., Phillipsburg, NJ: Presbyterian and Reformed Publishing, 2004.

— "Ecological 'Blind Spots' in the Structure and Content of Recent Evangelical Systematic Theologies." *Journal of the Evangelical Theological Society* 43.2 (June 2000): 273-86.

De la Croix, David and Axel Gosseries "The Natalist Bias of Pollution Control." *Journal of Environmental Economics and Management* 63.2 (2012): 271-87.

Deane-Drummond, Celia. "Response to James A. Nash 'The Bible vs. Biodiversity: The Case against Moral Argument from Scripture'." *Journal for the Study of Religion, Nature and Culture* 3.2 (2009): 271-78.

Demeny, Paul. "European Parliament on the Need for Promoting Population Growth." *Population and Development Review* 10.3 (1984): 569-70. http://dx.doi.org/10.2307/1973535

Dever, William G. *Who Were the Early Israelites and Where Did They Come From?* Grand Rapids, MI: Eerdmans, 2003. http://dx.doi.org/10.1179/003103204225014256

— *What Did the Biblical Writers Know, and When did they Know It?* Grand Rapids, MI: Eerdmans, 2001.

Doriani, Daniel M. "Birth Dearth or Bring on the Babies? Biblical Perspectives on Family Planning." *Journal of Biblical Counseling* 12.1 (Fall 1993): 24-35.

Eberstadt, Nicholas. "Demographic Exceptionalism in the United States: Tendencies and Implications." American Enterprise Institute, January 2007. http://www.aei.org/publication/demographic-exceptionalism-in-the-united-states

Eijkemans, Marinus, et.al. "Too old to have children? Lessons from natural fertility populations." *Human Reproduction* 29.6 (2014) 1304–1312.

Eldredge, Niles. *Life in the Balance: Humanity and the Biodiversity Crisis.* Princeton, NJ: Princeton University Press, 1998.

Ellison, Christopher and Patricia Goodson. "Conservative Protestantism and Attitudes toward Family Planning in a Sample of Seminarians." *Journal for the Scientific Study of Religion* 36.4 (1997): 512-29. http://dx.doi.org/10.2307/1387687

Erikson, Erik H. *Young Man Luther: A Study in Psychoanalysis and History.* London: Norton, 1993. http://dx.doi.org/10.2307/2504318

Esslemont, Tom. "Church Leader Sparks Georgian Baby Boom." BBC, 26 March 2009. http://news.bbc.co.uk/1/hi/world/europe/7964302.stm

Estes, Daniel J. "Like Arrows in the Hand of a Warrior (Psalm 127)." *Vetus Testamentum* 41.3 (July 1991): 304-11. http://dx.doi.org/10.1163/156853391x00289

EuroStat. European Commission. http://epp.eurostat.ec.europa.eu/

Eusebius. *The Proof of the Gospel, Being the Demonstratio Evangelica of Eusebius of Cæsarea.* Trans. William J. Ferrar. London and New York: SPCK, 1920.

Evans, Robert. *Reception History, Tradition and Biblical Interpretation: Gadamer and Jauss in Current Practice*. London: T&T Clark, 2014.

Fagley, Richard. *The Population Explosion and Christian Responsibility*. New York: Oxford University Press, 1960. http://dx.doi.org/10.2307/3510831

Fewell, Danna Nolan and David M. Gunn. "Shifting the Blame: God in the Garden." *Reading Bibles, Writing Bodies*. ed. Timothy K. Beal and David M. Gunn. New York: Routledge, 2003: 16-33.

Fitzgerald, Allan, ed. *Augustine Through the Ages: An Encyclopedia*. Grand Rapids, MI: Eerdmans, 1999. http://dx.doi.org/10.2307/3169408

Fleming, Daniel E. "Psalm 127: Sleep for the Fearful, and Security in Sons." *Zeitschrift für die alttestamentliche Wissenschaft* 107.3 (January 1995): 435-44. http://dx.doi.org/10.1515/zatw.1995.107.3.435

Forde, Gerhard. "Law and Gospel in Luther's Hermeneutic." *Interpretation* 37.3 (July 1983): 240-52. http://dx.doi.org/10.1177/002096438303700303

Fotion, Nick and Jan Christian Heller, eds. *Contingent Future Persons: On the Ethics of Deciding Who Will Live, or Not, in the Future*. Dordrecht: Kluwer Academic, 1997.

French, James and Shannon French. *Quiverx Children: God's Special Blessing*. Longwood, FL: Xulon Press, 2006.

Frymer-Kensky, Tikva. "The Atrahasis Epic and its Significance for Our Understanding of Genesis 1-9." *Biblical Archaeologist* 40.4 (1977): 147-55. http://dx.doi.org/10.2307/3209529

Gaca, Kathy. *The Making of Fornication: Eros, Ethics, and Political Reform in Greek Philosophy and Early Christianity*. Berkeley, CA: University of California Press, 2003. http://dx.doi.org/10.1525/california/9780520235991.001.0001

Gadamer, Hans Georg. *Truth and Method*. 1989. trans. Joel Weinsheimer, and Donald G. Marshall, 2nd edn., London: Continuum, 2004. http://dx.doi.org/10.2307/302234

Garrison, Vyckie. "No Longer Quivering." 2011. http://NoLongerQuivering.com

Gerstenberger, Erhard. *Psalms Part 2 and Lamentations*. Grand Rapids, MI: Eerdmans, 2001.

GFN. *Ecological Footprint Atlas 2010*. Oakland, CA: Global Footprint Network, 2010. http://www.footprintnetwork.org/en/index.php/GFN/page/publications/

Gifford, Paul. "Prosperity: A New and Foreign Element in African Christianity." *Religion* 20.4 (1990): 373-88. http://dx.doi.org/10.1016/0048-721x(90)90119-q

Goldstein, Joshua R., Tomas Sabotka, and Aiva Jasilioniene. "The End of Lowest-Low Fertility?" *Population and Development Review* 35.4 (December 2009): 663-99. http://dx.doi.org/10.1111/j.1728-4457.2009.00304.x

Goldstone, Jack A., Eric Kaufmann, and Monica Duffy Toft, eds. *Political Demography: How Population Changes are Reshaping National Politics and International Security*. Oxford: Oxford University Press, 2012.

Goodson, Patricia. "Ethics of Contraception: A Recurring Debate." *Presbyterion* 18.1 (1992): 34-49.

— "Protestants and Family Planning." *Journal of Religion and Health* 36.4 (December 1997): 353-66.

Gottlieb, Roger S. *The Oxford Handbook of Religion and Ecology.* New York and Oxford: Oxford University Press, 2006. http://dx.doi.org/10.1093/oxfordhb/9780195178722.001.0001

Goulder, Michael D. *The Psalms of the Return: Book V, Psalms 107-150.* Sheffield: Sheffield Academic Press, 1998.

Gourley, Bruce T. "In Response to: Albert Mohler on Singleness and Childlessness." *Baptist Studies Bulletin* 5.2 (February 2006). http://www.centerforbaptiststudies.org/bulletin/2006/february.htm

Graebner, Alan. "Birth Control and the Lutherans: The Missouri Synod as a Case Study." *Journal of Social History* 2.4 (Summer 1969): 303-32. http://dx.doi.org/10.1353/jsh/2.4.303

Green, R. P. trans. and ed. *On Christian Teaching.* By Augustine of Hippo. Oxford: Oxford University Press, 1997.

Greksa, Lawrence P. "Population Growth and Fertility Patterns in an Old Order Amish Settlement." *Annals of Human Biology* 29.2 (2002): 192-201. http://dx.doi.org/10.1080/03014460110075684

Gritsch, Eric W. "The Cultural Context of Luther's Interpretation." *Interpretation* 37.3 (July 1983): 266-76. http://dx.doi.org/10.1177/002096438303700305

Gruber, Mayer I. "Breast-feeding Practices in Biblical Israel and in Old Babylonian Mesopotamia." *Journal of the Ancient Near Eastern Society* 19 (1989): 61-83.

Grüneberg, Keith N. *Blessing: Biblical Meaning and Pastoral Practice.* Vol. B27, Cambridge: Grove Books, 2003.

— *Abraham, Blessing, and the Nations: A Philological and Exegetical Study of Genesis 12:3 in its Narrative Context.* Berlin: Walter de Gruyter, 2003. http://dx.doi.org/10.2307/3268468

Gudorf, Christine E. "Resymbolizing Life: Religion on Population and Environment." *Horizons* 28.2 (Fall 2001): 183-210.

Habel, Norman C. *The Land is Mine: Six Biblical Land Ideologies.* Minneapolis, MN: Fortress Press, 1995. http://dx.doi.org/10.2307/3266232

— "The Challenge of Ecojustice Readings for Christian Theology." *Pacifica* 13.2 (2000): 125-41.

Hackett, Conrad. "Religion and Fertility in the United States: The Influence of Affiliation, Region, and Congregation." PhD thesis. Princeton University, 2008.

Haines, Michael R. and Richard H. Steckel. *A Population History of North America.* New York: Cambridge University Press, 2000. http://dx.doi.org/10.2307/2700618

Hallo, William W. *The Context of Scripture.* Leiden: Brill, 2003.

Hamilton, Victor P. *The Book of Genesis: Chapters 1-17.* Grand Rapids, MI: Eerdmans, 1990.

Harrison, Carol. *Augustine: Christian Truth and Fractured Humanity.* Oxford: Oxford University Press, 2000. http://dx.doi.org/10.2307/3301156

Hart, David Bentley. *In the Aftermath: Provocations and Laments.* Grand Rapids, MI: Eerdmans, 2009.

Harte, John. "Human Population as a Dynamic Factor in Environmental Degradation." *Population and Environment* 28 (2007): 223-36. http://dx.doi.org/10.1007/s11111-007-0048-3

Hartley, John E. *Genesis*. Peabody, MA: Hendrickson, 2000.

Hauerwas, Stanley and Samuel Wells, eds. *The Blackwell Companion to Christian Ethics*. Oxford: Blackwell, 2004. http://dx.doi.org/10.1002/9780470996690

Hayford, Sarah R. and S. Philip Morgan. "Religiosity and Fertility in the United States: The Role of Fertility Intentions." *Social Forces* 86.3 (March 2008): 1164-88. http://dx.doi.org/10.1353/sof.0.0000

Headley, John M. *Luther's View of Church History*. New Haven, CT: Yale University Press, 1963.

Heine, Max. *Children: Blessing or Burden? Exploding the Myth of the Small Family*. Gresham, OR: Noble, 1989.

Hendel, Ronald S. "Of Demigods and the Deluge: Toward an Interpretation of Genesis 6:1-4." *Journal of Biblical Literature* 106.1 (March 1987): 13-26. http://dx.doi.org/10.2307/3260551

Hendrix, Scott. "Luther against the Background of the History of Biblical Interpretation." *Interpretation* 37.3 (July 1983): 229-39. http://dx.doi.org/10.1177/002096438303700302

— "The Future of Luther's Theology." *Dialog* 47.2 (July 2008): 125-35. http://dx.doi.org/10.1111/j.1540-6385.2008.00378.x

Henry, Matthew. *Commentary on the Whole Bible*. http://www.ccel.org/ccel/henry/mhc3.Ps.cxxviii.html

Hess, Richard S. and M. Daniel Carroll, eds. *Family in the Bible: Exploring Customs, Culture and Context*. Grand Rapids, MI: Baker Academic, 2003.

Hess, Richard S. and David Toshio Tsumura, eds. *"I Studied Inscriptions from Before the Flood": Ancient Near Eastern, Literary, and Linguistic Approaches to Genesis 1-11*. Winona Lake, IN: Eisenbrauns, 1994.

Hess, Rick and Jan Hess. *A Full Quiver: Family Planning and the Lordship of Christ*. Brentwood, TN: Wolgemuth and Hyatt, 1996.

Hessel, Dieter T., ed. *Theology for Earth Community: A Field Guide*. Maryknoll, NY: Orbis Books, 1996.

Hornok, Richard. "An Evaluation of a Program to Investigate Four Views of Birth Control." D.Min. thesis. Dallas Theological Seminary, 1993.

Horrell, David. "Introduction." *Ecological Hermeneutics: Biblical, Historical, and Theological Perspectives*. ed. David G. Horrell, Cherryl Hunt, Christopher Southgate and Francesca Stavrakopoulou. London and New York: T&T Clark, 2010: 1-12.

— *The Bible and the Environment: Towards a Critical Ecological Biblical Theology*. London: Equinox, 2010.

— "The Ecological Challenge to Biblical Studies." *Theology* CXII.867 (May/June 2009): 163-71.

Horrell, David, Cherryl Hunt, and Christopher Southgate. "Appeals to the Bible in Ecotheology and Environmental Ethics: A Typology of Hermeneutical Stances." *Studies in Christian Ethics* 21.2 (August 2008): 219-38. http://dx.doi.org/10.1177/0953946808094343

Houghton, Craig. *Family Unplanning: A Guide for Christian Couples Seeking God's Truth on Having Children*. Longwood, FL: Xulon Press, 2007.

Hout, Michael, Andrew M. Greeley, and Melissa J. Wilde. "The Demographic Imperative in Religious Change in the United States." *American Journal of Sociology* 107.2 (September 2001): 468-500. http://dx.doi.org/10.1086/324189

Hunter, Alastair G. *Psalms*. London: Routledge, 1999. http://dx.doi.org/10.1093/oxfordhb/9780199544486.003.0015

Hunter, David G. "Reclaiming Biblical Morality: Sex and Salvation History in Augustine's Treatment of the Hebrew Saints." *In Dominico Eloquio - In Lordly Essence: Essays on Patristic Exegesis in Honor of Robert Louis Wilken*. ed. Paul M. Blowers, Angela Russell Christman and David G. Hunter. Grand Rapids, MI: Wm. B. Eerdmans Publishing, 2002: 317-35.

— *Marriage, Celibacy, and Heresy in Ancient Christianity: The Jovinianist Controversy*. Oxford: Oxford University Press, 2007.

— "Resistance to the Virginal Ideal in Late-Fourth-Century Rome: The Case of Jovinian." *Theological Studies* 48.1 (March 1987): 45-64. http://dx.doi.org/10.1177/004056398704800103

Hussain, R. "The Role of Son Preference in Reproductive Behaviour in Pakistan." *World Health Organization Bulletin* 78.3 (2000): 379-88.

Hynes, Patricia. "Taking Population Out of the Equation: Reformulating I=PAT." *Dangerous Intersections: Feminist Perspectives on Population, Environment, and Development*. ed. Jael Silliman and Ynestra King. Cambridge, MA: South End Press, 1999: 39-73.

Inhorn, Marcia C., and Frank van Balen, eds. *Infertility Around the Globe: New Thinking on Childlessness, Gender, and Reproductive Technologies*. Berkeley, CA: University of California Press, 2002.

Ipsen, Carl. *Dictating Demography: The Problem of Population in Fascist Italy*. Cambridge: Cambridge University Press, 1996.

Istituto nazionale di statistica (ISTAT). "Geodemo." 2011. http://demo.istat.it/uniprev/

Johnson, Todd and Brian Grim, *The World's Religions in Figures: An Introduction to International Religious Demography*. Malden MA, Wiley, 2013

Jones, G. and M. Karim, eds. *Islam, the State and Population*. London: Hurst, 2005.

Jones, Jeffrey M. "In U.S., 3 in 10 Say they Take the Bible Literally." Gallup, 2011. http://www.gallup.com/poll/148427/Say-Bible-Literally.aspx

Jordan, James B. "The Bible and Family Planning: An Answer to Charles Provan's the Bible and Birth Control." *Contra Mundum* 9 (Fall 1993): 2-14.

Joyce, Kathryn. *Quiverfull: Inside the Christian Patriarchy Movement*. Boston, MA: Beacon Press, 2009.

Juttë, Robert. *Contraception: A History*. London: Polity Press, 2012. http://dx.doi.org/10.1080/19419899.2011.590628

Kahn, Susan M. "Rabbis and Reproduction: The Uses of New Reproductive Technologies Among Ultraorthodox Jews in Israel." *Infertility around the Globe: New Thinking on Childlessness, Gender and Reproductive Technologies*. ed. Marcia C. Inhorn and Frank van Balen. Berkeley and Los Angeles: University of California Press. 2002: 283-97.

Kaminski, Carol M. *From Noah to Israel: Realization of the Primaeval Blessing After the Flood*. Edinburgh: T&T Clark, 2004.

Karant-Nunn, Susan C. and Merry E. Wiesner, eds. *Luther on Women: A Sourcebook*. Cambridge: Cambridge University Press, 2003. http://dx.doi.org/10.1017/cbo9780511810367

Kaufmann, Eric. *Shall the Religious Inherit the Earth? Demography and Politics in the Twenty-First Century*. London: Profile, 2010.

Kaufmann, Eric P., Anne Goujon and Vegard Skirbekk. "American Political Affiliation 2003-43: A Cohort Component Projection." *Population Studies* 66.1 (March 2012): 53-67. http://dx.doi.org/10.1080/00324728.2011.628047

Kaufmann, Eric P., and William Bradford Wilcox. *Whither the child?: Causes and Consequences of Low Fertility*. Boulder, CO: Paradigm Publishers, 2012.

Keller, Catherine. "A Christian Response to the Population Apocalypse." *Population, Consumption and the Environment: Religious and Secular Responses*. ed. Howard Coward. Albany, NY: State University of New York Press, 1995: 109-21. http://dx.doi.org/10.1177/004057369705400217

Kidner, Derek. *Psalms 73-150*. London: Inter-Varsity Press, 1975.

Kikawada, Isaac, and Arthur Quinn. *Before Abraham Was: The Unity of Genesis 1-11*. Nashville, TN: Abingdon Press, 1985. http://dx.doi.org/10.2307/3260648

Kilmer, Anne. "The Mesopotamian Concept of Overpopulation and its Solution as Reflected in the Mythology." *Orientalia* 41.2 (1972): 160-77.

King, Karen L., ed. *Images of the Feminine in Gnosticism*. Philadelphia, PA: Fortress Press, 1988.

King, Philip J. and Lawrence E. Stager. *Life in Biblical Israel*. Louisville, KY: Westminster John Knox Press, 2001.

Kingdon, Robert M. *Adultery and Divorce in Calvin's Geneva*. Cambridge, MA: Harvard University Press, 1994. http://dx.doi.org/10.1080/03612759.1996.9951306

Klint, Stefan. "After Story – a Return to History?: Introducing Reception Criticism as an Exegetical Approach." *Studia Theologica* 54 (2000): 87-106. http://dx.doi.org/10.1080/003933800750059756

Kolb, Robert. *Martin Luther as Prophet, Teacher, Hero: Images of the Reformer, 1520-1620*. Grand Rapids, MI: Baker Academic, 1999.

Koltun-Fromm, Naomi. "Sexuality and Holiness: Semitic Christian and Jewish Conceptualizations of Sexual Behaviour." *Vigiliae Christianae* 54.4 (2000): 375-95. http://dx.doi.org/10.2307/1584608

Kosova, Gülüm, Mark Abney, and Carole Ober. "Heritability of Reproductive Fitness Traits in a Human Population." *Proceedings of the National Academy of Science* 107 (2010): 1772-78. http://dx.doi.org/10.1073/pnas.0906196106

Kraus, Hans-Joachim. *Psalms 60-150: A Commentary*. trans. Hilton C. Oswald. Minneapolis, MN: Augsburg, 1989.

Krause, Elizabeth L, and Milena Marchesi. "Fertility Politics as 'Social Viagra': Reproducing Boundaries, Social Cohesion and Modernity in Italy." *American Anthropologist* 109.2 (June 2007): 350-62. http://dx.doi.org/10.1525/aa.2007.109.2.350

Kretzmann, Norman and Eleonore Stump, eds. *The Cambridge Companion to Augustine*. Cambridge: Cambridge University Press, 2001. http://dx.doi.org/10.1017/ccol0521650186

Lang, Hartmut and Ruth Gohlen. "Completed Fertility of the Hutterites: A Revision." *Current Anthropology* 26.3 (June 1985): 395

Lehrer, Evelyn L. "Religion as a Determinant of Economic and Demographic Behavior in the United States." *Population and Development Review* 30.4 (December 2004): 707-26. http://dx.doi.org/10.1111/j.1728-4457.2004.00038.x

Lewis, Donald M. *Christianity Reborn: The Global Expansion of Evangelicalism in the Twentieth Century.* Grand Rapids, MI: Eerdmans, 2004.

Lino, Mark. *Expenditures on Children by Families.* Washington DC: USDA, 2012.

Livi Bacci, Massimo. *A Concise History of World Population.* 4th edn., Oxford: Blackwell, 2007. Loh, Jonathan et al. *Living Planet Report.* Gland, Switzerland: World Wildlife Fund, 2010. http://dx.doi.org/10.1002/hpm.964

Lohfink, Norbert. *Theology of the Pentateuch: Themes of the Priestly Narrative and Deuteronomy.* Edinburgh: T&T Clark, 1994.

Lohse, Bernhard. *Martin Luther's Theology: Its Historical and Systematic Development.* Edinburgh: T&T Clark, 1999.

Longman, Phillip. *The Empty Cradle: How Falling Birthrates Threaten World Prosperity and What to Do about it.* New York: Basic Books, 2004. http://dx.doi.org/10.2307/20034158

— "The Return of Patriarchy." *Foreign Policy* 153 (March/April 2006): 56-65.

Louth, Andrew, ed. *Genesis 1-11.* London: Fitzroy Dearborn, 2001.

Lovett, Laura. *Conceiving the Future: Pronatalism, Reproduction, and the Family in the United States, 1890-1938.* Chapel Hill, NC: University of North Carolina Press, 2007.

Lutz, Wolfgang and Vegard Skirbekk. "Policies Addressing the Tempo Effect in Low-Fertility Countries." *Population and Development Review* 31.4 (December 2005): 699-720. http://dx.doi.org/10.1111/j.1728-4457.2005.00094.x

Macbeth, Helen M. and Paul Collinson, eds. *Human Population Dynamics: Cross-Disciplinary Perspectives.* Cambridge: Cambridge University Press, 2002.

Madsen, Catherine. "Scarcity and Plenitude: Thoughts on Some Recent Jewish Books." *Cross Currents* 50.1-2 (2000): 145-53.

Magnuson, Kenneth T. "Marriage, Procreation and Infertility: Reflections on Genesis." *Southern Baptist Journal of Theology* 4.1 (2000): 26-42.

Maguire, Daniel C. "Population, Religion and Ecology." *The Oxford Handbook of Religion and Ecology.* ed. Roger S. Gottlieb. Oxford: Oxford University Press, 2006: 313-25. http://dx.doi.org/10.1093/oxfordhb/9780195178722.003.0014

Maier, Harry. "The Greening of American Fundamentalism and its Detractors." *Ecological Hermeneutics: Biblical, Historical and Theological Perspectives:* 246-65.

Malanima, Paolo. *Pre-Modern European Economy: One Thousand Years (10th-19th Centuries).* Leiden: Brill, 2009. http://dx.doi.org/10.1163/ej.9789004178229.i-428

Mangina, Joseph L. "Bearing Fruit: Conception, Children and the Family." *The Blackwell Companion to Christian Ethics.* ed. Stanley Hauerwas and Samuel Wells. Oxford: Blackwell Publishing, 2004: 246-65. http://dx.doi.org/10.1002/9780470996690.ch35

Markus, Robert A. *Saeculum: History and Society in the Theology of St Augustine.* Revised edn., Cambridge: Cambridge University Press, 1988.

— *Christianity and the Secular.* Notre Dame, IN: University of Notre Dame Press, 2006.

Marlow, Hilary. *Biblical Prophets and Contemporary Environmental Ethics: Re-Reading Amos, Hosea, and First Isaiah.* Oxford: Oxford University Press, 2009.

Martin-Schramm, James B. *Population Perils and the Churches' Response.* Geneva: World Council of Churches Publications, 1997.

Matheson, Peter. *The Rhetoric of the Reformation.* Edinburgh: T&T Clark, 1998.

— *The Imaginative World of the Reformation.* Minneapolis, MN: Fortress Press, 2001.

Mattox, Mickey L. *"Defender of the Most Holy Matriarchs": Martin Luther's Interpretation of the Women of Genesis in the Enarrationes in Genesin, 1535-45.* Leiden: Brill, 2003. http://dx.doi.org/10.2307/20477158

— "Luther on Eve, Women and the Church." *Lutheran Quarterly* 17.4 (Winter 2003): 456-74.

May, Elaine Tyler. *Barren in the Promised Land: Childless Americans and the Pursuit of Happiness.* Cambridge, MA: Harvard University Press, 1995. http://dx.doi.org/10.2307/2077295

Mays, James Luther. *Psalms.* Louisville, KY: Westminster John Knox Press, 1994.

McAfee, Gene. "Ecology and Biblical Studies." *Theology for Earth Community.* ed. Dieter Hessel. Maryknoll, NY: Orbis, 1996: 31-44.

McKee, Jeffrey K. *Sparing Nature: The Conflict Between Human Population Growth and Earth's Biodiversity.* New Brunswick, NJ: Rutgers University Press, 2003.

McKeown, John. *Christian Faith and the Environment: module manual.* University of Gloucestershire, Open Theological College: Cheltenham, 2005.

— "Receptions of Israelite Nation-building: Modern Natalism and Martin Luther." *Dialog: A Journal of Theology* 49.2 (2010): 133-140. http://dx.doi.org/10.1111/j.1540-6385.2010.00517.x

McKibben, Bill. *Maybe One: A Personal and Environmental Argument for Single-Child Families.* New York: Simon and Schuster, 1998. http://dx.doi.org/10.2307/2808166

McQuillan, Kevin. "When Does Religion Influence Fertility?" *Population and Development Review* 30.1 (March 2004): 25-56. http://dx.doi.org/10.1111/j.1728-4457.2004.00002.x

Mesaros-Winckles, Christy. "TLC and the Fundamentalist Family: A Televised Quiverfull of Babies." *Journal of Religion and Popular Culture* 22.3 (Fall 2010). http://dx.doi.org/10.3138/jrpc.22.3.007. http://dx.doi.org/10.3138/jrpc.22.3.007

Meyer, Lester. "Luther in the Garden of Eden: His Commentary on Genesis 1-3." *Word and World* 4.4 (Fall 1984): 430-36.

Meyers, Carol L. "The Family in Early Israel." *Families in Ancient Israel.* ed. Leo G. Perdue, Joseph Blenkinsopp, John J. Collins, and Carol Meyers. Louisville: Westminster John Knox, 2005: 1-47.

— "Procreation, Production, and Protection: Male-Female Balance in Early Israel." *Journal of the American Academy of Religion* 51.4 (December 1983): 569-93. http://dx.doi.org/10.1093/jaarel/li.4.569

Meyers, Jeffrey J. *Does the Bible Forbid Family Planning? A Biblical and Theological Evaluation of Mary Pride's Arguments against All Forms of Birth Control.* Niceville, FL: Biblical Horizons, January 1997.

Milgrom, Jacob. Review of "Before Abraham Was: The Unity of Genesis 1-11." *Judaism* 35.3 (Summer 1986): 371-74.

Miller, Patrick D. "Psalm 127: The House That Yahweh Builds." *Journal for the Study of the Old Testament* 22 (February 1982): 119-32. http://dx.doi.org/10.1177/030908928200702211

Mitchell, David C. *The Message of the Psalter: An Eschatological Programme in the Book of Psalms.* Sheffield: Sheffield Academic Press, 1997. http://dx.doi.org/10.2307/3268017

Moberly, R.W.L. *The Theology of the Book of Genesis.* Cambridge: Cambridge University Press, 2009.

Mohler, R. Albert. "Deliberate Childlessness: Moral Rebellion With a New Face." October 2003. http://www.albertmohler.com/2003/10/13/deliberate-childlessness-moral-rebellion-with-a-new-face-4/

— "Can Christians Use Birth Control?" March 2004. http://www.albertmohler.com/2004/03/30/can-christians-use-birth-control-3/

— "The Mystery of Marriage." August 2004. http://www.albertmohler.com/2004/08/01/the-mystery-of-marriage-part-1/

— "Deliberate Childlessness Revisited." August 2005. http://www.albertmohler.com/2005/08/15/deliberate-childlessness-revisited/

— "Falling Birthrates, Empty Cribs, and Collapsing Worldviews." October 2007. http://www.albertmohler.com/blog_read.php?id=1021

— "Of Babies and Believers." May 2007. http://www.albertmohler.com/2007/05/03/of-babies-and-believers/

— "Put a Stop to Large Families?" September 2008. http://www.albertmohler.com/2008/09/18/put-a-stop-to-large-families/

— "The Real Population Threat." March 2009. http://www.albertmohler.com/2009/03/26/the-real-population-threat-2/

Montgomery, John Warwick. "How to Decide the Birth Control Question." *Birth Control and the Christian.* ed. W. Spitzer and C. Saylor. Carol Stream, IL: Tyndale House Publishing, 1969: 576-83.

Moran, William. "Atrahasis: The Babylonian Story of the Flood." *Biblica* 52.1 (1971): 51-61.

Morecraft, Joseph. "The Bible on Large Families." *The Counsel of Chalcedon* 11.8 (October 1989): 9-10.

Mosher William D, Linda B Williams, and David P Johnson. "Religion and fertility in the United States: New patterns". *Demography* 29.2 (May 1992): 199–214

Moss, Robert, Adam Watson, and John Ollason. *Animal Population Dynamics.* London: Chapman and Hall, 1982. http://dx.doi.org/10.2307/2531356

Muers, Rachel. "It Takes at Least Two to Reproduce." *Cross Currents* 55.2 (Summer 2005): 162-71.

— "The Gender of Generations: Future Generations and the Social Maternal." *Ecotheology* 11.3 (2006): 311-25. http://dx.doi.org/10.1558/ecot.2006.11.3.311

Murtagh, Paul A. and Michael G. Schlax. "Reproduction and the Carbon Legacies of Individuals." *Global Environmental Change* 19.1 (2009): 14-20. http://dx.doi.org/10.1016/j.gloenvcha.2008.10.007

Myers, Norman, and Julian L. Simon. *Scarcity or Abundance?: A Debate on the Environment.* New York: W.W. Norton, 1994.

Nash, James A. "The Bible vs. Biodiversity: The Case against Moral Argument from Scripture." *Journal for the Study of Religion, Nature and Culture* 3.2 (2009): 213-37. http://dx.doi.org/10.1558/jsrnc.v3i2.213

Nestingen, James Arne. "The End of the End: The Role of Apocalyptic in the Lutheran Reform." *Word and World* 15.2 (Spring 1995): 195-205.

— "Luther in Front of the Text: The Genesis Commentary." *Word and World* 14.2 (Spring 1994): 186-94.

New Evangelical Partnership for the Common Good. "A Call to Christian Common Ground on Family Planning, and Maternal and Children's Health." 2012. www. newevangelicalpartnership.org.

Newport, Kenneth. *Apocalypse and Millennium: Studies in Biblical Eisegesis.* Cambridge: Cambridge University Press, 2000. http://dx.doi.org/10.1177/004057360205800437

North, Gary. *The Dominion Covenant: Genesis.* Tyler, TX: Institute for Christian Economics, 1987.

Oberman, Heiko. *The Reformation: Roots and Ramifications.* trans. Andrew C. Gow. Edinburgh: T&T Clark, 1994. http://dx.doi.org/10.2307/2544306

— *Luther: Man Between God and the Devil.* trans. Eileen Walliser-Schwarzbart. New Haven, CT: Yale University Press, 2006. http://dx.doi.org/10.2307/2864431

ONS. "Population Trends." 2011. http://www.statistics.gov.uk/

Owen, Samuel A. *Letting God Plan Your Family.* Wheaton, IL: Crossway, 1990.

Ozment, Steven E. *When Fathers Ruled: Family Life in Reformation Europe.* Cambridge, MA: Harvard University Press, 1983.

Pagels, Elaine. "The Politics of Paradise: Augustine's Exegesis of Genesis 1-3 versus that of John Chrysostom." *Harvard Theological Review* 78.1-2 (1985): 67-99.

— "Freedom from Necessity: Philosophic and Personal Dimensions of Christian Conversion." *Genesis 1-3 in the History of Exegesis: Intrigue in the Garden:* 67-98.

Parkerson, Donald and Jo Parkerson. "'Fewer Children of Greater Spiritual Quality': Religion and the Decline of Fertility in 19th Century America." *Social Science History* 12.1 (Spring 1988): 49-70. http://dx.doi.org/10.2307/1171296

Parris, David Paul. *Reading the Bible With Giants: How 2000 Years of Biblical Interpretation Can Shed New Light on Old Texts.* Carlisle: Paternoster Press, 2006.

— *Reception Theory and Biblical Hermeneutics.* Eugene, OR: Pickwick, 2009.

Parsons, Michael. "The Apocalyptic Luther: His Noahic Self-Understanding." *Journal of the Evangelical Theological Society* 44.4 (December 2001): 627-45.

Patte, Daniel. *Ethics of Biblical Interpretation: A Reevaluation.* Louisville, KY: Westminster John Knox Press, 1995.

Payette-Bucci, Diane. "Voluntary Childlessness." *Direction* 17.2 (1988): 26-41.

Pelikan, Jaroslav. *Luther the Expositor: Introduction to the Reformer's Exegetical Writings.* Saint Louis, MO: Concordia, 1969.

Perdue, Leo G., Joseph Blenkinsopp, John J. Collins, and Carol L. Meyers, eds. *Families in Ancient Israel.* Louisville, KY: Westminster John Knox Press, 1997. http://dx.doi.org/10.2307/604854

Petersen, David L. "Genesis and Family Values." *Journal of Biblical Literature* 124.1 (Spring 2005): 5-23. http://dx.doi.org/10.2307/30040988

Pew Forum. *Faith in Flux: Changes in Religious Affiliation in the U.S.* Washington DC: Pew Research, 2009.

Pew Forum. *U.S. Religious Landscape Survey.* Washington DC: Pew Research, 2008.

Poulson, Anna. "An Examination of the Ethics of Contraception With Reference to Recent Protestant and Roman Catholic Thought." PhD thesis. King's College London, 2006.

Price, Richard M. "Celibacy and Free Love in Early Christianity." *Theology and Sexuality* 12.2 (2006): 121-41. http://dx.doi.org/10.1177/1355835806061426

Pride, Mary. *The Way Home: Beyond Feminism, Back to Reality.* Wheaton, IL: Crossway, 1985.

Provan, Charles. *The Bible and Birth Control.* Monongahela, PA: Zimmer Press, 1989.

Quiverfull discussion forum. http://www.quiverfull.com/

Räisänen, Heikki. "The Effective 'History' of the Bible: A Challenge to Biblical Scholarship?" *Scottish Journal of Theology* 45.3 (1992): 303-24. http://dx.doi.org/10.1017/s0036930600038047

Ranta, Esa, Veijo Kaitala, and Per Lundberg. *Ecology of Populations.* Cambridge: Cambridge University Press, 2006. http://dx.doi.org/10.1017/cbo9780511610752

Reid, Darrel R. "Luther, Muntzer and the Last Day: Eschatological Hope, Apocalyptic Expectations." *Mennonite Quarterly Review* 69.1 (January 1995): 53-74.

Rivkin-Fish, Michele. "Pronatalism, Gender Politics, and the Renewal of Family Support in Russia: Towards a Feminist Anthropology of 'Maternity Capital'." *Slavic Review* 69.3 (Fall 2010): 701-24.

Robbins, Gregory A., ed. *Genesis 1-3 in the History of Exegesis: Intrigue in the Garden.* Lewiston: Edwin Mellen Press, 1988. http://dx.doi.org/10.2307/1519143

Rockwood, Larry L. *Introduction to Population Ecology.* Oxford: Blackwell, 2006.

Rotelle, John, ed. *The Works of Saint Augustine: A Translation for the 21st Century.* Hyde Park, NY: New City Press (1990-2014).

Rowland, Christopher, and Mark Corner. *Liberating Exegesis: The Challenge of Liberation Theology to Biblical Studies.* London: SPCK, 1990.

Ruether, Rosemary Radford. *Christianity and the Making of the Modern Family.* London: SCM Press, 2001.

Rushdoony, Rousas J. *The Myth of Over-Population.* Fairfax, VA: Thorburn Press, 1974.

Sailhamer, John H. *The Pentateuch as Narrative: A Biblical-Theological Commentary.* Grand Rapids, MI: Zondervan, 1992.

Sánchez, Edesio. "Family in the Non-Narrative Sections of the Pentateuch." *Family in the Bible.* ed. Richard S. Hess and M. Daniel Carroll. Grand Rapids: Baker, Academic, 2003: 32-58.

Sarna, Nahum M. *Genesis: The Traditional Hebrew Text with New JPS Translation.* Philadelphia, PA: Jewish Publication Society, 1989.

Sawyer, J. F. A. "Introduction" The Blackwell Companion to the Bible and Culture. ed. J. F. A. Sawyer. Malden, MA: Blackwell, 2006. http://dx.doi.org/10.1002/9780470997000

— "The Role of Reception Theory, Reader-Response Criticism and/or Impact History in the Study of the Bible: Definition and Evaluation." *Evangelische Kreditgenossenschaft Kassel (EKK) consultation*, Germany, 2004. http://dx.doi.org/10.1002/9780470752142.ch31

SBC. "The Great Commission Resurgence." 2009.

Schlabach, Gerald. "Continence, Consumption and Other Abuses: Or Why an Augustinian Ethic is Worth the Bother." *Annual Meeting of the Society of Christian Ethics*. 8 January 2000. http://personal2.stthomas.edu/gwschlabach/docs/2000sce.htm

Schreiner, Susan E. "Eve, the Mother of History: Reaching for the Reality of History in Augustine's Later Exegesis of Genesis." *Genesis 1-3 in the History of Exegesis*. Lewiston, N.Y. and Queenston, Ont: Edwin Mellen Press, 1988: 135-186.

Schüssler Fiorenza, Elisabeth. "The Ethics of Biblical Interpretation: Decentering Biblical Scholarship." *Journal of Biblical Literature* 107.1 (March 1988): 3-17. http://dx.doi.org/10.2307/3267820

Schwartz, Regina M. *The Curse of Cain: The Violent Legacy of Monotheism*. Chicago, IL: University of Chicago Press, 1997.

Schwingl, Pamela J. and Harry A. Guess. "Safety and Effectiveness of Vasectomy." *Fertility and Sterility* 73.5 (May 2000): 923-36.

Segovia, Fernando. "Cultural Studies and Contemporary Biblical Criticism: Ideological Criticism as Mode of Discourse." *Reading From This Place, Volume 2: Social Location and Biblical Interpreation in Global Perspective*. ed. F.F. Segovia and M.A. Tolbert. Minneapolis: Fortress, 1995: 1-20.

Segovia, Fernando and Mary Ann Tolbert, eds. *Reading from This Place: Social Location and Biblical Interpretation in Global Perspective*. Minneapolis, MN: Fortress Press, 1995. http://dx.doi.org/10.1177/030908929702207514

Shepherd, David. "'Strike His Bone and His Flesh': Reading Job from the Beginning." *Journal for the Study of the Old Testament* 33.1 (2008): 81-97. http://dx.doi.org/10.1177/0309089208094461

Shi, Anqing. "The Impact of Population Pressure on Global Carbon Dioxide Emissions, 1975-1996: Evidence from Pooled Cross-Country Data." *Energy Economics* 44 (2003): 29-42.

Sideris, Lisa H. *Environmental Ethics, Ecological Theology, and Natural Selection*. New York: Columbia University Press, 2003.

Silliman, Jael, and Ynestra King, eds. *Dangerous Intersections: Feminist Perspectives on Population, Environment, and Development*. Cambridge, MA: South End Press, 1999.

Ska, Jean Louis. *Introduction to Reading the Pentateuch*. Winona Lake, IN: Eisenbrauns, 2006.

Skirbekk, Vegard, Eric Kaufmann, and Anne Goujon. "Secularism, Fundamentalism, or Catholicism? The Religious Composition of the United States to 2043." *Journal for the Scientific Study of Religion* 49.2 (June 2010): 293-310. http://dx.doi.org/10.1111/j.1468-5906.2010.01510.x

Sleeth, J. Matthew. "6.5 Billion and Counting: A Christian Case for Small Families." *Books and Culture: A Christian Review* 8.36 (2007).

Smith, Andy. "Christian Responses to the Population Paradigm." *Dangerous Intersections: Feminist Perspectives on Population, Environment, and Development.* ed. Jael Silliman and Ynestra King. Cambridge, MA: South End Press, 1999: 74-88.

Spitzer, Walter O. and Carlyle L. Saylor, eds. *Birth Control and the Christian: A Protestant Symposium on the Control of Human Reproduction.* Wheaton IL: Tyndale House, 1969.

Sproul, R.C. Jr. *Believing God: Twelve Biblical Promises Christians Struggle to Accept.* Lake Mary, FL: Reformation Trust, 2009.

Stalker, David. *Genesis 1-11.* Edinburgh: Church of Scotland, 1957.

Statistics Canada. 2011. http://www.statcan.gc.ca/

Stavrakopoulou, Francesca. *Land of Our Fathers : The Roles of Ancestor Veneration in Biblical Land Claims.* London: T&T Clark, 2010.

Strand, Paul. "Back to the Future: The Growing Movement of Natalism." Christian Broadcasting Network, 2006. Archived at http://www.freerepublic.com/focus/f-religion/1437791/posts (originally at cbn.com).

Tanner, Kenneth and Christopher A. Hall, eds. *Ancient and Postmodern Christianity: Paleo-Orthodoxy in the 21st Century.* Downers Grove, IL: InterVarsity Press, 2002.

Thiselton, Anthony. *Can the Bible Mean Whatever We Want it to Mean?* Chester: Chester Academic Press, 2005.

Thompson, John Lee. *Reading the Bible With the Dead: What you Can Learn from the History of Exegesis that you Can't Learn from Exegesis Alone.* Grand Rapids, MI and Cambridge: Eerdmans, 2007.

— "Hagar, Victim or Villain? Three Sixteenth-Century Views." *Catholic Biblical Quarterly* 59.2 (April 1997): 213-33.

Toft, Monica Duffy. "Wombfare: The Religious and Political Dimensions of Fertility and Demographic Change," in *Political Demography: How Population Changes Are Reshaping International Security and National Politics,* ed. Jack Goldstone, Eric P. Kaufmann and Monica Duffy Toft. Oxford University Press, 2012. 213-225.

Torode, Sam and Bethany Torode. *Open Embrace: A Protestant Couple Rethinks Contraception.* Grand Rapids, MI: Eerdmans, 2002.

Torre, Miguel de la. *A Lily Among the Thorns: Imagining a New Christian Sexuality.* San Francisco, CA: Wiley, 2007.

Tucker, Gene M. "Rain on a Land Where No One Lives: The Hebrew Bible on the Environment." *Journal of Biblical Literature* 116.1 (Spring 1997): 3-17. http://dx.doi.org/10.2307/3266743

Turner, Adair. "Population Ageing: What Should We Worry about?" *Philosophical Transactions of the Royal Society* 364 (2009): 3009-21. http://dx.doi.org/10.1098/rstb.2009.0185

Turner, Laurence B. *Announcements of Plot in Genesis.* Sheffield: JSOT Press, 1990.

United Nations. *World Population to 2300.* New York, 2004. http://www.un.org/esa/population/publications/longrange2/WorldPop2300final.pdf

— *World Population Prospects: 2012 Revision.* http://esa.un.org/unpd/wpp/

— *Live births, deaths, and infant deaths, latest available year.* November 2011. http://unstats.un.org/unsd/demographic/products/vitstats/serATab3.pdf

Van Leeuwen, Raymond. "'Be fruitful and multiply': Is this a Command, or a Blessing?" *Christianity Today* 45.14 (12 November 2001): 58-61.

Vandermeer, John H., and Deborah E. Goldberg. *Population Ecology: First Principles.* Princeton NJ: Princeton University Press, 2003.

Viands, Jamie. *"I will surely multiply your offspring" An Old Testament Theology of the Blessing of Progeny with Special Attention to the Latter Prophets.* Eugene, OR: Pickwick, 2014.

Voas, David. "Does religion belong in population studies?" *Environment and Planning A 39* (2007): 1166-80. http://dx.doi.org/10.1068/a38154

Watters, Steve and Candice. *Start Your Family: Inspiration for Having Babies.* Chicago, IL: Moody Publishers, 2009.

Wax, Trevin. "Turning Around the SBC: An Interview with Dr Danny Akin." 2 June 2009. http://thegospelcoalition.org/blogs/trevinwax/2009/06/09/turning-around-the-sbc-decline-an-interview-with-dr-danny-akin-2/

Weigel, George. *The Cube and the Cathedral: Europe, America, and Politics Without God.* New York: Basic Books, 2005. http://dx.doi.org/10.2307/20031738

Wendebourg, Dorothea. "Luther on Monasticism." *Lutheran Quarterly* 19.2 (Summer 2005): 125-52.

Wenham, John. "Large Numbers in the Old Testament." *Tyndale Bulletin* 18 (1967): 19-53.

Wenham, Gordon J. *Genesis 1-15.* Milton Keynes: Word, 1987. http://dx.doi.org/10.2307/1517668

— "Sanctuary Symbolism in the Garden of Eden Story." *I Studied Inscriptions from Before the Flood: Ancient Near Eastern, Literary, and Linguistic Approaches to Genesis 1-11.* ed. Richard S. Hess and David Toshio Tsumura. Winona Lake, Ind: Eisenbrauns, 1994: 399-404.

— "Family in the Pentateuch." *Family in the Bible: Exploring Customs, Culture and Context.* ed. R.S. Hess and M.D. Carroll. Grand Rapids: Baker Academic, 2003: 17-31.

Westermann, Claus. *Blessing in the Bible and the Life of the Church.* Trans. Keith Crim. Philadelphia, PA: Fortress Press, 1978. http://dx.doi.org/10.2307/3265202

— *Genesis 1-11.* trans. John J. Scullion. London: SPCK, 1983. http://dx.doi.org/10.1017/s0036930600044744

White, Katherine J. Curtis. "Declining Fertility Among North American Hutterites: The Use of Birth Control within a Dariusleut Colony." *Social Biology* 49.1 (2002): 58-73. http://dx.doi.org/10.1080/19485565.2002.9989049

White, L. Michael, and O. Larry Yarbrough, eds. *The Social World of the First Christians.* Minneapolis, MN: Fortress Press, 1995. http://dx.doi.org/10.1093/jcs/39.2.352

White, Lynn. "The Historical Roots of Our Ecologic Crisis." *Science* 155.3767 (10 March 1967): 1203-07. http://dx.doi.org/10.1126/science.155.3767.1203

Whybray, R. Norman. *The Good Life in the Old Testament.* London: T&T Clark, 2001.

Williams, Daniel H. *Evangelicals and Tradition: The Formative Influence of the Early Church.* Grand Rapids, MI: Baker Academic, 2005.

Wilson, Douglas. *Reforming Marriage.* Moscow, ID: Canon Press, 1995.

Wink, Walter. "Ecobible: The Bible and Ecojustice." *Theology Today* 49.4 (January 1993): 465-77. http://dx.doi.org/10.1177/004057369304900403

Wood, James W. *Dynamics of Human Reproduction: Biology, Biometry, Demography.* New Brunswick, NJ: Transaction, 1994.

Wright, Christopher J. H. *God's People in God's Land: Family, Land, and Property in the Old Testament.* Exeter: Paternoster Press, 1990.

Wrigley, E. A. and R. S. Schofield, *The Population History of England, 1541–1871. A Reconstruction.* London: Edward Arnold, 1989.

Yarbrough, O. Larry. *Not Like the Gentiles: Marriage Rules in the Letters of Paul.* Atlanta: Scholars Press, 1986. http://dx.doi.org/10.2307/3267847

Yegerlehner, David. "'Be Fruitful and Multiply, and Fill the Earth.': A History of the Interpretation of Genesis 1:28a." PhD thesis. Boston University, 1974.

Zerjal, Tatiana et al. "The Genetic Legacy of the Mongols." *American Journal of Human Genetics* 72.3 (2003): 717-21. http://dx.doi.org/10.1086/367774

Zimmerman, Anthony. *Natural Family Planning: Nature's Way – God's Way.* Milwaukee, WI: De Rance, 1980.

Index

abortion 3, 32, 38, 182
Abraham 40, 50, 79, 95, 96, 99, 118, 119, 121, 134, 135, 162, 198
abstinence 4, 35, 160, 164
Adam 50, 69, 89, 90, 94, 95, 102, 105, 120, 154, 159, 162, 168, 170, 189, 190, 199
Adam and Eve 21, 66, 68, 70, 94, 125, 126, 149
ageing 65, 201, 202
Akin, Daniel 13, 39, 49
Ambrose of Milan 55, 146, 148, 151, 152, 160
Amish 14, 46, 206
Anglican 11, 18, 24, 34, 35
anthropocentrism 179
Athanasius 148
Athenagoras 71
Atrahasis 127-130
Augustine of Hippo 4, 25, 27, 28, 43, 145-175

Beisner, Calvin 16, 17, 18, 49, 64, 65, 69, 75, 134-137, 137, 180, 190
biocapacity 201, 204, 205, 207
biodiversity 29, 143, 177, 178, 179, 180, 184, 186, 188, 189, 207
birth rate 2, 4, 5, 6, 8, 9, 13, 15, 21, 33, 36, 45, 51, 57, 63, 65
breastfeeding 2, 45, 111

Cain 95, 125, 126, 127, 165
  Cainites 125
Calvinism 17, 65
  Calvinists 64
  New Calvinist Movement 212
  Orthodox Calvinists of the Netherlands 16

Calvin, John 96, 138, 190, 211
Canaan 116, 119, 126, 137, 192
  Canaanites 116, 122-124, 135, 192, 194
Carlson, Allan 14, 16, 17, 18, 37, 39, 50, 78, 85, 106, 132, 203, 204, 209, 215
Catholicism 4, 10, 11, 20, 27, 35, 59, 77, 81, 107, 145, 146, 147, 174, 182
childfree 66
childlessness 4, 31, 39, 47, 56, 63, 66, 87, 97, 115, 173
Cohen, Jeremy 27
consumption 8, 113, 163, 177, 182, 184, 195
contraception 4, 20, 32, 33, 34, 35, 43, 46, 76, 139, 142, 150, 209, 212
cornucopia 64
cornucopian ideology 64-65, 85, 100, 102, 134, 136, 165, 197

eco-Bible hermeneutic 184
ecofeminism 179, 181, 183
ecological footprint 14, 22, 29, 177, 184, 186, 205, 207. See also natalism, ecological critique of
ecological hermeneutic 178
ecological sustainability. See sustainability
eschatology 52, 100, 101, 107, 132, 147, 148, 155, 165, 167, 175, 188
eugenics 4, 34, 147
Eusebius of Caesarea 60, 70
Evangelicalism 11, 14-15, 29, 35-38
Evangelicals 1, 14, 17, 79, 182, 213
Eve 89, 95, 98, 126
extinction 87, 116, 142, 180, 185, 186, 189, 198, 199, 201, 207, 210

family
  planning 2, 4, 9, 10, 12, 17, 19, 20, 34,
    35, 36, 43, 44, 74, 75, 182, 209
  values 77
fertility treatment 3, 20, 45

Gadamer, Hans-Georg 23, 26, 27
genetic 52, 55, 119, 122, 148, 166, 181,
    185

homeschooling 13, 59
Hutterite 14, 45-46, 206

immortality 56, 114, 128, 141, 143, 155,
    156, 164, 206
inerrancy 11, 42, 211
infertility 2, 3, 20, 31, 32, 40, 45, 54, 95,
    96, 97, 98, 99, 111, 127, 128, 130, 171

Jacob (Israel) 79, 96, 113, 118, 119, 122,
    135, 136, 138, 144, 192
Jauss, Hans Robert 22, 28
Jovinian 86, 146, 149, 152, 153, 157, 166,
    174, 175

Leah 96, 99, 115
Lutheran Church Missouri Synod 34,
    35, 211, 213
Lutheranism 16, 17, 37, 43, 79, 211
Luther, Martin 23, 28, 29, 42, 77-108, 145,
    172, 173, 175, 180, 209, 212

Manicheism 145, 146, 149, 150, 151, 152,
    153, 164, 174
Melancthon, Philipp 93
Mohler, Albert 16, 17, 37, 39, 44, 49, 54,
    59, 66, 74, 204
Mormon 9, 15, 49, 212
Moses 66, 70, 110, 115, 116, 120, 121, 122,
    137, 161, 192, 193, 194
Muslim 38, 50, 51, 86
Mussolini, Benito 33

natalism
  Catholic 15-16, 77, 211
  ecological critique of 177-208
  Evangelical 75, 132

limited 4, 12, 17-19, 18, 23, 44, 49, 52,
    75, 78, 212
  modern 29, 32-39, 143
  Protestant 3, 4, 9, 23, 31-76
  state 32, 214
  unlimited 4, 6, 17, 17-19, 23, 38, 40, 44,
    45, 45-49, 52, 62, 65, 70, 74-76, 78, 129,
    212
Natural Family Planning 3, 4, 145
Noah 70, 123, 125, 191, 194

Origen 148
Orthodox Catholic Church (Eastern) 15,
    20

patriarchy 56, 211
Paul of Tarsus 68, 71
Pentecostal 14
population 6
procreationism 4, 199
prosperity 14, 26, 40, 53, 63, 73, 124, 134
  economic 65, 133-134
Protestantism 6, 20, 34, 42
Protestants 4, 9, 12, 16, 38, 43
  fundamentalist 9

Quiverfull 4, 9, 12, 16, 18, 23, 37, 38, 45,
    46, 48, 49, 62, 69, 211, 212

Rachel 79, 87, 96, 96-100, 123, 138
reception 1, 5, 11, 14, 14-16, 20-29, 39-44,
    75, 77-81, 106, 118, 123, 144, 178, 179,
    184, 196, 211, 212, 216
ressourcement 27-29, 145, 163-174, 175,
    177, 180, 210, 211

Sarah 96, 97, 99, 121, 123
Seth 125, 165, 166
Southern Baptist 18
  Convention 13
Sproul, R. C., Jr. 36, 41, 50, 51
sustainability 8, 14, 21, 29, 163, 177, 187,
    204, 205, 207, 212, 214

Tertullian 56, 63, 67, 161

vasectomy 3, 72

This book need not end here...

At Open Book Publishers, we are changing the nature of the traditional academic book. The title you have just read will not be left on a library shelf, but will be accessed online by hundreds of readers each month across the globe. We make all our books free to read online so that students, researchers and members of the public who can't afford a printed edition can still have access to the same ideas as you.

Our digital publishing model also allows us to produce online supplementary material, including extra chapters, reviews, links and other digital resources. Find *God's Babies* on our website to access its online extras. Please check this page regularly for ongoing updates, and join the conversation by leaving your own comments:

http://www.openbookpublishers.com/isbn/9781783740529

If you enjoyed this book, and feel that research like this should be available to all readers, regardless of their income, please think about donating to us. Our company is run entirely by academics, and our publishing decisions are based on intellectual merit and public value rather than on commercial viability. We do not operate for profit and all donations, as with all other revenue we generate, will be used to finance new Open Access publications.

For further information about what we do, how to donate to OBP, additional digital material related to our titles or to order our books, please visit our website: http://www.openbookpublishers.com

OpenBook Publishers

Knowledge is for sharing

Lightning Source UK Ltd.
Milton Keynes UK
UKOW02f0226301214

243722UK00009B/26/P

9 781783 740529